# ROE v. WADE:
## Unraveling the Fabric of America

**(Revised & Expanded 2012)**

### Front Cover:

Blind Lady Justice – The personification of the moral force that underlies the rule of law – gazing from atop the so-called Wall of Separation (of Church and State) upon the reality that she has been misled by our United States Supreme Court into bringing about the opposite of the ultimate principle for which she stands.

The quote in graffiti on the Front Cover Wall:
The great 19th century, American legal commentator and compiler, Joel Prentiss Bishop (1814-1901)

Originally Titled (and with a different cover design):
## What's Really Going On With Pro-Roe V. Wade Catholic Politicians
(Tate Publishing & Enterprises, LLC. 2011)

*Front Cover design by Daniel Williams*

PHILIP A. RAFFERTY

# ROE v. WADE:
## Unraveling the Fabric of America

**(Revised & Expanded 2012)**

TATE PUBLISHING
AND ENTERPRISES, LLC

Published by Tate Publishing & Enterprises, LLC
127 E. Trade Center Terrace | Mustang, Oklahoma 73064 USA
1.888.361.9473 | www.tatepublishing.com

Tate Publishing is committed to excellence in the publishing industry. The company reflects the philosophy established by the founders, based on Psalm 68:11,
*"The Lord gave the word and great was the company of those who published it."*

Published in the United States of America

ISBN: 978-1-62295-678-4
1. Law / Constitutional
2. Law / General
12.11.19

# DEDICATION

I dedicate this work to the memories of my father, Owen Rafferty, and my mother, Lilly Rafferty, and to my friends Sherilyn Patrick and Stephen Price.

# ACKNOWLEDGMENTS

Sir John H. Baker, retired Professor of English Legal History, University of Cambridge, former Downing Professor of the Laws of England, and Fellow of Saint Catharine's College, provided invaluable assistance in producing many of the cases set forth in the appendices of this book. His generous contribution included responding to my countless questions, as well as providing background and critical commentary on (and in many instances, locating and translating) many of the cases set forth in the appendices of this book. He is, in my opinion, the embodiment of legal scholarship. I am forever grateful to him in rendering to me such kind assistance.

I am grateful also to the staff and research librarians of the Los Angeles County Public Library (and particularly to Peter Rosenwald, retired), the Los Angeles County Law Library, and the Huntington Library (San Marino, California) for the kind and patient assistance they rendered to me over the course of several years. Stephen Price and Theresa Bouvier provided invaluable and very timely assistance in finalizing the MS for submission to Tate.

Sherilyn Patrick computer-typed, formatted, and assisted in editing countless versions of the project which gave rise to *Side B* of this book. Her contribution extended continuously for over a twenty-five-year period. She remained gracious and patient throughout. A person who possessed these virtues to a lesser degree would have long since thrown the manuscript and me into the deepest portion of the Los Angeles River. I am forever grateful to her.

Tate Publishing's staff remained available and helpful from the beginning to the end of the composition and construction of this book from ms. form. Its director of production, Melanie Harr-Hughes, conceptual editor, James D. Bare, two of its layout designers, Joey Garrett and Christina Hicks and one of its cover designers, Kellie Southerland graciously directed me through the world of book writing. Would that every novice be gifted with just such true guides. Tate's actions in producing this book more than matched its advertising assertions. What a delightful surprise and outcome.

# CONTENTS

# EPIGRAPHS

"There's been a bit of debate lately on what the early Church thought of abortion. That's surprising when you think about it, because we'd give a lot to have the kind of documentary record for other doctrines that we have for the Church's condemnation of this practice.... No other moral issue has such a detailed paper trail. Even the earliest documents—most of them very brief—take time to state an unqualified condemnation of the practice. The Fathers spoke with such certainty, clarity, and consistency on the issue that it's hard to find any seams in the argument. That's all the more remarkable when we consider how the...[Roman] culture of the time treated children... Infanticide was a common... practice."

—Mike Aquilina, *Roots of the Faith: From the Church Fathers to You* 121-122 (2010)

"The [early] Church is worried about its public image and concerned to show that it is not a subversive organization threatening the well-being of [Roman] society...

In just two respects are the first Christians recorded as having been consciously different from their neighbours. First, they were much more rigorous about matters of sex [which includes marriage] than the prevailing attitudes in the Roman Empire. [Secondly], abortion and...[infanticide or the] abandonment of unwanted children were accepted as regrettable necessities in Roman society, but, like the Jews before them, Christians were insistent that these practices were completely unacceptable. Even those Christian writers who were constructing arguments to show how much Christians fitted into normal society made no effort to hide this deliberate difference."

—Diarmaid MacCulloch, *Christianity: The First Three Thousand Years* 119 (2009)

—"Self-interest is not the only thing that tempts us to commit injustice. One of the strongest motives to do wrong is to make everything go right... Sometimes justice requires allowing bad things to happen to other people... [Let us, therefore, put Paul in reverse, and make evil good]: Let us do evil for the sake of good."

—J. Budziszewski, *What We Can't Not Know: A Guide* 67 (Spence Publishing Co., 2003)

Our "holding, we feel, is consistent with the... demands of the profound problems of the modern day."

—*Roe v. Wade*, 410 U.S. 113, 165 (1973)

Here is the most profoundly preposterous statement ever uttered by the United States Supreme Court: "Our holding... is consistent with the lenity of the [English] common law."

—Anonymous (quoting *Roe v. Wade*, 410 U.S. at 165)

"'I assert that the hundreds of thousands of abortions performed in America each year are a disgrace to civilization.'"

—Ellen Chesler (Margaret Sanger biographer and Planned Parenthood board member), quoting Margaret Sanger, proponent of eugenics, and founder of America's largest elective abortion provider, Planned Parenthood. (Quoted in the *Los Angeles Times*, Tuesday, March 2, 2010, at p. A10.)

"Every woman who undergoes amniocentesis is a eugenicist."

—*Ellen Chesler, id.*

"If the opponents of *Roe* expect to see it overruled, they had better learn to speak the language of the Court. They must exchange their impassioned moral rhetoric for the rather more sterile language of Constitutionalism."

—Gary L. McDowell

"For years I adopted, without bothering to think, the attitude common among secular, affluent educated people who took the propriety of abortion for granted, even when it was illegal. Though punitively illegal, like that of drinking alcohol during Prohibition, it was thought to reflect merely unenlightened prejudice or religious conviction, the two being regarded as much the same."

—*Robert Bork, infra,* note 35 (of *Side A*) at 173

"Several times I have taken issue with those who entertain the ambition of adopting a neutral, non-partisan approach in theology and similar fields. All who endorse such an approach have to learn that personal commitment and critical reflection can and should mutually support each other. As Paul Griffiths has stated, 'to be confessional is simply to be open about one's historical and religious locatedness, one's specificity, an openness that is essential for serious theological work and indeed for any serious intellectual work that is not in thrall to the myth of the disembodied and unlocated scholarly intellect.'"

—Gerald O'Collins, *Christology: A Biblical, Historical, and Systematic Study of Jesus* 357 (2nd Edition, 2009) (quoting P.J. Griffiths, "The Uniqueness of Christian Doctrine Defended," in G. D'Costa (ed.), *Christian Uniqueness Reconsidered* (Maryknoll, NY: Orbis Books, 1990) 169.

"The Constitution was a very plainly written document, and when it used phrases like "an establishment of religion," for example, it referred to something well known to people who had already lived under an established church, the Church of England. The prohibition against an establishment of religion had nothing to do with a "wall of separation" between church and state, which appears nowhere in the Constitution, but was a phrase from Thomas Jefferson, who was not even in the country when the Constitution was written."

—Thomas Sowell, *Intellectuals and Society* 178 (2009)

"Do we …, in the name of separation of church and state, box up our faith so that it doesn't give full expression to the gospel?"

—Michael Lee

"The very concept of ordered liberty precludes allowing every person to make his own standards on matters of conduct in which society as a whole has important interests."

—*Wisconsin v. Yoder*, 406 U.S. 205, 215–216 (1971)

"We repeat … that the State does have an … important and legitimate interest in protecting [unborn or potential] … human life [from the beginning of the process of human conception]."

—*Roe v. Wade*, 410 U.S. 113, 162 (1973)

"The absolute worst violation of the judge's oath of office is to decide a case based on a partisan political or philosophical [or personal] bias, rather than what the law requires."

—Justice Antonin Scalia

"Our task … is to resolve the issue [of whether the 14th Amendment's due process clause guarantees to an unmarried woman a right to undergo a physician-performed abortion], by constitutional measurement, free of emotion and predilection. We seek earnestly to do this."

—*Roe v. Wade,* 410 U.S. at 116

"All they [the *Roe* majority and concurring justices] wanted was to get those [state, criminal abortion] statutes off the books."

—Harvard law professor, Mark Tushnet (who was clerking for *Roe* majority justice, Thurgood Marshall, when *Roe* was being decided)

"Many among the intelligentsia create their own reality—whether deliberately or not—by filtering out information contrary to their conception of how the world is or ought to be. Some have gone further. J.A. Schumpeter said that the first thing a man will do for his ideals is lie. It is not necessary to lie, however, in order to deceive, when filtering will accomplish the same purpose. This can take the form of suppressing some facts altogether."

—Thomas Sowell, *Intellectuals and Society* 119 (2009)

"The power of the modern state [including one of its arms, such as its highest court] makes it possible for it to turn lies into truth by destroying the facts which existed before, and by making new realities to conform to what until then had been ideological fiction."

—Hannah Arendt

"It is thus apparent that at Common Law..., [throughout Colonial America to] the time of the adoption of our Constitution and, [from that point, throughout the several states and territories of the United States, to approximately the mid-19th century]..., a woman enjoyed a right to [an abortion]."

—*Roe v. Wade,* 410 U.S. at 140–141

"At common law the unborn child is generally considered to be in being … in all cases where it will be for the benefit of such child to be so considered."

—*Hall v. Hancock* (1834), 32 Mass. 255, 257–58

"The Supreme Court is based on the reasons we give in our opinions.'"

—Helen J. Knowles, *The Tie Goes to Freedom: Justice Kennedy on Liberty* 9 (2009) (quoting Justice Kennedy).

"People do things for reasons … , and people give reasons for things they do. But the reasons they do them and the reasons they give frequently are not the same."

—Jon Franklin

"'When politics comes in the door, truth flies out the window.' Historians who want to influence politics with their history writing have missed the point of the craft; they ought to run for office."

—Douglas Brinkley (quoting Rebecca West)

Success in politics, the latter having taken its cue from the world of advertising, and from the folks in public relations, is inversely related to the willingness of the voting public to think critically, and to demand substance.

—Anonymous

"A full understanding of truth is to understand the errors it corrects."

—Mortimer Adler

"Truth can be error to minds unprepared for it."

—Cardinal J.H. Newman

"Often, it takes a book to set straight a paragraph of falsehoods, half-truths, facts, and innuendos."

—G.K. Chesterton

"In a time of universal deceit, telling the truth is a revolutionary act."

—George Orwell

"There is no sadder sight in the world than to see a beautiful theory killed by a brutal fact."

—William James

"Catholics who claim to be privately convinced of [the truth] of the Church's teaching on ... [abortion] while voting [or working] to make abortions possible are not credible ... The truth is, they do not believe what the Church teaches."

—James Carroll, *Practicing Catholic* 168 (2009)

"Even those anti-Catholic bigots who embrace [the] ... view ["that the Church should accept the norms of secular society on ... issues ... such as abortion"], if they are honest, should admit that their ... advances in these debates have come not when they defeated the Catholic opposition in intellectual combat, but when their rivals left the field without a fight."

—Philip F. Lawler

"Secularists, who reject religion, should also look for signs of secular fundamentalism [such as their unscientific belief that whatever banged (a virtually unimaginable outpouring of matter and energy from a mere speck) or got banged in the original big bang somehow managed to pop itself into existence from void or nothingness, or else somehow managed to maintain itself so that it was never non-existent], which is often as stridently bigoted about religion as some forms of religion are about secularism. In its own brief history, secularism has also had its disasters: Hitler, Stalin, and Saddam Hussein show that a militant exclusion of religion from public policy can be as lethal as any pious crusade."

—Karen Armstrong

"Life in this day and age is cheaper than a piece of meat in the meat market. People will haggle over the cost of steak more than they will consider the worth of a human life."

—Judge Earl Strayhorn

"With each different criterion of personhood, a different set of beings is welcomed [or turned away at]...the gates of others regards...The one over there says that some [unborn] human babies are persons, but only if their mothers [want them].

"Denial of the *imago Dei* is something new, and much more dangerous than a simple return to paganism...This puts such a strain...on moral knowledge that justice flips upside down. Refusing to learn, they finally distort even what they already know."

—*Budziszewski supra,* at p. 73–74

"Everything turns away–Quite leisurely from the disaster."

—W.H. Auden

"Over and over and over again, the Synoptic Gospels show us how he valued every individual...as unique and irreplaceable."

—Gerald O' Collins

"When God creates, he creates out of love for the creature; his purpose is that the intelligent creature should share in some way or other in his own joy."

—Roch A. Kereszty, *Jesus Christ: Fundamentals of Christology*, 449 (revised ed., 2002)

"Our Lord Jesus Christ, the Word of God, from out of his boundless love, became what we are that he might make us what he himself is (*Divine*)."

—Irenaeus, *Adversus Haereses*

"[W]hile Christians should not ignore the claims of other religions, they should not play down or misrepresent their own claims about Jesus as universally present to mediate revelation and salvation everywhere. In my experience, adherents of other faiths find such dissimulation, even when adopted by Christians for 'the best of reasons,' dishonest and even disrespectful towards partners in inter-religious dialogue."

—Gerald O'Collins, *Christology, supra* at p. 350.

To claim that the religion of a crucified Jew condemned under a legitimate Roman tribunal was the absolute and universal religion for all humankind seemed as absurd an undertaking for sophisticated intellects at that time as it seems today. Undeterred, the Fathers explained that Christianity...

—*Kereszty, supra*, p. 438.

The public ministry of Jesus itself shows that even the teaching [and] the powerful deeds of the incarnate God were not enough to change the hearts of his audience. All that Jesus could achieve through his life was to unmask and provoke the power of evil in

both the leaders and the crowds of his people so that they crucified him in the name of religion and the defense of public order.

—Kereszty, supra, at p. 341.

"If they do not listen to Moses and the prophets, neither will
they be convinced even if someone rises from the dead."

—Luke 16:31

"We are, all of us, always just one chronic illness or one mortal
misfortune away from eternity."

—Mary Eberstadt

Philosopher: Friend, which is the more "wondrous" or the "more
unlikely to have occurred (or to occur)": (1) That from void or
nothingness, inanimate matter and life should have come into
existence in the first place (and think, here, outside of the void and
of nothingness because, almost by definition, there can be no mystery in void and nothingness), or (2) that inanimate matter and life
having come, and then having passed away, should come again?

Friend: I will say number (1); and I say so because, while there
is a kind of partial precedent for number 2, number 1 is, by definition, unprecedented.

Philosopher: Well, my friend, since (1) has occurred already,
then, are you not compelled to agree that it is not unreasonable to
believe that you may come again to live after you have passed away?

—Anonymous philosopher

"This Jesus God raised up, and of that we all are witnesses."

—Acts 2:32

"The first fact in the history of Christendom is a number of people who say they have seen the Resurrection. If they had died without making anyone else believe this "gospel," no gospels would ever have been written."

—C.S. Lewis, *Miracles* 149 (1947)


"The message which electrified the world of the first century was not "love your enemies," but "He is risen.""

—Ronald Knox, *Caliban in Grub Street* 113 (1930)


"By believing in the resurrection of Christ [*i.e.,* by believing that God's love for us is more powerful than sin and death,] we all imitate the faith of Abraham, who believed that God is able to bring forth life from his "dead" body and from the "dead" womb of Sarah (*Rm.* 4:17–25)."

—*Kereszty, supra,* at 185.


To see a foetus is to see an adult human being " in potentia." If that is the way that you see the world, then it is not awfully important to establish whether the foetus can be properly defined as human now. The exact moment at which we begin to be human is not determinative when one is thinking about the morality of abortion. We look at what God has created to be human. To look at a human being is to see someone who is destined for God. To see human beings as created, rather just as the accidental product of evolution, is to see beings who are made for more than we can say.

Timothy Radcliffe,
What Is the Point of Being Christian?, 127 (2005)

# NOTE TO THE READER

You don't need religion to kill *Roe v Wade* constitutionally, although some pro-*Roe* politicians use religion (in reverse) to shield *Roe*. *Side A* argues that supporting abortion-access contradicts Jesus Christ, the giver of "abundant life". *Side B* argues that the fetus unquestionably qualifies as a *5th* (*14th*) *Amendment* person. (Elsewhere, I have argued that the embryo qualifies equally: See www.parafferty.com: click on *Roe v Wade*, and scroll to pp. 236-239. And see the asterisk (*) note of *Side B*, infra at pp. 195-196.) The two arguments are laid side by side so people will quit confusing them.

Legal commentators are unanimous in rejecting the *Roe* opinion (the *Roe* majority justices' publicly stated basis for their decision); and the *Casey* opinions do not affirm *Roe's* reasoning and fundamental premises, or offer alternative premises. What, then, keeps *Roe* standing? Only these: (1) unreason, and (2) the clinging to precedent by five justices in *Casey*.[1]

The conduct of anti-*Roe* opinion, pro-*Roe* decision persons, in arguing alternative justifications for *Roe*, without calling for its reconsideration, undermines judicial accountability, [2] and shields from view this great scandal of *Roe* (and *Casey*): they are implicated in the destruction of fifty million or so constitutional persons.[3] I will prove this by documenting that there is every good reason to believe that our Founding Fathers, the signers of the *Declaration of Independence* and framers of our *Constitution* (and it's *5th Amendment* Due Process Clause: "no person [or human being] shall be...deprived of [his] life without due process of law") thought of the fetus as a human being no less than themselves and therefore entitled to the security for its life that the "rule of law" can provide.

It has been said that "Scripture is silent on abortion [to which can be added, say, on the Trinity, and on the morality of using the big bomb], and there is no theological basis for con-demning...abortion." Not true! To state something "implicitly" is not to be silent, and so says John Paul II, in his <u>Evangelium Vitae</u> (*cap.* III, no. 61, 1995): "The texts of *Sacred Scripture*... show such great respect for the human being in the mother's womb that they require as a logical consequence that God's com-mandment 'you shall not kill' be extended to the unborn child". God is not silent here: "Even if a mother could forget her unborn child, I will not forget you. I have carved you in the palm of my hand." *Isaiah* 49:15-16. Jewish thought recognized the unborn child as God's most precious gift and, therefore, the thought of aborting it would have been foreign to the Jewish mentality. Murphy-O'Connor, in his *Jesus and Paul* (2007), p.41, and citing *Jeremiah 1:5*: "Before I formed you in the womb, I knew you", observed: "from the late 6th century (bc), it became a common belief that the child in its mother's womb is formed by God as proof of his loving care". Laws of prohibition get on the books due to existing bad practices, not non-existent ones.

Abortion is the most divisive issue of our day. If Judeo-Christian thought has nothing to say on this subject, then it must be true also that Jesus Christ (the very Word of God) and the Holy Spirit, are not relevant to our times. But it is not true: "Lo, I am with you always, to the close of the age" (*Mt. 28:20*); and *John* 14:16-17: "I will ask the Father and he will give you another advocate to dwell with you forever, the Spirit of truth." The Church's Living Tradition serves as the best theological basis for the condemnation of abortion. (<u>See</u>, <u>supra</u>, p. 9.)

The "Consistent Ethic of Life" principle seems to be employed chiefly as a means of separating its proponents from "pro-lifers" - portrayed in the media as narrow-minded. So, many Catholics, not wanting to be seen as narrow-minded, sup-press their outrage over abortion and, thereby, fail to act as wit-nesses to the "Gospel of Life". Great praise is heaped upon the City of Hope for its single-mindedness of purpose in fighting "only" cancer. Yet, no one would say that the City of Hope is acting narrow-mindedly in (just) fighting cancer, and not also the many other deadly human diseases.

# PREFACE

"The worst thing about…sloganeering is that it obscures, rather than clarifies, the facts of a situation".

—Michael Hiltzik

Here is the slogan of pro-*Roe*, Catholic politicians: "Because I am a committed Catholic, I am personally opposed to abortion; but being also a person of humility, I will not impose this religious belief on those persons who, in our pluralistic society, do not hold to that belief." I propose to demonstrate that this slogan, while politically expedient (and while fawned over by the information media and by the intellectual and academic communities), is wholly unsound morally speaking, theologically speaking, and constitutionally speaking.

Let us look at what these pro-*Roe* Catholic politicians are in effect saying (assuming, of course, they are being sincere – which I seriously doubt): What the Church says is indeed true: before our very eyes a pogrom — a holocaust against unborn children in the wombs of their mothers is occurring: a wholesale, massive slaughter of utterly defenseless human beings. Notwithstanding that this is true, and with the heavy heart of Jesus Christ, not only are we not going to lift a hand in opposition to this slaughter, but we are going to do all that we can (such as supporting *Roe* and supporting access to "partial-birth" abortion) to see that, at least for the time being, it continues unabated.

Implicit in that slogan are these three presuppositions: (1) Religion or religious belief has a monopoly on all that can be said and done in opposition to abortion or access to abortion, (2) "intentionally" supporting access to abortion is reconcilable to the Living Christ and Author of Life, and (3) *Roe* is constitutionally sound, and therefore, the human fetus, alive in the womb of his or her mother, is properly not recognized as a person within the meaning of the due process clauses in the Fifth and Fourteenth Amendments. I will explode to "kingdom come" these three (3) presuppositions. More specifically, I hope to demonstrate (1) that Christ, beginning at his "virginal conception" by the Holy Spirit, "is in solidarity or is one with" the conceived unborn always and in all ways, and (2), the post-embryonic human fetus, whether or not it can be proved to be a human being, unquestionably qualifies as a constitutional person.

I hope to demonstrate also that the supports for the foregoing slogan consist of nothing more than intellectual confusion (across the entire intellectual spectrum), and militant, anti-religious prejudice. No reasonable person would maintain that to argue that the principle of the inviolability of a human being should apply without exception to every human being, would be to argue from a view-point on which religion has a monopoly. And if that is true, then it constitutes pure anti-religious bigotry to argue that the extending of that principle to children in the wombs of their mothers (whether or not they are in truth human beings) would reflect what can be considered only as a religious viewpoint. As related by Philip Lawler:

> As the leading abortionist Bernard Nathanson would reveal after his dramatic conversion to the pro-life cause and the Catholic Church, strategists for the abortion lobby deliberately cultivated the notion that all public opposition to abortion was guided by the Catholic Church. The belief that a fetus is an unborn child, they argued, was based on a Catholic theological tenet, which non-Catholics could not be expected to accept. This argument *should* have been recognized immediately as a fraud. The humanity of a fetus is not a matter of theological speculation; it can be established by scientific tests. And opposition to abortion was never exclusively a Catholic affair.[1]

*Side A* offers a Christ-centered, biblically and theologically based argument against the position of the committed Catholic believer who impliedly maintains that his or her directly intended support for abortion access can be reconciled to the living Christ and Author of life. So, several of the authorities on which I will rely (mainly, Scripture and works on Christology), are not the traditional ones (which I accept fully), such as the Church fathers (and theologians), encyclicals, canons, and the *Catechism*. "Vatican II called for a renewal of moral theology to make it more personalistic, Scripture-based, and Christ-centered."[2] There has been, in my opinion, noncompliance by Catholic theologians with this Vatican II call on the question of the morality of committed, Catholic politicians supporting *Roe* and access to abortion. So, *Side A*, represents my offering to that question in response to this Vatican call.

The argument presented here is, of course, virtually wholly applicable to the non-Catholic, committed Christian believer who maintains this same position. And yes, this is precisely what I am arguing: being a committed Christian and "intentionally" supporting abortion access are always, and in all ways, mutually exclusive. This is particularly true, because, as I hope to demonstrate, Jesus Christ "is one with unborn children in the wombs of their mothers."[3] And if He is so, then "deliberated" abortion is, in no uncertain terms, a knife-stab into the very heart of Christ. But I will be even more to the point:

> The human person ... [is] created through the sharing of the love of God the Father. The Holy Spirit ... [makes] this love dwell in the person, imprinting the image of the Son. In fact, the Fathers of the Church say that we ... [are] created "in the Son." The creation of humanity [*i.e.*, of each and every human being] is thus the work of the love of the Three in One. Redemption itself is an act of the same love. It enables us to share in the full realization of God's love in the form of Christ, to the point of the fullness of our relationship as children of God, which is realized in communion with our brothers and sisters, among persons who live relationships as brothers and sisters because they are sons and daughters who, in Christ, turn to the Father.[4]

Given the truth of what is contained in the foregoing quote, then I say that no committed Christian mind can conceive of a greater heresy than that of a committed Christian believer maintaining that the practice of abortion (or the supporting of access to the same) is acceptable to Christ (the Author of Life and Conqueror of the domination of the human heart by the power of intrinsic evil). To maintain so, is to maintain that the Son is at war not only with His Church (which, from day one of its existence, has "continuously" and "consistently" taught that freely-induced abortion is always and everywhere a grave intrinsic evil, and therefore is never permissible, and can never be given direct or intended support), but also with His Father, and therefore is to maintain also that the Holy Spirit (whose mark is the love that proceeds from the Father to the Son and from the Son to the Father) is in truth a spirit of alienation and annihilation. From the perspective of the Magisterium, the Church's teaching on freely-induced abortion is considered no less inspired by the Holy Spirit than is the canon of inspired scripture.[5]

This means that a reader who lays no claim on making a sincere effort at being a "committed" Christian believer may as well skip *Side A* and go directly to *Side B*.

In *Side A*, I hope to demonstrate that pro-*Roe*, Catholic politicians are doing nothing less than encouraging the practice of (militant) anti-Catholic bigotry (by falsely implying that religion has a monopoly on all that can be said in opposition to abortion), and hiding behind their Catholic faith (instead of offering it as a light for the world). It may also be the case that they are unknowingly counter-witnessing God's gift of life to men as well as the purpose of the incarnation, passion, and resurrection of Jesus Christ as related in *Jn. 10:10*: "I came so that they may have life, and have it more abundantly", i.e., that they may have eternal life or live divinely or share in divine life. (Who can be safely excluded from John's "they"?)

President Obama can be reasonably said to be radically committed to upholding *Roe v. Wade*. This is particularly true because he has publicly committed himself to nominating to the United States Supreme Court only persons committed to upholding *Roe*. However, as long as a committed Christian who voted for Obama for President, did not do so because of Obama's radical pro-abortion-access position, then it cannot be said that such a person who voted so, thereby, "intentionally" supported (compelled) access to abortion. So, nothing in *Side A* is meant to apply to the committed Christian who voted for Obama but did not do so because of Obama's radical, pro-abortion-access position.[6]

In *Side B*, it will be demonstrated that pro-*Roe*, Catholic politicians are backing naked judicial tyranny or rule by men (instead of "by the rule of law"). It will be demonstrated also that in its *Roe opinion* the Court perpetrated a fraud on our constitutional community; and that — and contrary to the opinion in *Roe* — there is no question that the "formed" (post-embryonic) human fetus, living inside his or her mother's womb, qualifies as a person within the meaning of the due process clauses in the Fifth and Fourteenth Amendments.

The *Side B* arguments on "judicial fraud" and "judicial tyranny" are being put forth mainly to justifiably shame the United States Supreme Court into reconsidering *Roe v. Wade*, so that the issue, of whether the human fetus (alive in the womb of his mother) qualifies as a constitutionally recognized person, can be reconsidered.

To its everlasting disgrace, the *Roe* Court, in the course of holding that the human fetus, alive in his mother's womb, has no due process-guaranteed right not to be killed at the direction of his mother, failed to provide the human fetus with a due process-mandated, meaningful opportunity to be heard on the question of whether or not he or she qualifies as a Fourteenth Amendment, due process clause person. Roe's fetus in *Roe* was provided neither with a *guardian ad litem* nor with an attorney. *Roe's* fetus, who was incapable of defending himself or herself, was totally unrepresented in *Roe*. And this appears also to have been the case in all of the legal proceedings that culminated in the decision of *Roe v. Wade*.

The perspective of *Side B*, then, is that of an attorney arguing his client's position before the United States Supreme Court. *Side B* then, is not at all about discussing or debating or presenting a so-called balanced view on the legitimacy of *Roe's* fetal non-person holding. Rational discussion, here, is no longer possible (if it ever was possible). Also, pro-*Roe* advocates have no interest in debating an issue on which they have already won.[7]

*Side B* is an "argument" demonstrating that there is no question that the post-embryonic, human fetus (alive in the womb of his mother) is a person within the meaning of the due process clauses in the Fifth and Fourteenth Amendments. So, I am not concerned that many experts on constitutional law may disagree with such an argument. I would simply put these two questions to these experts: (1) What I want to know is whether you can demonstrate that my argument is seriously flawed in any material respect; and (2), if you cannot demonstrate so, then what, specifically, keeps you from accepting the argument?

Here is a final note to the reader regarding *Side A* and *Side B*: They absolutely do "not" presuppose or assume, and do "not" argue that, as a matter of fact, the formed (post-embryonic) human fetus, alive in the womb of his mother, is a human being. This, simply, cannot be conclusively proved. And because my opponent in argument does not accept the same as fact, and because I cannot prove this fact, then I chose to follow Aquinas: "If one chooses to argue a point with an opponent, then he must argue on his opponent's grounds, and not on his own grounds." (In any event, "review of law courts" such as the Supreme Court sitting in Roe v. Wade, and as distinguished from "trial courts," lack absolutely the jurisdiction to decide "disputed" questions of fact. But see www.parafferty.com: click on *Roe v. Wade* and scroll to pp. 250-276.)

The foregoing, of course, does not govern the constitutional legitimacy of state action. The Court, in *Marshall v. United States*

(1974), stated: "When Congress undertakes to act in areas fraught with medical or scientific uncertainties legislative options must be especially broad. The Court, in *Paris Adult Theater I v. Slaton* (1973), observed: "We do not demand of Legislatures 'scientifically certain criteria of legislation'"; and: "Nothing in the Constitution prohibits a state from reaching [, say,] ... [the] conclusion [that obscene materials have a tendency to debase society and to produce anti-social behavior], and acting on it legislatively simply because there is no conclusive evidence or empirical data."[8] The Court, in *Jacobson v. Massachusetts* (1905), in rejecting a personal liberty, due process challenge to a Massachusetts statute making smallpox vaccination compulsory, remarked:

> The legislature of Massachusetts was not unaware of these opposing theories [the then theory that smallpox vaccination is a preventative of smallpox, versus the then theory that smallpox vaccination does not serve as a preventive, and may even cause smallpox or other diseases to occur in the body], and was compelled ... to choose between them ....It is no part of the function of a court ... to determine which one of two modes was likely to be most effective for the protection of the public against disease. That was for the legislative department to determine ...
>
> ....The state legislature proceeded upon the theory which recognized vaccination as at least as effective, if not the best known way in which to meet and suppress the evils of a smallpox epidemic that imperiled an entire population. Upon what sound principles as to the relations existing between the different departments of government can the court review this action of the legislature? If there is any such power in the judiciary to review legislative action in respect of a matter affecting the general welfare, it can only be when that which the legislature has done comes within the rule that, if a statute purporting to have been enacted to protect the public health, the public morals, or the public safety, has no real or substantial relation to those objects, or is, beyond all question, a plain, palpable invasion of rights

secured by the fundamental law, it is the duty of the courts to so adjudge, and thereby give effect to the Constitution.[9]

The reader may be wondering about all the appendices in my book. They contain mainly unpublished (and heretofore, virtually unknown) abortion prosecutions at the English common law. (Many of them were translated from the Latin by Sir John H. Baker, arguably England's greatest scholar of English legal history.) These cases (and those in my earlier work: Roe v. Wade: The Birth of a Constitutional Right (1992): available online for free at www.parafferty.com; click on Roe v. Wade, and scroll to pp. 461-765) squarely, and authoritatively, refute absolutely, *Roe's* fundamental premise that under the English common law a woman enjoyed the right to do away with her unborn child. (They are keyed, for the most part, to the text of *Side B* accompanying notes 15-18, as well as those notes.) It was chiefly from this utterly false, fundamental premise that the *Roe* Court drew the conclusions that (1) a woman's right to an abortion qualifies as a fundamental right, "constitutionally speaking", and (2) that the unborn human fetus or child, alive in the womb of his mother, does not qualify as a person within the meaning of the Fourteenth (Fifth) Amendment due process clause.[10] And as observed by Justice Stevens: "the Court 'has not hesitated to overrule [its own] decisions [*stare decisis* notwithstanding] ..., where scholarship ... [has] demonstrated that their fundamental premises were not to be found [neither explicitly nor implicitly] in the Constitution'."[11]

If one compares what I write on (as well as the case authority, etc., which I cite in support of what I write on this subject) the history of the prosecution of abortion and unborn child-killing at the English common law to what Professor P. Mueller has to say on this subject (see his The Criminalization of Abortion in the West, pp. 12-13, 15, 18 & 134-148 [2012]: where in essence he argues that all such criminal prosecutions ceased by approximately 1348), then all reasonable and unbiased persons should conclude that the good Professor Mueller is a writer of legal fables, and may very well be the reincarnation of Cyril Means Jr. (See, infra, Unraveling at pp. 149-150, 206-209.)

My contention is no more than that around 1600, the child killed in its mother's womb (in contrast to the child that died from the in-womb killing act "after" being brought forth alive – which remained a capital felony: see Q v. West (1848), infra at p. 125) ceased to qualify as a victim of common law homicide (but said in-womb killing continued to be prosecuted as a very serious-but lesser crime) "only" because Bourton's Case (1326/7) was so fundamentally misinterpreted by leading English legal authorities, such as Staunford (d. 1558) and Coke (d. 1634). (See, infra, Unraveling at pp. 105-108 & 126-149.) Mueller has a certain theory of how a certain thing in legal history occurred in the West. What I have written explodes that theory – at least in reference to English common law. Unwilling to re-examine the validity of his theory as applied to English Law, he proceeds to re-write what I have written so that the exploding bomb I put to his theory actually becomes a small puff of wind pushing forward *his* theory. He writes (Mueller, supra at p.146): "Rafferty tried to prove that the eventual refusal of the common law to grant criminal protection to unborn human life did not come about until publication of Staunford's Treatise in 1557".

In the course of joining in the Court's majority and concurring opinions in *Washington v. Glucksberg* (1997), 521 U.S. 702, which holds that there is "no" constitutional right of an individual to physician-assisted suicide, Justice O'Connor stated: "'our Nation's history, legal traditions, and practices, do not support the existence of such a right.' [Therefore], I join the Court's [majority and concurring] opinions."[12] In *Side B*, it will be demonstrated beyond all reasonable doubt that not only do "our Nation's history, legal traditions, and practices" not support the existence of a woman's right to a physician performed abortion, but do in fact support the right of a woman's unborn fetus or child not to be aborted.

# SIDE A: ABORTION AND THE PRESENCE OF THE LIVING CHRIST AND AUTHOR OF LIFE

"The raising of Lazarus is the crowning *sign* that reveals Jesus to be *the* Life giver ('ubi Christus, ibi resurrection et vita')".

—Gerald O'Collins

"Christ died for all men without exception. There is not [now], never has been, and never will be a single human being for whom Christ did not suffer [and die].'"

—Mary Healy, *The Gospel of Mark* 214 (2008)
(quoting Council of Quiercy, CCC 605)

"nothing in the Bible suggests that killing human fetuses is the equivalent of killing human beings."

—Sam Harris, *The End of Faith* 167

"Scripture is silent on abortion, and there is no theological basis for condemning or defending abortion."

—Garry Wills, *Head and Heart: American Christianities* 526 (2007)

"Abortion is atheism in action."

—Father James Morrow

"When Jesus speaks of God, he never speaks of God as dealing both life and death, but only as dealing life."

-Father Ronald Rolheiser

"In the matters of life and death we are partners with God."

-President Obama

If *Roe v. Wade* is constitutionally true (not to be confused with being morally true), then it would be immoral for a Catholic to *knowingly* say otherwise (and as distinguished from, say, urging that Roe be nullified via a constitutional amendment). A first principle of Catholic moral teaching is the acknowledgment of "what is true" regardless of wherever that truth may lead: "There is nothing more profound in the life of the intellect than our eagerness to know, without tepidity and without fear, under conditions of a certitude totally determined by the power of truth." The truth of the matter is, however, the *Roe* decision is as far from being constitutionally true as is north from south.[1]

I know of no way to begin to be childlike and "to live as a son in the Son" other than to think that the person (and "a" person is always a singularity), the pre-incarnate Son of God, is so filled with ecstatic and vibrant joy by the beauty in the love that he receives from his Father (God being overwhelmed by God, so to speak), that he will not be still at the thought that a single human being (beginning with Adam and extending to all his descendants) might miss out on being loved so by his Father. And when he put on hold his beatific relationship with his Father, and became (and remains) a human being – but not a human person – since he already is a person, albeit a divine one (see infra, endnote 3 (p.173) of Preface), he did not flinch:

> Jesus enters into Satan's territory... to begin his campaign against the powers of evil. He is looking for a fight! Yet he will confront Satan not with a blast of divine lightning, but in his frail human nature, empowered by the Spirit.[2]

In *Jn. 17:3* Christ puts "eternal life" as "knowing" the Father, and Himself who the Father sends to human beings. The only way to really know another person is to be in an intimate relationship with that person. Benedict XVI observed: "friendship, true knowledge of the other person, needs closeness and indeed, to a certain extent, lives on it….Jesus chose the Twelve primarily 'to be with him'; that is, to share in his life and learn directly from him…who he really was."[3] Henry Wansbrough, general editor of *The New Jerusalem Bible* and a member of the Pontifical Biblical Commission, observed:

> Revelation… [can be] seen as a divine act of self-revelation, God's own self-disclosure, made not only to the mind but also to the heart. It is therefore God's self-giving, for in biblical language to 'know' is used of a warm and personal relationship….So, the revelation in scripture is the offering or communication of a person, the self-giving of a person, demanding a response in faith. God in his great love speaks to humankind as friends and enters into their life, so as to invite and receive them into relationship with himself.[4]

"Eternal life", then, means to be in a profoundly intimate relationship of life-enhancing "friendship" with the Trinitarian God (and all of their beloved).

The word "profound" hardly suffices to describe such a relationship because God, who before or at least until Christ was well into his public ministry could be thought of only as "Other", now is known as he really is. Arguably, then, a human being in such a relationship receives an ability or capacity for exercising a new way of knowing or relating, and by which way of knowing, he is able to participate in the very inner life of the Trinity.[5] Add to this human being (who possesses a "new way of knowing") a new or glorified body, i.e., a body that can manifest itself as physical, and that is impervious to the laws of physics, and to space, time, and non-existence, *etc.* The Gospels relate that after his resurrection, and before his ascension (and even after it in

Paul's case), Christ appeared or became perceptible to some of his disciples and disappeared at will.[6]

Now, assuming, without conceding, that the human fetus is "not" yet a human being, then, arguably the human fetus is to a human being what a human being is to his resurrected self, in which case, from the perspective of our ultimate or complete being, both the human fetus and the human being are not yet complete. No reasonable person would argue that a human being may be killed because it has yet to receive its future being. Yet, it is argued that a human fetus may be killed because it has not yet received the being that makes it a human being. And the irony here is that while the human being who is killed can continue towards resurrection and eternal life, that might not be the case for the aborted human fetus if, in fact, it is not yet a human being. So arguably, abortion has far greater adverse consequences than the deliberated killing of a human being because the aborted human fetus is deprived of the opportunity to "live divinely," which is the hope of every Christian: "We are promised... eternal life" [a sharing in] the inner life of God as our own... end [and]... the primary purpose of creation in the first place." So, if our conception and our final or resurrected state are "intimately connected", then does not intended abortion, in effect, attempt to sever this intimate connection?[7]

Pro-*Roe* Catholic politicians are, in effect and in the name of Jesus Christ, supporting the denial to another of what - eternal life in Jesus Christ - they would not think of denying to themselves. It is literally impossible to be more anti-Christ than that.

It is not being implied that if in truth the aborted human embryo or fetus is not a human being, then one cannot hope that God will preserve it for "eternal life." "Nothing is impossible for God." (I am thinking of spontaneous abortions, miscarriages, and the post-abortion-awakened conscience.) Also, and outside of human freedom (with which God does not compete out of his respect for the integrity of the human person), God's "eternal life" plan for man (which includes each and every individual human being who has "ever" lived and "will" live) will not be thwarted by man. Nevertheless, no person should test the loving kindness and generosity of God.[8] More importantly, God's gift of human freedom and responsibility should not be thrown back in his face.

I know that when the words or thoughts contained in *Jn.10:10* were originally conveyed to the witnesses to faith in Jesus Christ, it would not have entered into the thinking of *any* of those witnesses that Christ or John had in mind here (and I have no reason to think that Christ or John had this in mind), also the "conceived unborn," if only for the reason that it would not have entered into the mind of a "then" Jew or Christian to contemplate even having or bringing on an abortion. Then Jewish sensibility "saw every historical or natural event in terms of faithfulness or unfaithfulness to God." The Jews viewed the conception and birth of a child as signaling God's favor and childlessness as signaling God's punishment for sinfulness and unfaithfulness. Yet, suppose that a hearer of *Jn.10:10*, upon hearing Christ (or John) speak so, asked Christ (or John) if his "they" would include children in the wombs of their mothers. How would Christ (or John) have answered? I say he would have most certainly answered: "Yes." Since Jesus Christ is of the same mind of God (He and His Father are one), then Jesus Christ knows the unborn child in the womb of his mother, as God knows this child, *i.e.*, He knows more than any other human being, that His Father's act or process of creating a particular child is his Father's, and our Father's, act of communicating or sharing his very self with another. And God does not act against or work against himself. *And see* Jesus' *Jerusalem Lament* in *Luke 19:44*: "They will smash you to the ground and your children within you"; and this from *Jn.16:21*: "When a woman is in labor, she has pain because her hour has come. But when her child is born, she no longer remembers her anguish because of her joy [and God's joy] of having brought a human being into the world." *And see* also *Luke 1:15*: John "will be filled with the [prophetic] Holy Spirit even from [*i.e.*, while in] his mother's womb" (and as read in conjunction with *Luke 1:41*: "When Elizabeth heard Mary's greeting, the infant [John] leaped in her womb").[9] And as noted by Murphy O'Connor: "After [i.e., after approximately the latter part of the 6th century B.C.] *Jeremiah* [1:5: "Before I formed you in the womb I knew you."], it became a common belief that the young child in its mother's womb is formed by God as proof of his loving care (*e.g., Ps. 139:13; Job 10:8-9*)."[10]

Given (1) that Christ is all about all of life (always and in all ways), (2) that "relationship" gives and enhances life, (3) that abortion turns away life and relationship, and (4) that *Jn.10:10* turns towards life, and then carries it to "abundant life", then I am not convinced that I am citing "out of context". Before any human fetus came into existence it was an "eternally" unique thought of God (and which demonstrates, of course, that in the case of either intended support for access to abortion or the acceptance of deliberated abortion, one's thoughts here are not God's thoughts): "Long ago, even before he made the world, God chose us to be his very own through what Christ would do for us."[11]

The generic "they" in *Jn. 10:10* certainly would include generations of human beings (such as me and you) not yet then conceived in their mothers' wombs, if not also the "then already dead", such as Abraham, John the Baptist, and John and Mary Caveman. So, how is that the "they" would include the "then living" and dead, as well as "those not yet conceived", but not "those conceived but not yet born"? It doesn't make sense to exclude the conceived unborn, particularly given the good prospect of being born alive, since, and as will be established, abortion was out of the question.

The Judeo-Christian God is "a hands-on person." So, why do we often prefer to view God's act or process of creating a human being, which always springs from love — which is always personal and particular to the thing He loves - and, therefore, is "never" happpenstance, as being performed by a sort of "remote-control process"? God's Providence is always personal and intimate. "It is a premise of [the Christian] faith in the living God that God is at work in every circumstance [including his or her creation] of every person's life…, in the joys and sorrows, the pains and pleasures, the fears and frustrations of everyday life".[12]

A person "could object that…[the words in *Jn. 10:10*] are actually John's words, later developments of faith, and that they are not really from Jesus. But this is precisely the point. They are, in fact, the words of Jesus, certainly of the risen Jesus who now lives and speaks (in the) Spirit; they come from the same identical Jesus of Nazareth."[13]

The *Gospel of John* probably dates to around C.90-100 A.D. The *Didache* (or *Teaching of the Apostles*) dates to around C.50-100 A.D. Chapter 2 of the latter work states in part: you shall not murder a child by abortion, or commit infanticide.[14]

Considered as a whole, and in light of the *New Testament*, the *Old Testament* relates God's patient work of restoring into the being of every human being "His Image".[15] The process of human gestation is God's act of engaging in or of being "actively present" to the process of creating a new human being in his Image.[16] (If He were not active or present, then His Image could not hit its mark.) So, by what *Old Testament* precept can man justify appropriating to himself (and then destroying by abortion) what God is in the act of creating?[17]

The English translation of the *Septuagint* or *Greek* version of *Exodus 21:22-23* reads so:

> And if two men strive and smite a woman with child, and her child be born imperfectly formed [i.e., not yet formed into a recognizable human body and, therefore, not yet informed with a human or rational soul], he shall be forced to pay a penalty: as the woman's husband may lay upon him, he shall pay with a valuation. But if he be perfectly formed [i.e., organized into a human body and, therefore, also informed with a human or rational soul], he shall give life for life.[18]

Protestant minister and Harvard College President (from 1654-72) Charles Chauncy, in commenting on the Hebrew version of *Ex. 21:22-23*, observed:

In concluding punishments from the judicial law of Moses that is perpetual, we must often proceed by analogical proportion and interpretation, as *a paribus similibus, minore ad majus etc.* [roughly: by analogical comparison, proof of a lesser necessarily proves its greater: for e.g., if it is wrong to cause the destruction of an unborn child by an act of negligence, then, how much more so is it wrong to deliberately destroy an unborn child]; for there will still fall out some cases, in every commonwealth, which are not in so many words extant in Holy Writ, yet the substance of the matter in every kind (I conceive under correction) may be drawn and concluded out of the Scripture by good consequence of an equivalent nature. As, for example, there is no express law against destroying conception in the womb by potions, yet by analogy with *Exodus* xxi. 22, 23, we may reason that life is to be given for life.[19]

And, as observed by Rodney Stark in his *The Rise of Christianity* (1996):

From the start, Christian doctrine absolutely prohibited abortion and infanticide, classifying both as murder. These Christian prohibitions reflected the Jewish origins of the movement. Among Jews, according to Josephus: "The law, moreover, enjoins us to bring up our offspring, and forbids women to cause abortion of what is begotten, or to destroy it afterward; and if any woman appears to have done so, she will be a murderer of her child" [Josephus, Flavius, *The Complete Works*] (1960 ed. [p.632 at *Against Apion*, book 2, para. 25; 1998 *Wm. Whiston* edition at p.966, para. 24]). In similar fashion, the Alexandrian Jewish writing known as the *Sentences of Pseudo-Phocylides* [before 100 C.E.] advised: "A woman should not destroy the unborn babe in her belly, nor after its birth throw it before dogs and vultures as prey" (quoted in [Michael J.] Gorman [*Abortion & the Early Church,*] 1982:37).[20]

Currently, it is popular to attack religious bodies for their past bad practices. For example, law professor, Bruce J. Einhorn, in his *Holy Terror*, decries the many pogroms carried out under the auspices of a state-recognized religion (or at least without protest from the religious leaders or those in the know of the particular religion), with particular examples being Judaism and Christianity: "The people of the Book — of the Ten Commandments [and] Gospel…were no different in making the earth scream with the blood of the decimated."[21]

Yet, when religious bodies actively protest against abortion as a pogrom against the conceived unborn, they are told to keep their religious views to themselves.

The Church never has held as a doctrine of faith or morals that the human fetus is a human being. The Church knows full well that the pure question "when does a human being begin its existence as the same" is no more a religious or moral question (or a question of conscience) than is the question of whether life exists elsewhere in the universe. As is stated in the *Encyclopedia of Theology: The Concise Sacramentum Mundi* (1982): "The question as to the exact moment of the animation [or rational ensoulment] of the human embryo has not been decided by the magisterium of the Church."[22]

In a real sense, to maintain that religious belief has a monopoly on all that can be said in opposition to abortion contradicts scientific thinking. As is stated in *Van Nostrand's Scientific Encyclopedia*:

> The creation of an embryo and development of a fetus and finally the birth of an infant is a continuous physiological process commencing with conception and ending with the cutting of the umbilical cord. It is not in any way a digital, step-wise process with distinct periods ….
>
> Only for convenience in studying and teaching are certain rather fuzzily defined phases or stages of embryo and fetus development identified and given names …The embryo and later the fetus is an individual entity, imbued with individ-

ualistic qualities [genes] which affects its rate of progress, much as later the progress of the infant to a mature adult will be determined by individualistic qualities.

From a purely scientific standpoint, there is no question but that abortion represents the cessation of human life.[23]

Rudy Giuliani, while campaigning for the Republican presidential nomination in 2008, and upon hearing that Archbishop Raymond Burke would deny him Holy Communion because of his support for abortion rights, gave these replies: "There's freedom of religion in this country"; and, "how I practice my Catholic faith is between me and my priest."[24]

The "practice" of Catholicism is not a private matter. It is meant to serve as a light for the world. Father Walter Burghardt (d. Feb. 16, 2008) has observed: " 'Catholic social teaching [is] simply the church spelling out the second great commandment of love. The social dimension of the Gospel must be preached…because there is no such thing in Christianity as a privatized, me-and-Jesus spirituality'."[25] Secondly, the magisterium or teaching authority of the Church trumps any contrary authority of Giuliani's priest (although it is highly doubtful that any such priest exists here). Thirdly, only a person drowning in anti-Catholic bigotry and profoundly ignorant of constitutional law (and Giuliani is neither) would seriously maintain that under the First Amendment's religious freedom clause Archbishop Burke could be compelled to administer Holy Communion to Giuliani, or could be enjoined from excommunicating him.

Giuliani makes such statements, not because he believes them to be true, but only because he knows that it would not enter the minds of the members of the information media to challenge or question him on the truth of such statements. Also, such statements tend to demonstrate that Giuliani has an extremely low opinion of the mental capacities of the voting public.

The kindest thing that the Church can say here about Giuliani (as well as every other pro-*Roe* Catholic politician), is that if they are sincere, then their consciences are immature or not well-formed: "When concerning areas or realities that involve fundamental ethical duties - legislative or political choices contrary to Church principles and values are proposed or made, the Magisterium teaches that a well formed conscience does not permit one to vote for a political program or an individual law which contradicts the fundamental contents of faith and morals".[26]

It may very well be the case that Catholic bishops are scandalizing pro-life Catholics in not having put a hot poker to the Guilianis, Kerrys, Cuomos and Pelosis, etc. Raymond Cardinal Burke, in his *Divine Love Made Flesh* 177 (2012) observes: "We are witnesses to the scandal caused by Catholic politicians who present themselves to receive Holy Communion and, at the same time…support legislation…which permits procured abortion. Regarding such situations, the Holy Father declares plainly: 'There is an objective connection here with the Eucharist (citing 1 Cor. 11:27-29)'. The Holy Father reminds bishops of their duty to reaffirm the relationship of the Eucharist to the moral life, especially for those who have responsibility for the common good. For bishops to do less constitutes a failure to shepherd the flock entrusted into their care."

From its inception the Church has continuously condemned deliberated abortion as one of the worst crimes that a human being can commit or aid. Catholic bishops, then, should be doing far more than simply blowing hot air at these pro-Roe, Catholic politicians. At the very least, the bishops should set forth fully, clearly, and precisely why they are giving these Catholic politicians a pass. Putting this another way, the Catholic faithful should not be left at sea in trying to understand how this inaction by their bishops is somehow reconcilable to the absolute duty of the bishops to provide the faithful with "militant" moral leadership. And this seems particularly true since the Catholic woman who undergoes an induced abortion incurs an excommunication under canon law. By way of analogy, Mary Healy, in her *The Gospel of Mark* (2008), observed:

John recognized that the behavior of political leaders had a powerful impact on the moral environment of the country at large. The Herodian scandal would dull the consciences of the people and put obstacles in the way of the "straight path" God was preparing for the Messiah (1:3). Like the prophets of old, John was willing to risk his life for his message.[27]

The bishops should know that no provision of our Constitution prohibits either an executive officer or legislative officer from signing or not signing a bill or voting for or against a certain bill because of his or her religious convictions. This is true not only because there is no constitutional duty or legal requirement for a legislator to explain why he or she voted a certain way or why a governor or president signed or vetoed a bill, but because what matters here is legislative purpose, and not legislative motive. The Court in *Westside Community Schools v. Mergens* (1990), observed: "Even if some legislators were motivated by a conviction that religious speech in particular was valuable and worthy of protection, that alone would not invalidate the act, because what is relevant is the legislative *purpose* of the statute, not the possibly religious motives of the legislators who enacted the law."[28]

Pro-choice proponents should be very grateful indeed that the motivation card cannot be played, for it would certainly cause them to fold. As related by Paul Kengor:

> "This [i.e., the expedited FDA approval process for the RU-486 abortion pill] had been a longtime goal of abortion advocates like Ron Weddington, who with his wife, Sarah Weddington, had presented "Jane Roe" to the Supreme Court. Ron Weddington sent a four-page letter to President Clinton, urging: "I don't think you are going to go very far in reforming the country until we have a better educated, healthier, wealthier population". The new president could "start immediately to eliminate the barely educated, unhealthy and poor segment". "No, I'm not advocating some sort of mass extinction of these unfortunate people", wrote

Weddington. "The problem is that their numbers are not only not replaced but increased by the birth of millions of babies to people who can't afford to have babies. There, I've said it. It's what we all know is true, but we only whisper it." By "we" Weddington said he meant "liberals" like himself and the Clintons.[29]

In the course of the final two presidential 2004 debates, Senator John Kerry stated that it would violate the 1st Amendment's prohibition against governmental enactment of an "exclusively" religious belief by voting his Catholic anti-abortion belief, or otherwise acting against the *Roe*-compelled legalization of abortion.

If Kerry's position is constitutionally sound, then *Roe* is constitutionally immune from constitutional attack by virtue of the First Amendment. Kerry's position assumes that Catholic moral teaching (or religion in general) possesses a monopoly on all that can be said in opposition to abortion. (Of course, religion no more possesses a monopoly here, than does it possess a monopoly on stealing or killing.) This monopoly means that any argument, *etc.*, against *Roe* is necessarily religiously based, and is therefore automatically excluded from consideration by virtue of the First Amendment's prohibition of religion in government.

Such a position or argument proves too much. Atheism (or secularism, as the case may be), for purposes of the First Amendment, qualifies as the equivalent of a religion or religious belief. Now, atheism holds or believes or argues that any opposition to abortion access is religiously based. Therefore, and constitutionally speaking, such an argument is necessarily prohibited by the First Amendment's prohibition of religion in government, in this case, the religion of atheism.[30]

It is thought that Kerry mimicked thoughts expressed by Mario M. Cuomo in his September 13, 1984 address to the Department of Theology at the University of Notre Dame. Not true. Cuomo clearly and correctly relates that there is no First Amendment prohibition for a holder of a political office to vote his religious convictions. Cuomo simply states that such a person should not vote so, if the position at which his convictions are directed is not supported by a community consensus. He states: "Our public morality …, the moral standards we maintain for everyone … depends on a consensus view of right and wrong. The values derived from religious belief … should not be accepted as part of the public morality unless they are shared by the pluralistic community at large, by consensus".[31] Which "pluralistic community" has Cuomo in mind here: That of the State of New York, or perhaps Indiana, or perhaps the State of Texas in 1973 (when the *Roe* Court knocked Texas' criminal abortion statute - as well as those of virtually all of the other states - off the face of the earth), or the Federal Republic of the United States? If it is the latter, then Cuomo is surely very wrong.

One could refer Cuomo to (1) the Tenth Amendment, which provides in part for a qualified right of the people of each state to enjoy self-government, (2) to the principle that constitutional adjudication is not "the mere reflex of the popular opinion or passion of the day", and (3), to *Addington v. Texas* (1979): "The essence of federalism is that states must be free to develop a variety of solutions to problems and not be forced into a common, uniform mold."[32] Notwithstanding what the *Roe* majority justices evidently believed to be the case, Supreme Court justices do not serve as our Nation's roving problem-solvers in the sky.[33]

The *Roe* Court, without so much as a "single dot" of recognizable constitutional interpretation or authority, humiliated the several states by shoving down their throats the compulsory legalization of physician-performed abortion. *Roe* is an assault upon federalism. It is "tyrannical uniformity" imposed upon the several states by lawless justices, who possessed no conviction that they held the Constitution "only" as a sacred trust. It is *Roe*, and only *Roe*, that has divided our Nation on the issue of access to abortion.

Cuomo would be undoubtedly surprised to learn that in *Lawrence v. Texas* (2003), the Court held (without identifying, and without demonstrating, the nature of and source of this individual right of freedom from the constraints of State imposed morality, and also without putting forth so much as a single dot of recognizable constitutional authority in support of this right) that the majority of citizens or residents of a state may not constitutionally enact into law its morality on a minority that does not accept the majority's morality. Putting this another way, a very ambitious *Lawrence* Court has outlawed public morality (and cured legal insanity in the process) under the guise of interpreting the Fourteenth Amendment liberty. (I say "under the guise of" because what is really going on here is a brand of "private judicial morality" overruling a brand of "public morality".)[34] Persons oblivious to their own moral ignorance, and over-inflated with a sense of their ability to think cleverly and impartially, and to effectuate desired social change, may harbor such an ambition. Sane judges and justices do not.[35]

A person of faith or a religious body (such as the Roman Catholic Church) has no less a First Amendment, free-speech right than, for example, the ACLU to advance constitutional arguments not grounded or dependent on doctrines, beliefs, or opinions on which religion has a monopoly. As *Side B* demonstrates, constitutional grounds for burying *Roe* exceed the farthest horizon.

John Farmer, Jr., has observed: "Anyone raised Roman Catholic in America in the past fifty years has had to confront this reality: The central tenets of his faith, if followed strictly, will leave him estranged from the culture of his daily life."[36] This is no real loss when compared to the loss of an utterly self-giving God who sets before us life and death, and then leads us to choose life[37] by living for others, and by engaging the culture of death.

Gerald O'Collins, in his *Jesus: A Portrait* (2008), observed:

> Deliverance from evil spirits features prominently in the ministry … of Jesus…. But how should we interpret this activity of Jesus in opposition to Satan? … Should we simply translate the *New Testament* language in terms of various forms of … mental ailments that hold people helplessly captive? Two recurrent experiences encourage me to continue

thinking that Jesus was engaged against personal powers of evil from which we need deliverance: First, the massively destructive and self-destructive folly of savage conflicts continues to hint at the existence and influence of invisible satanic evil that inspires the visible human protagonists.... Second ... [is how] "good" people ..., with the best of intentions, can be mysteriously led astray into doing [and supporting] things that are in fact evil.[38]

A good example here of a combination of the two foregoing "recurrent experiences" is: "committed" Christians supporting abortion access.

In my opinion, from the perspective of an alert, committed Catholic, the following observation serves as perhaps the greatest precedent (with the exception, of course, of the execution of God the Son) in support of the truthfulness of this proposition: humanity's capacity to deceive itself (or to be deceived) in the name of humanity transcends humanity:

> In 1933 Hitler promised peace between Church and state. Shortly after [in the same year, German Catholic] ... bishops agreed to allow Catholics to join the Nazi party. Nazi members could now attend services in uniform and be admitted to the sacraments. The statement of the bishops constituted a formal recognition of Nazism and of Catholic membership in the party which gave the Nazis a certain respectability.[39]

Almost, by definition, a committed Catholic cannot knowingly cooperate with intrinsic evil. The German bishops, in 1933, did not know that the Nazi Party was intrinsically evil. Pro-*Roe* *(committed)* Catholic politicians know that abortion is intrinsically evil. And they know this because their Church, on the authority and inspiration of the Holy Spirit, tells them as much. So, their moral culpability is infinitely more profound than that of the German bishops in 1933. And it may be that U.S. Catholic bishops, in not excluding pro-*Roe* Catholic politicians from the sacraments are giving to abortion an unwarranted, perceived respectability.

The Catholic Church, despite all the serious failings of its individual members (both lay and clerical), retains (as the sinless body of Jesus Christ) the promise of the Holy Spirit in opposing the intrinsic evils of induced abortion and the giving of support to maintaining access to it. Pro-*Roe* Catholic politicians give a certain respectability to the intrinsic evil of abortion. By their actions, here, they are in fact maintaining that in the opinion of the Holy Spirit, running after political office trumps discipleship and the promise of eternal life.

However Jesus may have understood intrinsic evil (*e.g.*, as a spiritual person-Satan, or simply as a malignant cancer on the moral order, or both), he certainly considered it as "non-divisible." This means, for *e.g.*, that if a person devotes all of his or her available time and energy fighting the intrinsic evil of abortion (so that he is left without any energy or time to fight against, say, poverty, social injustice, or unnecessary capital punishment), the fact remains, he is fighting intrinsic evil on all of its innumerable fronts. Conversely, a person who cooperates with or actively supports abortion fortifies intrinsic evil on all of its innumerable fronts.

Mary Healy, in her *The Gospel of Mark* (2008), states: "The trial [or informal hearing on whether Jesus should be turned over to Pontius Pilate] is rigged from the start, since the [Jewish Supreme Court — the Sanhedrin or] chief priests, scribes, and elders have already decided that Jesus must die. But as many a corrupt... [court] has done before and since, they [the persons constituting the Sanhedrin] seek at least an appearance of legal propriety to justify their action."[40] In *Roe v. Wade*, the majority justices made the same sorry attempt to create an appearance of legal propriety [*i.e.*, of being decisively impartial]: "Our task... is to resolve the issue [of whether the Fourteenth Amendment's due process clause guarantees to an unmarried woman a right to undergo a physician-induced abortion], by constitutional measurement, free of emotion and predilection. We seek earnestly to do this."[41] However, and thanks to Harvard law professor Mark

Tushnet (who, when *Roe v. Wade* was being decided, was clerking for Justice Marshall — one of *Roe's* majority justices), it is now known that *Roe v. Wade* also was "rigged from the start": "All they [the Roe majority and concurring justices] wanted was to get those [state, criminal abortion statutes] off the books".[42]

This means – and this is real tragedy because it doesn't have to be so - that every person and organization that supports Roe, as well as those persons and organizations that are on record as opposing Roe but have effectively given up the fight to destroy it are, in effect, ratifying "case rigging" by our Nation's highest court. And now, in *Side B*, not only will I prove that as true, but I will do so, not on my grounds, but on the Roe Court's "own rigged grounds".

But before I do this, I wish to make it clear that not for a second do I hold the Court to be solely responsible for what Roe (Casey)[43] has wrought. As observed by Alan Jacobs, in his *Original Sin: A Cultural History* 236 (2008):

> The doctrine of original sin stands in judgment of *every* political system. This happens, in part, because [so many] sinful human individuals lack the will to resist the transformation of all social orders – past, present, and future – into something corrupt....Even people who in their daily lives do little harm will, nevertheless, allow great harm to be done by their institutions.

# SIDE B:
# THE POST-EMBRYONIC HUMAN FETUS AS A CONSTITUTIONALLY RECOGNIZED PERSON*

"our holding... is consistent... with the lenity of the [English] common law [on abortion]."

—*Roe v. Wade* 410 U.S. at 165.

"Law counts for little against the cause of the moment."

—Lord Acton

In relevant part the Fifth Amendment provides that "no person shall be deprived of life... without due process of law". If it can be demonstrated that the "formed" (i.e., the post-embryonic) human fetus qualifies as a Fifth Amendment, due process clause person, then it should follow that the "formed", human fetus qualifies also as a Fourteenth Amendment, due process clause person.[1] And if that is the case, then not only does *Roe v. Wade* and all of its progeny fall[2], but it would now violate Fifth and Fourteenth Amendment due process (which, in essence, protect a person from arbitrary federal action, and from arbitrary state action, respectively) for the federal government and the states to fail to enact laws safeguarding the formed, human fetus from being aborted. As observed by Justice Stevens: "The permissibility of terminating the life of a fetus could scarcely be left to the will of the state [and federal] legislatures [if] a fetus is a person within the meaning of the [Fifth and] Fourteenth Amendment[s].[3]

It is true that in *Roe* the Court held that the fetus does not qualify as a Fourteenth Amendment, due process clause person. However, that holding, if it is not void *ab initio*, is certainly voidable at any time, for the simple reason that the *Roe* Court, in its rush to judgment, forgot to appoint independent, sagacious counsel (let alone, a *guardian ad litem*) to represent the fetus in the course of holding that the fetus has no right to life or to be born under the Fourteenth Amendment's due process clause.[4]

Suppose that a "federally" condemned woman was impregnated by her prison guard eight (8) weeks to the day before her scheduled date of execution, and that the dirty deed was uncovered through a DNA analysis of semen contained in a used prophylactic found in her bedding on the eve of her scheduled date of execution. Suppose also that the condemned woman does not request a stay of execution until the birth of her child, but that an obstetric ultrasound or dating scan confirms the existence in her womb of a live, walnut-size, formed fetus. Finally, suppose that the "sole" (I repeat: "sole") issue before the Court is whether a federal statute, which bars, without exception (other than the exception of the person's inability to appreciate that his or her death is imminent), all reprieves, violates the Fifth Amendment's due process clause (enacted in 1791), in that the condemned woman's live fetus qualifies as a Fifth Amendment, due process clause person. Who would argue to uphold the statute barring the granting of a fetus's petition for a stay of his mother's execution?

In Massachusetts, in 1778, the governing body that presided over Mrs. Spooner's execution for murdering her husband was, itself, looked upon as a child-murderer by its own citizenry after an autopsy on the body of Mrs. Spooner (who pleaded her belly upon being sentenced to hang — claiming to be "quick with child", but was found not to be so) revealed that Mrs. Spooner was then five months pregnant with a "perfectly formed child."[5]

Justice Stevens observed that Supreme Court justices, in interpreting the text of the Constitution, "must, of course, try to read ... [the] words [used by the framers of the Constitution] in the context of the beliefs that were widely held in the late eighteenth century".[6]

Charles Leslie, in his *Treatise of the Word Person* (1710), observed that a fetus or man becomes "a *Person* by the Union of his Soul and [formed] Body ... This, is the acceptance of a person among men, in all common sense, and as generally understood."[7] Similarly, Walter Charleton, a fellow of the Royal College of Physicians, in his *Enquiries into Human Nature* (1699), observed "That the life of man doth both originally spring, and perpetually depend from the intimate conjunction and union of his reasonable soul with his body, is one of those few assertions in which all Divines [theologians] and natural philosophers [scientists] unanimously agree."[8] This union was then understood to occur at "fetal formation" (and not at "quickening" — the pregnant woman's initial perception of the movement of her fetus). This understanding was not based on any religious belief, be it Catholic, Protestant, theistic, or otherwise, rather on the opinion or teaching of Aristotle as set forth in his *Historia Animalium*.[9] That most celebrated, American physician Benjamin Rush (1745-1813), a founding father and signer of the Declaration of Independence, in his *Medical Inquiries* (1789), observed: "No sooner is the female ovum thus set in motion, and the fetus formed, then its capacity of life is supported."[10]

In *Smith v. Alabama* the Court observed that "the interpretation of the Constitution ... is necessarily influenced by the fact that its provisions are framed in the language of the English common law, and are to be read in light of its history."[11] In *Plyer v. Doe*, the court observed: "The [Fifth Amendment] term person is broad enough to include ... every human being within the jurisdiction of the republic."[12]

Blackstone (whose four-volume *Commentaries* on the English common law, served as "a primary legal authority on the common law for 18th ... century American lawyers", magistrates, and judges), in the course of discussing the fundamental or inalienable rights of persons (in this instance, *the right to life* — "a right inherent by nature in every individual" and confirmed in the "Declaration of Independence"), at common law, observed:

> Life [*i.e.*, the principle by which a human fetus becomes a living human being] is the immediate gift of God [, i.e., just as soon as the product of human conception develops into a fetus, God creates that particular fetus' human soul and joins it to this newly-formed human fetus] ... It begins in contemplation of law as soon as the infant is able to stir [then understood to occur at "fetal formation," and "not" at the pregnant woman's "quickening": <u>See</u> the discussion in the endnote (13) to this quote.] For if a woman is *Quick with child* [i.e., is pregnant with a live child or formed fetus] ... and [she], by a potion or otherwise, kills it in her womb ... [, so that it is brought forth dead, instead of alive, then, she is guilty of committing] a very heinous misdemeanor".[13]

Add to these observations of Blackstone, Justice Stevens, and the Court in *Smith v. Alabama* and in *Plyer v. Doe*, the fact that at common law, in Colonial America, and throughout the states and territories of the United States from their inceptions, a condemned woman who is found to be pregnant with a live child or simply pregnant, as the case may be, is reprieved so that her child is not also executed. In *Baynton's Case* (1702), the condemned, on being sentenced to death, successfully "pleaded her belly":

> Baynton: "I am with child."
> Court: "Let a jury of matrons be sent for."
> Clerk : "Matrons: enquire whether Baynton be quick with child."
> Court (to the matrons): "enquire whether this woman be quick with child: if she be with child, but not quick ... give your verdict so; and if she be not quick with child, then she is to undergo the execution."
> Court (to the matrons): "Do you find the prisoner to be with child, with quick child, or not?"
> Forewoman (to the Court): "Yes ... she is quick with child."[14]

Add also here the fact that at the English common law, intended or induced abortion was subject to criminal prosecution not only after the pregnant woman became "quick with child" (or with "quick child"), but also "before" she became "quick with child."

In Derby, England, in August of 1732, in the case of *Rex v. Beare*, Eleanor Beare was convicted of (1) the common law misdemeanor offense of destroying, through intended abortion, the "foetus in the womb of Grace Belford" (it was not alleged, and no evidence was presented that Belford was then "quick with child", i.e., was pregnant with a live fetus or child), and (2) the misdemeanor offense of encouraging a husband to administer a poison to his wife. Beare received two or separate sentences of two days on the pillory and three years imprisonment. The "populace ... gave her no quarter, but threw such quantities of eggs, turnips, etc., that it was thought she would hardly have escaped with her life." The *Beare* trial judge, in the course of commenting on the evidence to the *Beare* jury relative to the abortion indictment, related that "he never met with a case so barbarous and unnatural."[15]

Another case on point (and there are many more such cases on point), is the case of *R. v. Jane Wynspere* (Nottingham, England, 1503):

> On inquisition taken at Basford ... before [coroner] Richard Parker ... upon the view of the body of Jane Wynspere ... by The oath of ... [names of fourteen jurors omitted], who say Upon their oath that ... Jane Wynspere ... single woman, Being pregnant ... drank ... various ... poisons in order to kill and destroy the Child in her body; from which the said Jane then and there died. And thus the same Jane ... feloniously, as a "felo de se," killed ... herself.[16]

What, then, can be said of *Roe's* contention (and it is chiefly this contention that the *Roe* Court relied upon in concluding that the human fetus, alive in the womb of the mother, does not qualify as a due process clause person) that intended abortion was recognized as a right or liberty at the English common law?[17] Hannah Arendt's description of the modern state says it best: "'the power of the modern state [and the United States Supreme Court is but an arm of our Federal Government] makes it possible for it to turn lies into truth by destroying the facts which existed before and by making new realities to conform to what until then had been ideological fiction'."[18]

The problem is not so much that the *Roe* Court erred in concluding that the human fetus is not a due process clause person. The real problem is that the consequences of this erroneous conclusion seem too enormous (the destruction of some fifty million constitutional persons) so as to admit the error.

The opinion in *Roe* not only displays full-blown, judicial incompetence; it is without question the most poorly reasoned, unprofessional, and ridiculous judicial opinion in the entire history of Anglo-American law. Thomas Woods, Jr., said of the *Roe* opinion:

> Every aspect of … [it] was faulty — the constitutional arguments, the biological arguments, and the historical arguments — as even many proponents of abortion rights acknowledge. For instance, legal scholar John Ely … condemned the *Roe* decision "because it is bad constitutional law, or rather because it is *not* constitutional law and gives almost no sense of an obligation to try to be."

Yet, the *Roe* opinion is even worse than all of that: this opinion not only unwittingly establishes the constitutional "nonexistence" of a right to privacy – the very right which *Roe* says gives rise to a "fundamental right" to an abortion (and which is undoubtedly why the right of privacy has been continuously, "wholly" silent in the forty years since *Roe* was decided), but also unwittingly proves the "constitutionality" of the very Texas, criminal abortion statute the opinion says is unconstitutional.[19] And the *Roe* opinion gets worse still: it is, in no uncertain terms, a fraud committed by the Court upon our constitutional community. The Court's written opinion serves as an explanation of *why* and *how* the Court arrived at its decision. It is supposed to be a reasoned elaboration, publicly stated, that justifies the Court's decision. Suppose it can be demonstrated that the *Roe* opinion fails to set forth the true reason for *Roe's* central holding (which is, that prior to fetal viability, a woman's right to abort her fetus is unbridled — and contrary to popular belief — remains very nearly unbridled even after fetal viability), and sets forth here, instead, spurious and nonsensical reasons. If that can be demonstrated, then one can reasonably state that, in *Roe,* our United States Supreme Court perpetrated a fraud upon our constitutional community.

*Roe* author Justice Blackmun expressly admitted that *Roe's* central holding represented nothing more than "arbitrary action" by the Court. In a *Roe* memorandum (1972) to the *Conference of Supreme Court Justices* he stated: As can be seen in my *Roe* draft opinion, "the end of the first trimester is critical." He added: "this is arbitrary, but perhaps any other selected point, such as quickening or viability, is equally arbitrary."[20]

In the actual *Roe* opinion, Blackmun arbitrarily substituted "fetal viability" in place of "the end of the first trimester" as the so-called critical point, i.e., as the point until which the state's "legitimate" interest in safeguarding the unborn child, alive in the womb of his mother, remains "nonoverriding" or "non-compelling" — vis-a-vis its mother's interest in aborting him (and therefore, this unborn child cannot be safeguarded through the use of criminal abortion sanctions.). The "covert" reason why Blackmun arbitrarily made this substitution was his adopted belief "that many women, particularly young women in distressed circumstances, might deny to themselves and everyone else that they were pregnant until their pregnancies were reasonably well advanced." Blackmun got this belief from Mark Tushnet (via Justice Marshall), who was then clerking for Justice Marshall, and which means or demonstrates that we are a nation still being ruled by a former law clerk.[21]

Also of relevance here is this memo (Dec. 12, 1972) from Justice Marshall to Justice Blackmun:

"Dear Harry: I am inclined to agree that drawing the line at viability accommodates the interest at stake better than drawing it at the end of the first trimester. Given the difficulties which many women may have in believing that they are pregnant and in deciding to seek an abortion, I fear that the earlier date may not in practice serve the interest of those women, which your opinion does seek to serve."[22]

The Constitution mandates that the *Roe* opinion serve "only" (I repeat "only") the Constitution. The reader should, therefore, understand that there can be no real doubt that the *Roe* opinion's failure to disclose the "true" reason for the Court's selection of "fetal viability" (as the so-called abortion cutoff point) was a "calculated" move to keep hidden from the *Roe* parties (particularly, *Roe* defendant Henry Wade, then Attorney General for the State of Texas) an unconstitutional - because it contradicts the due process-mandate of "judicial impartiality" - "operating bias" in favor of plaintiff Roe.[23]

The reader should also understand that the *Roe* opinion could not very well have stated that the *Roe* decision represents nothing more than "arbitrary action" by the federal government, in this case by Supreme Court justices. To have stated so, would have been tantamount to stating that the *Roe* decision is unconstitutional because it violates the Fifth Amendment's prohibition of "arbitrary action" by the Federal Government.[24]

Here is the entirety of what the *Roe* opinion offers in support of its holding concerning "fetal viability" as the so-called abortion cut-off point: State regulation protective of pre-viable fetal life is lacking in logical and biological justifications. However, "State regulation protective of fetal life after viability ... has both logical and biological justifications." So far as is known, the terms "logical justifications" and "biological justifications" are foreign to the English language. They are simply nonsense. And, even assuming they have some real meaning, the *Roe* opinion gives no clue as to "what" is lacking and "what" is supported by "logical and biological justifications".[25] Logic deals simply with the proper relationship between "concepts" (without reference to their underlying truth); and biology has as its proper subject all living things, including the previable human embryo or fetus.

Is the pro-*Roe* reader still not convinced that *Roe* is a fraud? Well, then, reverse the scenario: *Roe v. Wade* is decided against *Roe*, and subsequently, a *Roe* Court memo is discovered which reveals that the *Roe* majority justices had cast their votes for *Wade* because of their "arbitrary" beliefs that a human being is so at its conception. Who, here, would not cry out "foul play and fraud"!

The reader should contrast Blackmun's *Roe* memorandum with this court observation in *Borass* (1979): "When it is seen that a ...point there must be, and that there is no ...logical way of fixing it precisely, the decision of the legislature must be accepted unless we can say that it is very wide of any reasonable mark."[26] In *Roe* the Court expressly conceded that the state's interest in safeguarding unborn human life is reasonable, legitimate, real and important throughout the gestational process.[27]

The Court, in *Lawrence v. Texas* (2003), overruled its holding in *Bowers v. Hardwick* , that the state may criminalize homosexual sodomy when committed in private. *Lawrence* left fully intact *Hardwick's* holding that homosexual sodomy does not, and cannot, qualify constitutionally as a "fundamental right." In the course of denegrating *Bowers*, and notwithstanding the principle of *stare decisis*, the *Lawrence Court* observed: "criticism of *Bowers* has been substantial, and continuing, disapproving of its reasoning in all respects, not just its historical assumptions."[28] Compared to the extensive and "unanimous", and ongoing criticism directed at the *Roe* opinion, the criticism directed at the *Bowers* opinion is less than minuscule.[29] And the only reason why the *Roe* Court cannot be accused of "intentionally" misrepresenting the history of the fetus (fully protected) and of abortion (completely outlawed) at the English common law is because judicial bias cannot be ruled out here. "Bias is impervious to reason". Yet, notwithstanding having repeated opportunities, the Court has never acknowledged that its *Roe* opinion has been "unanimously" condemned. All that our constitutional community gets here is *Casey* and its adolescent reliance on the much abused principle of *stare decisis* and its babblings on coping with the mystery of human existence and life. That is hypocrisy, and not constitutional law.

Elizabeth Drew, in her piece, *Why Watergate Matters*, observes: "All of this matters ... because it is a cautionary tale about overreaching for power, abuse of the office of the presidency, and about protecting the Constitution. Such things matter a lot."[30] Not really. And the reason why is because the virtual equivalent of those things occurred also in *Roe v. Wade*: the abuse of the office of the United States Supreme Court, the overreaching for power by Supreme Court Justices, a judicial cover-up (of the admittedly arbitrary — and therefore unconstitutional - basis for *Roe's* central holding), and the undermining of the Constitution by polluting it with the small-minded (not that it would make a difference here if they were large-minded) personal beliefs of justices who can't wait to toss judicial impartiality out of the constitutional decision-making process, and who think that their competence knows no bounds. The *Roe* decision is the Supreme Court's Watergate (only more so: President Nixon, unlike the *Roe* majority justices, did not commit the act or acts he sought to cover up).

This means that Watergate matters "only" because the media decided to make it matter. Watergate, then, can be reduced to nothing more than a media event.

It is doubtful that any legitimate constitutional law scholar would challenge the validity of this observation of Justice Brennan: "The integrity of the process through which a [constitutional] rule [or decision] is forged and fashioned is as important as the result itself; if it were not, the legitimacy of the rule [or decision] would be doubtful".[31]

Since the process in *Roe* is flawed beyond recognition, and yet *Roe* still stands, then, very arguably, *Roe* has begun the ruination of constitutional law, and the ascent of supreme law by judicial predilection. Or, just as doctors who do not seek to make their patients healthy by standards to which they are obligated, are highly dangerous men and women, so also are Supreme Court justices who do not seek to hand down constitutional law by standards to which they are obligated. And it is the height of irresponsibility for persons (particularly anti-*Roe* opinion, pro-*Roe* decision legal commentators) to create covers for such justices, and to give them a pass simply because he or she favors the law that such justices hand down.[32]

# A LONG CONCLUSION (TO SIDE B): CONTAINING SOME PARTING SHOTS AND FINAL THOUGHTS

The damage caused by the fraud of *Roe v. Wade* seems too enormous to admit the fraud: the possible destruction of more than fifty million human lives. Vested interests would also preclude such an admission. The Supreme Court and the ACLU, commonly referred to as defenders of the Constitution, would have to be referred to as great enemies of the Constitution.

There can be no question that in *Roe*, the Court handed down the most poorly reasoned, unprofessional, and dishonest opinion in the entire history of Anglo-American law. What is more, the following quote from that utterly contrived opinion only compounds the dishonesty that underlies this opinion: "Our task ... is to resolve the issue [of whether the Fourteenth Amendment's due process clause guarantees to an unmarried woman a right to undergo a physician-performed abortion], by constitutional measurement, free of emotion and predilection. We seek earnestly to do this."[1] And leading professors of constitutional law, such as Erwin Chemerinsky, in seeking to defend the *Roe* opinion, are in reality defending the indefensible practice of grave judicial dishonesty: "The obligation to write an opinion justifying its conclusion as being principled, not arbitrary, and consistent with precedent, substantially limited the Court in deciding [the] ... issue presented in *Roe*."[2]

Professor Chemerinsky, in criticizing the Court's five to four decision in *Gonzales v. Carhart* (2007),[3] which upheld a federal ban on partial-birth abortion, let go this unprofessional appeal to militant, anti-Catholic bigotry: The decision rests on nothing more than the "view of five aging male justices - all Catholic."[4] Insert "Black" or "Persian" in place of "Catholic," here, and the good professor would be deemed as a racist and anti-ethnic bigot. Don Imus got kicked off radio for his racial remarks; yet Chemerinsky gets published for doing the immoral equivalent. Or, shall it remain politically correct behavior to appeal to anti-Catholic bigotry in the context of sounding off for abortion rights?

That the information media is no less biased than Chemerinsky, is easily demonstrated. Justice Powell, after retiring from the Court admitted to NPR's Nina Totenberg not only that he entered into the *Roe v. Wade* decision-making process with a pro-compelled, legalization-of-abortion bias, but also that this bias compromised his impartiality there because it "strongly influenced" his decision to join in the *Roe* majority opinion. What is more, Powell engaged in judicial deceit by concealing this "strong bias" from the Roe litigants. Here is what Totenberg related on "Nightline" regarding how Powell compromised his duty to decide impartially in *Roe v. Wade*:

> Lewis Powell … told me that one of the things that had influenced him strongly in his decision to join *Roe v. Wade* was an experience he'd had when he was a … senior partner in a … law firm … [H]e got called one night from one of his office boys, and went back to the office to find this young man in tears, distraught. The kid [had been] living with … an older woman. She had become pregnant and, acting on her instructions, the office boy … aborted her … She … hemorrhaged, and he had run to … Powell for help. The two men … found her dead … Powell had to turn his office boy over to the local prosecutor, but he persuaded the prosecutor not to bring charges … Powell told me…: 'Ever after that, I thought this was the business of private choice, and not of the government.'[5]

A prosecutor's office does not contain a jail cell, but a police department does. So Powell did not "turn over" his clerk to the prosecutor. And it may be that Powell, the prosecutor, the local coroner, and chief of police, committed "misprision of felony" (a felony) if they conspired or aided in the concealing of a criminal homicide.

Totenberg did not realize what she was disclosing here, because she presented Powell's decision to join *Roe*, not as a glaring instance of applied judicial bias, but as a courageous justice voting his conscience as formed from a personal experience. Powell's sympathy and compassion for the plight of his office clerk and sadness over the tragic death of the clerk's girlfriend are highly commendable; but any such feelings are "forbidden" tools of constitutional interpretation as would have been Powell's sadness over the death of the girlfriend's aborted child. Powell had an absolute Fifth Amendment, due process-mandated duty to recuse himself from participating in the deciding of *Roe v. Wade.* He did not recuse himself there. For that reason alone, as long as *Roe* stands, it stands on judicially tainted grounds. (Subsequently, Powell underwent a sea change of heart – relating that *Roe v. Wade* and its companion case, *Doe v. Bolton* were "the worst opinions I ever joined.")[6]

Here is the question that raises the real probability of pro-*Roe* media bias: Why is it that not one television or radio commentator or editorial board of a legal newspaper or of one of our nation's largest or major newspapers or magazines has uttered so much as a single word on Powell's operating bias and deceit in *Roe v. Wade* (a monumental decision, to say the least), while every one of those people and entities talked or wrote incessantly on the so-called "perceived" bias of Justice Scalia (who fiercely continues to state that *Roe* is an illegitimate and lawless decision at best) in the Cheney energy policy task force case, a less than monumental decision? (The reader will recall that Scalia and Cheney were caught holding hands in a duck blind.)[7] The obvious answer here is that these people and entities suffer from pro-*Roe* bias. And here is the source of this media bias: pro-*Roe* Catholic politicians and certain special interest organizations (including certain legal organizations, at least one of which parades itself as a champion of individual liberties) continuously put out to our constitutional community a message to the effect that any and every anti-*Roe* position reflects nothing more than a religious belief. Such a message constitutes nothing less than a rank appeal to militant, anti-religious bigotry.

The presence of anti-religious prejudice in the context of sounding off for abortion rights has even infected the Supreme Court. Justice Stevens, in his concurring opinion in *Thornburg v. American College of Obstetricians* (1986), stated:

> Unless the religious view that a fetus is a 'person' [or human being] is adopted ..., there is a fundamental and well-recognized difference between a fetus and a human being; indeed, if there is not such a difference between a fetus and a human being, the permissibility of terminating the life of a fetus could scarcely be left to the will of the state legislatures.[8]

Note that Justice Stevens neither articulated the so-called "fundamental difference" between a formed human fetus and a live-born human being (and this is because it almost certainly cannot be done)[9], nor identified the persons or bodies of thought that recognize this difference as a "fundamental" difference. Furthermore, the so-called religious view or opinion that Justice Stevens has in mind is not at all a religious view or opinion. It is a "philosophical" opinion. It states that the human soul is infused into the product of human conception at conception ("immediate animation") or at the completion of the process of fetal formation ("mediate or delayed animation"), depending on the particular opinion. But further, Justice Stevens is presupposing here (and also in his concurring opinion in *Webster* (1989),[10] where he makes an impoverished attempt to elaborate on his foregoing *Thornburg* statements) a certain definition of what constitutes a human being. Then, without articulating this definition (which means that all a person can infer from this unarticulated definition is that both the formed (post-embryonic) and unformed human fetus would not fall within this definition), he commences to argue that the Constitution dictates that this unarticulated definition of a human being is the only definition that can pass constitutional muster. Any definition of a human being that would be broad enough to include the human fetus would be, to that extent, substantially, if not only religiously based, and therefore would run afoul of the First Amendment's prohibition of religion in government. It is a pity that Justice Stevens, before launching his foregoing escapade in anti-religious bigotry, did not consult *Van Nostrand's Scientific Encyclopedia*.[11]

Assuming, without conceding, that an honest person may reasonably state that in his or her opinion a conceived, unborn human fetus (or embryo) is not a human being, that same person, to remain honest, must admit here "that for all it may be known, every time a doctor aborts a fetus (or embryo) an innocent, defenseless human being is thereby killed." Therefore, every doctor who performs an abortion demonstrates a willingness to kill an innocent human being. And every person who would argue or vote for, etc., legalized abortion condones this willingness to kill an innocent human being (which is, of course, the virtual equivalent of "implied malice" or a "depraved heart" as those concepts appear in the common law of criminal homicide. If the matter, here, was not so serious, then it would be almost hilarious how pro-choice persons simply refuse to come to terms with this inescapable truth. "Out of sight, here, is indeed out of mind.") "That a conclusion satisfies one's private conscience does not attest to its reliability."[12] Also, neither science nor medicine offers solace to the pro-choice conscience: "From a purely scientific standpoint, there is no question but that abortion represents the cessation of human life";[13] and: "Our knowledge of fetal development, function and environment has increased remarkably. As an important consequence, the status of the fetus has been elevated to that of a patient who should be given the same meticulous care by the physician that we long have given the pregnant woman."[14]

No post-*Roe*, pro-*Roe* Supreme Court justice has come up with even a semblance of "constitutional" justification for the *Roe* decision. All that has been offered here is so much wind-scattered chaff, such as this hippy babble offered by Justice Kennedy in a (joint) lead opinion in *Casey* (1992), which upheld *Roe* by a five (5) to four (4) vote (and which offering constitutes an implicit rejection of *Roe*'s right to privacy holding): "At the heart of [14th Amendment guaranteed] liberty is the right to define [and act on] one's own concept of existence, of meaning, of the universe, and of the mystery of human life."[15] The inference, here, is that one way for a pregnant woman to deal with the mystery of the life of her unborn child is to simply obliterate it.[16]

Kennedy articulated not a dot of constitutional authority to support his version of how the Constitution guarantees abortion. Yet, he had such authority at the end of his fingertips in the form of "judicial fan mail" (*i.e.*, letters written to Blackmun from women thanking him for *Roe v. Wade*).

Kennedy had voted with the minority to overrule *Roe v. Wade* in the Court's 1989 *Webster* decision,[17] which upheld *Roe* by a vote of five to four. While Chief Justice Rehnquist was working on his majority opinion in *Casey* (to which Kennedy had committed to joining, and which would be announcing the total overruling of *Roe*), *Roe* author Justice Blackmun spoke privately with Kennedy and, in a highly unethical move, showed to Kennedy letters that Blackmun had received from women "who spoke of how the right to choose abortion had been important in their lives." Kennedy subsequently switched sides, and *Roe* was upheld in *Casey* by a vote of five to four.[18]

Kennedy also failed to cite here a secondary authority that was readily available: his own private or personal moral beliefs. Very shortly after *Casey* was published, Kennedy related the following to over five hundred state and federal judges at an ABA dinner honoring the judiciary:

> We, of course, are bound by the facts, the law, the rules of
> logic, legal reasoning and precedent....But we are also bound
> by our own sense of morality and decency....We must never
> lose sight of the fact that the law has a moral foundation, and
> we must never fail to ask ourselves not only what the law is,
> but what the law should be.[19]

What happens to logic, the law, legal reasoning, and precedent when they conflict "irreconcilably" with a justice's own sense
of morality, decency, and belief of "what the law should be?" The
answer is that the former are tossed out of the constitutional
decision-making process. Otherwise, justices could not make the
law conform to their private sense of morality, decency, and belief
of "what the law should be."

Whether or not Kennedy realized this in making the above
statements, he conveyed to our constitutional community that he
rejects "the principle of the impartiality of the judiciary." Coke
(1552-1634) puts it: "no man out of his own <u>private</u> reason ought
to be wiser than the law;"[20] and Blackstone (1723-1780) has it
that the judge "is sworn to decide, not according to his own <u>pri-
vate</u> judgment, but according to the known laws and customs of
the land."[21] Furthermore, although a party in making his or her
case before the Supreme Court, can argue the facts, apply logic,
cite precedent and present a reasoned legal argument, he or she,
nevertheless, cannot possibly divine, let alone argue the merits
of such items as the various justices' private or personal views
on morality, decency, justice, and how they would contemplate
"what the law should be." Kennedy's approach to constitutional
interpretation contains, then, an unknowable and, therefore, hidden agenda. This violates procedural due process because litigants arguing before the court are not given "notice" of the contents of this hidden agenda.

There exists virtual unanimity among *Roe* legal commentators that the *Roe* opinion does not justify the *Roe* decision. Fried
described *Roe* as "twisted judging," and Posner called the *Roe*
opinion "unprofessional".[22] Philip Bobbitt, one of many anti-*Roe*

opinion, pro-*Roe* decision legal commentators, referred to the *Roe* opinion as "a doctrinal fiasco" and questioned whether the *Roe* Court believed in its own opinion.[23] What Bobbitt and every one of the anti-*Roe* opinion, pro-*Roe* decision legal commentators are saying, in effect, is that the Court need not reconsider *Roe* (*i.e.*, and unlike the legislative and executive branches of government, the Court need not be accountable), because they have come to the Court's aid by developing sound constitutional supports for *Roe*. These commentators have conveniently overlooked the crucial fact that it is the Court, and not the commentators, who decide whether or not those supports are sound. However, the Court cannot make such a determination without reconsidering *Roe*. And it is highly worth noting that nowhere in either the *Gonzales v. Carhart* (2007) or *Casey* opinions is even one of these anti-*Roe* opinion, pro-*Roe* propaganda commentaries mentioned.

It may be fairly concluded that such commentators do not have confidence in the soundness of their pro-*Roe* arguments, or they do not trust the Court to consider impartially their pro-*Roe* arguments, or they fear being shunned by their colleagues and the members, *etc.*, that constitute the information media. They qualify, here, as nothing more than abortion-access advocates masquerading as constitutional law scholars. Also, these commentators, in not calling on the Court to reconsider *Roe* - and this is why their pro-*Roe* commentaries should be burned at the stake, undermine the principle that "the authority of the Court's construction of the Constitution ultimately 'depend[s] altogether on the force of the reasoning [i.e., the Court's written opinion] by which it is supported.'"[24] More specifically, Justice Brennan observed:

> [I]n our legal system judges have no power to *declare* law...That, of course, is the province of the legislature. Courts *derive* legal principles, and have a duty to explain *why* and *how* a given rule has come to be. This requirement...restrains judges and keeps them accountable to the law and to the principles that are the source of judicial

authority. The integrity of the process through which a rule is forged and fashioned is as important as the result itself, if it were not, the legitimacy of the rule would be doubtful.[25]

In *Casey's* joint lead opinion Justices Kennedy, Souter, and O'Connor mimicked Rodney King's infamous lament ("can't we all just get along") in putting forth this extra-judicial statement: We now call upon "the contending sides of... [our] national [abortion] controversy to end their national division by accepting a common mandate rooted in the Constitution." Inasmuch as pro-choice persons obviously accept *Roe's* mandate on abortion, then this extra-judicial statement can "only" be targeted at pro-life persons, who I expect are righteously laughing out loud at *Casey's* Rodney-Kings lament. In any event, who appointed these justices as our Nation's roving peacemakers in the sky? Unreasoned injustice and judicial predilection do not make for a convincing or acceptable constitutional mandate. Constitutional law scholars are virtually "unanimous" in voicing the opinion that the *Roe* opinion is a far, far cry from dictating the *Roe* decision. And the *Casey* opinion is even less convincing than the *Roe* opinion, if that is possible.[26]

All that these three justices have demonstrated, in making the foregoing extra-judicial statement, is that, besides being seriously naïve and out of touch with reality, they remain woefully and culpably ignorant of the two principles or beliefs that motivate *Roe's* opponents: (1) an inflamed desire to be out from under the thumb of outrageous judicial tyrants, or putting it another way, an utter disdain for judicial power grabs under the guise of detached constitutional analysis or decision-making (and this is what initially ignited, and continues to fuel our nation's abortion controversy); and (2) the fundamental moral imperative to seek to protect the most defenseless of beings belonging to the human family. No reasonable and unbiased person would maintain that the foregoing two (2) principles and beliefs lack a firm foundation in reason and human experience. Yet, every informed and unbiased person, who looks at the *Roe-Casey* opinions, is forced to conclude that they serve simply as one more monument to humanity's infinite capacity to deceive itself, in the name of humanity, as always, of course. "Unreasoned injustice" rules in *Roe-Casey*.

And so, what David Gelernter so clearly has observed remains in clear view: "The abortion issue is a catastrophic wound in U.S. cultural life. It has inflicted unending battles on American society ever since the Supreme Court seized control of the issue from state legislatures in 1973 - in one of the grossest power grabs American democracy ever faced."[27]

Justice Kennedy (and in reference to a proposal to televise Court hearings), observed: "We teach that we're judged by what we write."[28] Then, let the *Roe-Casey* opinions be their judge.

Unless our constitutional community is to continue suffering from (Court-induced) "battered-constitutional-community syndrome", it had better start railing against *Roe v. Wade*.

The movement in the United States to grant American culture a divorce from moral judgment, in effect, presupposes that the human person is neither relational nor a moral agent by nature, and has no real reason or need to exercise analytical and critical judgment in viewing or participating in human-based activities.

The *Roe*, *Casey*, and *Lawrence* justices, together with pro-*Roe* Catholic politicians, pro-*Roe* legal scholars, virtually all journalists and members of the information media, the Democratic platform committee, and such organizations as the ACLU, *etc.*, look upon the reader as a potential moral idiot. To accept *Roe v. Wade* requires at the least the suspension of moral judgment (without which true critical and analytical judgment fade from human consciousness). Think about listening to Paul: "Do not conform yourselves to this age, but be transformed by the renewal of your mind, that you may discern ... what is good."[29]

# APPENDIX 1

## REPRODUCTION (WITH AUTHOR'S COMMENTARY AND ANNOTATION: HEREINAF-TER "WITH ACA") OF

## REX V. ELEANOR BEARE (AKA., ELEANOR MERRIMAN) (DERBY, ENGLAND, AUGUST 15, 1732)[1]

*Eleanor Merriman*, now the wife of *Ebenezer Beare*, indicted for a misdemeanor, in endeavoring to persuade Nich Wilson to poison his wife, and for giving him poison for that end.

Indicted a second time by the name of Eleanor Beare, for a misdemeanor, in destroying the foetus in the womb of Grace Belfort [Belford], by putting an iron instrument up into her body, and thereby causing her to miscarry.

Indicted a third time, for destroying the foetus in the womb of a certain woman, to the jury unknown, by putting an iron

---

1   Reproduced from 2 *Gentleman's Magazine* 931-32 (August 1732). This case is mentioned also in Audrey Eccles, *Obstetrics and Gynaecology in Tudor and Stuart England* 69-70 (1982) (my initial source), and in 2 J.C. Cox, *Three Centuries of Derbyshire Annals* 48 (London, 1890) (mentions only the first indictment). This case came under the jurisdiction of the Midland Circuit; but according to Professor Sir J.H. Baker, the 1732 Midland Circuit records evidently have not survived (related in a letter to the author from professor Sir John H. Baker).

instrument up her body, or by giving her something to make her miscarry. Pleaded not guilty.

## [EVIDENCE ON THE FIRST INDICTMENT]

*COUNSEL FOR THE KING.* Gentlemen of the jury, you have heard the indictment read, and I must observe to you, that the crime for which the prisoner stands indicted, is an offence of the highest nature, next to murder itself; it is the instigation of a man to kill his wife, in the most secret manner, in order to keep it from the eyes of the world, and thereby to escape the punishment due to such a crime, by giving her poison in drink, of such a nature as should not work suddenly but by degrees, and thereby to kill her without any suspicion of murder; and it is owing to the good providence of God that the man did not give his wife the poison, for if he had, and she had died, the prisoner would have been tried for the murder.

## CALL NICHOLAS WILSON

*COURT:* Do you know the prisoner?

*WILSON:* Yes.

*COURT:* How long?

*WILSON:* It is about three years since I unfortunately met with the prisoner at a publick house at Wirksworth; after some conversation, she told me I was young, and could not take my liberty for fear of having uneasiness with my wife, but if I would be ruled by her, she would put me in a way to be rid of it. I asked her how? She said she would give me something to give my wife in her drink which would do her job. I told her that we would both be hanged. She said I need not fear that, for it would not kill her suddenly but by degrees, and that it would never be suspected. In a few days I met with the prisoner again, and she gave me something in a paper to give my wife in her drink, and told me it would quickly do her job. I took the paper and buried it, and went home and told my wife what had passed between me and the prisoner, and she desired me to keep out of her company; and I have never seen her since, till I now see her at the bar.

*PRISONER*: Did not you hire one Mary Yeomans to poison your wife, and did not you receive some poison (if it was poison) from her, and afterwards send for me, and tell me the stuff you had from Mary Yeomans would do no good?

*EVIDENCE* [i.e., N. Wilson]: No, I had the stuff from you and no other, and I buried it as above.

## CALL JOHN WILSON

*COURT*: What have you to say to the prisoner?

*J. WILSON*: Since she was in prison, she sent for me, and told me she had something against my brother which would touch his life, and desired he would keep out of the way at the Assizes.

*COUNSEL*: Your Lordship will observe, that the prisoner, fearing N. Wilson might be an Evidence against her, had that contrivance to send him out of the way.

## CALL HANNAH WILSON

*H. WILSON*: My husband told me he had received something from the prisoner, which she bid him give me in some drink, and it would shut me quickly.

# TO THE SECOND INDICTMENT

COUNSEL: Gentlemen, you have heard the indictment read, and may observe, that the misdemeanor for which the prisoner stands indicted, is of a most shocking nature; to destroy the fruit in the womb carries something in it so contrary to the natural tenderness of the female sex, that I am amazed how ever any woman should arrive at such a degree of impiety and cruelty, as to attempt it in such a manner as the prisoner has done, it has really something so shocking in it, that I cannot well display the nature of the crime to you, but must leave it to the evidence: It is cruel and barbarous to the last degree.

## CALL GRACE BELFORT [BELFORD]

GRACE BELFORD: I lived with the prisoner as a servant about ten days, but was not hired, and I was off and on with her about fourteen weeks: When I had been with her a few days there came company into the house, and [the company] made me drink ale and brandy (which I was not used to drink) and it overcame me; my mistress sent me into the stable to give hay to some horses, but I was not capable of doing it, so [I] laid me down in the stable; and there came to me one Chr, a young man that was drinking in the house, and after some time I feared I was with child, I told her [Beare] I thought I was; then she said if I could get 30 shilling from Chr, she would clear me from the child without giving me physick. A little time after, some company gave me cider and brandy, my mistress and I were both full of liquor, and when the company was gone, we could scarce get up stairs; but we did get up; then I laid me on the bed, and my mistress brought a kind of an instrument, I took it to be like an iron skewer, and she put it up into my body a great way, and hurt me.

COURT: What followed upon that?

EVIDENCE: Some blood came from me.

COURT: Did you miscarry after that?

*EVIDENCE*: The next day after I went to Allesiree, where I had a miscarriage.

*COURT*: What did the prisoner do after that?

*EVIDENCE*: She told me the job was done. I then lodged two or three nights with one *Ann Moseley* (now *Ann Oldknowles*); and [I] coming one morning to see the prisoner, I called for a mug of ale and drank it, and told her I was going home; then came in *John Clark*, and on the prisoner's saying I was going home, he said he would give me a glass of wine, to help me forward, which accordingly he did, out of a bottle he had in his pocket; then I took my leave of him; and when I was a little way out of town, I fell down at a style, and was not well, I lay a little while, then got up, and went to Nottingham that night.

## CALL JOHN CLARK

*COURT*: Do you know the prisoner?

*CLARK*: Yes, I have frequented her house.

*COURT*: Did you ever hear her say anything that she had used means to make a woman with child miscarry, by putting any kind of instrument up their bodies, or by giving them any thing to take inwardly?

*CLARK*: Yes, I have.

*COURT*: Have you seen her instrument for that purpose, or have you seen her use any means to make any woman with child miscarry?

*CLARK*: No, but I have heard her say she had done it, and that she then had under her one *Hannah*, whose other name [Hewit?[2]] I know not.

---

2    See 2 *Gentleman's Magazine* 722 (April, 1732), in which the following appears:

*COURT*: Have you heard her say she had been sent for these wicked practices, or had any reward for causing any one to miscarry?

*CLARK*: I heard her say she had been once sent for to Nottingham, and, as I remember, she said she had five pounds for the journey.

---

*March 29.* Were executed at *Derby*: *John Hewet*, a butcher, and *Rosamond Oherenshaw*, widow, and servant to Mrs. Eleanor Beare at the Crown on *Nans-green Derby*, for poisoning the said *Hewet's* wife [Hanah]. They walked to the tree in shrowds and died very penitent, confessing their guilt, and that *Hewet* had criminal familiarity not only with his fellow sufferer, but her mistress [Beare], who was the principal promoter of this murder; for which she will be tried next Assizes. *Hewet* said he had been married to the deceased seven years, but in short time differing, they parted, and that he, being persuaded by Beare, sent the poison to her by her servant.

Oherenshaw said, her wicked mistress fixed up the poison in a pancake, and ordered her (while her self was ironing in the parlour) to give it [to] *Hannah Hewit* to eat, she being sick after [eating] it [and] cast some of it up on the yard, which a pig eat of and died, and did the woman in great agony at the end of three hours. She confessed they had given her poison before in broth; and that since her widowhood she had a child by one H.S. before she came to live at the Crown at *Nan's-Green*. Tis added, that the bones of a child about 7 months growth were found buried in the garden of the said house; and a great deal of *Mrs. Beare's* wicked practices were discovered.

This account not being come to hand before our last was published, we took a false relation of the Assizes at Derby, from the Lond. Evening Post March 21, which we hope our readers will take as a sufficient excuse, it being as far from our intentions to insert a false fact, as impossible for us to know the exact truth of what we are obliged to take in a hurry from the news papers.

*PRISONER*: Did you not say you never heard me say any thing of using any means to cause miscarriage in any person, or saw me use any means for that end?

*CLARK*: No, I said I never saw you do any thing that way, but had heard you say you had done it. Would you have me forswear myself?

*PRISONER*: No, but I would have you speak the truth.

*CLARK*: I do.
Then the prisoner called several persons to speak in her behalf, but only two appeared, and they only gave her friend a reputable character, and said the prisoner had had a good education, but they knew nothing of the latter part of her life.

*MR. MAYOR*: The prisoner at the bar has a very bad character, and I have had frequent complaints against her for keeping a disorderly house.

Many evidences were ready in Court to have proved the facts she stood charged with in the third indictment; but his Lordship, observing that the second indictment was proved so plainly, he thought there was no necessity for going upon the third.

His Lordship summed up the evidence in a very moving speech to the jury, wherein he said, he never met with a case so barbarous and unnatural. The jury, after a short consultation, brought the prisoner in guilty of both indictments, and she received sentence to stand on the pillory, the two next market-days, and to suffer close imprisonment for three years.

*Derby, August 18, 1732.* This day Eleanor Beare, pursuant to her sentence, stood for the first time in the pillory in the marketplace; to which place she was attended by several of the Sheriff's officers; notwithstanding which, the populace, to show their resentment of the horrible crimes wherewith she had been charged, and the little remorse she has shown since her commitments, gave her no quarter, but threw such quantities of eggs, turnips, etc. that it was thought she would hardly have escaped with her life: she disengaged herself from the pillory before the time of her standing was expired, jumped among the crowd, whence she was with difficulty carried back to prison.

Unlike every one of the other known English common law abortion presentments or indictments, neither of the *Beare* common law misdemeanor abortion indictments allege that the pregnant woman was *quick with child* or *with quick child* or big or great with child or pregnant with a live child. This means that Beare was indicted for destroying, through deliberated abortion, the pre-human being product of human conception. The prosecutor referred to the product of Belford's miscarriage, not as a living child, but rather as the "fruit in the womb". The terms "kill" and "destroy" are not necessarily synonymous, for while both a living and a non-living thing can be destroyed, only the former can be killed. No evidence appears to have been offered to show that Belford's fetus had acquired life, and was still in life when it was aborted. Belford simply stated that she miscarried soon after the abortion was performed. She did not say that she had "quickened".

If a reader remains unconvinced that the two *Beare* abortion indictments do "not" allege the destruction of a live child, then let that reader compare those indictments to the following indictment alleging a (non-abortion related) unborn child killing in the case of *Rex v. Evans* (London, 1724):

> Flemming Evans, of S. Katharine's, was indicted for the murder of a male infant (unborn) on the 6th of May last [1724], by striking and kicking on the belly, Susan, the Wife of John Davis, then quick with the said infant. The Child was stillborn, very much bruised, and one of its Arms [had been] broken. But the Law supposing it impossible for a Child to be murdered before it is born,[3] the Court directed the Jury

---

3    This supposition became a part of the common law "only" because of Coke's misinterpretation of *Bourton's Case. See supra* note 18 of *Side B.* The liveborn, aborted child remained a murder victim. *See, e.g., Q v. West* (1848), *infra* in *Appendix 4.*

to acquit the Prisoner of this Indictment, but ordered the Prosecutor to bring another against him for the assault.[4]

It is difficult to understand with reasonable certainty what the word *foetus* was meant to convey as it was employed in the *Beare* abortion indictments. The common law rule is that technical or scientific words are to be understood in their technical or scientific sense, and not in their popular sense. Edith Boyd, in her *Origins of the Study of Human Growth* (1980), observed:

> In the early eighteenth century, physicians had begun to distinguish between *embryo* and *fetus*, using the Greek term *embryo*... to designate the organism in the early stages of prenatal growth and the Latin term *fetus*... to designate the developing organism after it had acquired all its members, including digits (for example, *see Ruysch*, 1724, p.54). This is still the usual but not universal custom. *In a Treatise on Midwifery* [1752], William Smellie (1697-1763), a leading obstetrician of London and teacher of William Hunter, recognizing this distinction, set the time for the dividing line at the [end of the] third month.[5]

John Quincy, in his *Lexicon Physico-Medicum Or, A New Physical Dictionary* (1719), defined *fetus* as "[t]he child in the womb... after it is perfectly formed, before that, it being called *Embryo*."[6] Chitty, in his *Treatise on Medical Jurisprudence* (1834), observed: "From the commencement of the impregnation or con-

4   *Old Bailey Session Proceedings*, December 4-9 (Harvester Press Microform Collection (1984) for the period 1714-1743) (1725), p.10.

5   P.273. *See* 1 Wm. Smellie, *A Treatise on the Theory and Practice of Midwifery* 74 & 110 (8th ed. corrected, Lon., 1774) (1st ed., 1732): "The conception is called Embryo until all the parts are distinctly formed, generally in the third month; and from that period to delivery is distinguished by the appellation *Foetus*."

6   P.158. *See also, e.g.*, J. Kersey, *Dictionarium Anglo-Britanicum, or A General English Dictionary sub tits. Embryo* & *Foetus* (1708); and S. Blanchard, *The Physical Dictionary* 96 (*Foetus*) (London, 1697).

ception, until the end of the *third month*, the embryo is termed an *ovum*, afterwards it is to be called *foetus* until the termination of gestation. But the most accurate physiologists use the term *foetus* indiscriminately during the time of gestation."[7] E. Chambers, in his *Cyclopaedia: Or An Universal Dictionary of Arts and Sciences* (London, 1728), gave the following definitions of *foetus* and *embryo*, respectively: "Foetus: in medicine, denotes the child while yet contained in the mother's womb; but particularly after it is perfectly formed — till which time it is properly called embryo;" "Embryo: in medicine, foetus; the first beginning or rudiments of the body of an animal, in its mother's womb, before it... [has] received all the dispositions of parts necessary to become animated — which is supposed to happen to a man on the 42nd day, at which time the embryo commences [to be] a perfect foetus."[8]

It seems, then, that in England in the eighteenth century, the term *fetus*, in its popular, as well as in its technical or scientific sense, could refer to either the product of human conception when it is in a state of fetal formation or the product of human

7    2 Chitty, *A Practical Treatise on Medical Jurisprudence* 400 (London, 1834). *See also id.* at 401.

8    E. Chambers, *Cyclopaedia: Or, An Universal Dictionary of Arts and Sciences* (London, 1728) *sub tits. Foetus* & *Embryo. But see* John Quincy, *The New Dispensatory sub. tit* Foetus/Embryo (London, 1753) (embryo becomes a fetus after the completion of the fourth month after conception). Some 19th century works state that the human embryo does not develop into a fetus until after the fourth or fifth month from conception. *See e.g.*, 4 *Pantologia: A New Cabinet Cyclopaedia sub. tit Embryo* (1819); *The American Medical Dictionary sub. tit Foetus* & *Embryo* (1811); and *Midwife's Practical Directory* 56 (1834) (embryo ceases and fetus commences at the middle of the fourth month from conception). *But see* 3 *Paris & Fonblanque, Medical Jurisprudence* 224 (fn.) (1823) (a foetus can be born alive as early as 3 months after its conception); *Chitty, supra* note 7 (of this *Appendix*) at 400-401 (human embryo becomes a fetus three months after conception); and Michael Ryan, *A Manual of Jurisprudence* 128 (1832) (the foetus is about four inches long at three months).

conception from the moment of its conception. It therefore cannot be reasonably stated that the term *foetus*, as used in the *Beare* abortion indictments, was meant to refer only to the product of human conception when it is in a state of fetal formation.

It is probably true that in England in the eighteenth century, it was generally received medical or scientific opinion that the product of human conception achieved fetal formation at about the end of the third month after conception.[9] It is also true that according to Belford's unchallenged statement, she was approximately thirteen to fourteen weeks into her pregnancy when Beare performed the abortion on her. Belford stated the following: (1) she worked for Beare for about fourteen weeks; (2) she had sexual intercourse with Chr a few days after she began to work for Beare; and (3) she miscarried the day after she left her employment with Beare (which means that the abortion was performed the day before Belford left her employment with Beare). However, it does not appear that in *Beare*'s trial evidence was offered to show that Belford miscarried of a "formed fetus". It may be that the product of Belford's miscarriage appeared to Belford as nothing more than a lump of blood or flesh.

Why was not Belford indicted as an accessory? The reason seems to be that it was a then and there legal custom (but not a binding legal rule) not to charge or not to prosecute an accomplice who agreed to fully cooperate in the prosecution of the principal. Justice Gould in *R v. Rudd* (1775) stated:

> *All* the judges were of opinion, that in cases not within any statute, an accomplice, who fully and truly discloses the joint guilt of himself and of his companions, and truly answers all questions that are put to him, and is admitted by justices of the peace as a witness against his companions, and who, when called upon, does give evidence accordingly, and appears under all the circumstances of the case to have acted a fair and ingenuous part, and to have made a full and true

---

9    *See supra*, note 8 (of this *Appendix 1*).

information, ought not to be prosecuted for his own guilt so disclosed by him.[10]

Regarding the punishments Beare received for her two misdemeanor convictions, they might be explained in *Regina v. Wright* (1705). It is stated there that if a person is convicted of two misdemeanors, and has no goods to forfeit, then the authorized sentence or punishment can include a jail sentence on one of the convictions and to be placed in the pillory on the other.[11]

I am at a loss to offer an explanation as to why the *Beare* trial court recommended to the *Beare* prosecutor not to bother proceeding on the second abortion indictment. A wild guess is that in common law misdemeanor prosecutions, a defendant could not be sentenced on more than two misdemeanor convictions because there existed only two types of punishment (not counting a fine or monetary punishment) in such cases: imprisonment and corporal punishment. The foregoing assumption itself assumes that consignment to the pillory falls under corporal punishment (which included whipping), and that consecutive same-punishments were illegal.

A person may want to argue that *R v. Beare* is not to be given much weight as it represents the judgment of but one judge. But from the American perspective, the same can be said of the pro-therapeutic abortion case of *R v. Bourne* (1939).[12] Yet, the Court in *Roe v. Wade* spoke approvingly of the decision in *Bourne*.[13] In any event, the California Court of Appeal in *Gardner v. Superior Court* (1986) observed: "in the development of the common law, the analysis of printed decisions of appellate courts is only part of the show. Development of the law begins in the trial courts ..."[14]

---

10   1 *Cowper's Rpts.* (Boston, 1809) 331, 339. *See also, e.g., R v. Lord Gray*, 3 *State Trials* 519.

11   2 Ray. 1189, 1195-96. An illustration of a pillory appears in S. Robbins, *Law: A Treasury of Art and Literature* 144 (1990).

12   [1938] 3 All E.R. 615, 1 K.B. 687.

13   *See Roe v. Wade*, 410 U.S. at 137.

14   182 C.A. 3d 335, 339; 227 Cal. Rptr. 78.

Some may want to argue also that in England, *R v. Beare* (on abortion) was never followed. That argument presupposes that the post-*Beare*, English judiciary was presented with an opportunity to follow or reject *Beare* (on abortion). However, no one knows if such an opportunity ever existed. Available evidence suggests that the post-*Beare*, English judiciary, in fact, accepted *Beare* on abortion.[15] Also, in 1803 the English Parliament implicitly accepted *Beare* on abortion.[16]

---

15   *See R v. Russell* (1832), *infra* in *Appendix 6*.

16   *See* 43 Geo. 3, ch. 58, sec. 1 & 2 (1803) in 44 *The Statutes at Large* 203-205 (1804).

# APPENDIX 2

## REPRODUCTION (WITH ACA) OF

## COLONY OF RHODE ISLAND AND PROVIDENCE PLANTATIONS V. DEBORAH ALLEN (1683)[1]

On Indictment by the Gen. Attorney against Deborah Allen, Daughter of Mather Allen of the Towne of Dartmouth in the Colony of New Plymouth for fornication [resulting in the birth of a bastard child], and for Indeavouringe the Dithuction [destruction] of the Child in her womb: being brought into the Court, her Charge Read, and asked whithyer Guilty or not, Ownes Guilty. The Court doe

---

1   Reproduced from *General Court of Trials: Newport County 1671-1724.A.* n.p. (4 Sept. 1683 Session). As of 1987, this volume was housed in the Providence, Rhode Island College, Phillips Memorial Library Archives *sub nom. Rhode Island Court Records Collection.* The staff of Phillips Memorial Library Archives, per my request, searched their *Rhode Island Court Records Collection* in an attempt to locate the *Allen* indictment and any depositions, *etc.*, that may have been taken in connection with the *Allen* case. The search proved fruitless: "The search turned out to be a *wild goose chase*; there is nothing further on the [*Deborah Allen*] case in our Records. As I am sure you can imagine, the records going back 300+ years are rather incomplete." Jane M. Jackson, Assistant Archivist for Phillips Memorial Library Archives, in a letter to Philip A. Rafferty (February 18, 1987). I am grateful to the staff of the Phillips Memorial Library Archives for conducting this search on my behalf. My original source for *Allen's Case* is Lyle Koehler, *A Search for Power: The "Weaker Sex" in Seventeenth-Century New England* 329 & 336 n. 132 (1980).

Sentence Deborah Allen for her Transgression forthwith to be severly whipped in the Towne of Newport with fifteen stripes on the naked back and pay officer's fees.

Some readers may want to argue that the *Allen* abortion allegation was added only to put Allen in an even more unfavorable light. More specifically, they might argue that because in colonial America a whipping was the common punishment that was or could be imposed on a woman who committed fornication, or on a woman who gave birth to a bastard child, then it hardly can be said that the attempted abortion related in *Allen's Case* is set forth there as a charge separate from the charge of fornication (resulting in the birth of a bastard child).

In Rhode Island in 1683 the mother and the father of a bastard child could be whipped for their fornication. *The Rhode Island Code of 1647*, which was in force in 1683, provided that the punishment for fornication or for producing a bastard child shall be the punishment that the English law proscribes for the same.[2] The 1683 edition of Dalton's *The Country Justice* sets forth this punishment:

> By the Statute 7 Jac. [1, c.iv, sec.7 1609)] it appeareth that the Justice of Peace shall now commit such leud Woman to the House of Correction, there to be punished, etc. And *quaere* if the Justices of Peace may not punish (by corporal punishment [, in this instance, by whipping]) the Mother by force of this Statute of 18 Eliz., [X, c.3 (1576], and then send them to the House of Correction....
>
> But such corporal punishment or commitment to the House of Correction is not to be until after the Woman is delivered of her child; neither are the Justices of Peace to med-

---

2    *The Rhode Island Code of 1647*, in expressly outlawing fornication, stated that the punishment for fornication shall be "what penaltie the Wisdom of the State of England have or shall appoint touching these transgressions [adultery and fornication]." 1 *Records of the Colony of Rhode Island and Providence Plantations in New England: 1636-1663* 173 (Providence, R.I., 1856).

dle with the Woman until that Child be born and wherewith she is [pregnant] happen to miscarry: For you shall find that about 31 Eliz. [1589] a Woman great with child, and suspected of incontinency, was commanded (by the Masters of Bridewell in London) to be whipped there, by reason whereof she travelled, and was delivered of her Child before her time, etc. And for this, said Masters of Bridewell were in the said case fined to the Queen at a great Sum, and were farther ordered to pay a sum of money to the said woman.[3]

*18 Eliz. 1, c.3* (1576) made it discretionary, not mandatory, that a woman be whipped for giving birth to a bastard child. Also, it appears to have been a well-established judicial custom, if not, for the most part, the law throughout the English North American colonies to permit a convicted fornicator to pay a fine in lieu of being whipped. Indeed, in 1683 in Rhode Island, the same Court that sentenced Deborah Allen to be whipped permitted each of three other female fornicators to pay a fine in lieu of being whipped ("one pound, Six Shillings, Eight pence ..., or [else] ... fifteen stripes on the Naked back")[4] Deborah Allen was

---

3   M. Dalton, *The Countrey Justice* 41 (London, 1682). On the influence of Dalton's *Countrey Justice* on Colonial American judicial officers, *see e.g.*, Peter C. Hoffer and N.E.H. Hull, *Murdering Mothers: Infanticide in England and New England 1558-1803* 13-17 (1981);. *See also* R. Chamberlain, *The Compleat Justice Enlarged* 37-42 (London, 1681); *A Manuall or Analecta Formerly Called the Compleat Justice* 31-32 (6th ed., London, 1648); and W. Nelson *The Office and Authority of a Justice of Peace* 92 (9th ed., 1726). 18 Eliz. I, c.3 (1576) is reproduced in 6 *Statutes at Large (I Mary. 35 Eliza.)* 311 (Cambridge, 1763). It reads in pertinent part: "justices of the peace ... may, by their discretion, take order ... for the punishment of the mother ... of such bastard child". *7 James 1 c. IV. Sec. 7* (1609) is reproduced in 7 *Statutes at Large (39 Eliza. 12 Chas. 2)*, 225 (Cambridge, 1763). It provides for one year in house of correction, "there to be punished and set on work" for a first offence of bastardy. *See also id.* at 327, *sec.* 15.

4   *See General Court of Trials, supra* note 1. These three were Hannah Archer, Rebechah Hobson and Sarah Dye. *See also, e.g., The Earliest Printed Laws*

ordered to be whipped "forthwith", and was not permitted to pay a fine in lieu of being whipped.

By virtue of what law was Deborah Allen prosecuted for having attempted to destroy her unborn child? So far as is known, Rhode Island did not then have on its books a criminal abortion statute. *The Rhode Island Code of 1647* expressly adopted the English common law on indictable offenses, but apparently, or at least arguably, it did so only to the extent that those indictable offenses were expressly or implicitly set forth there.[5] An example of the latter would be an attempt to commit one of the express offences. While the offense of murder was set forth in that code,[6] deliberated abortion was not. The last paragraph of this code provided as follows:

> These are the Lawes that concern all men, and these are the Penalties for the transgression thereof, which by common consent are Ratified and Established throwout this whole Colonie; and otherwise than thus what is herein forbidden, all men may walk as their consciences perswade them, every one in the name of his God. And lett the Saints of the Most

---

*of Delaware* 1704-1741, 62 (Wilmington, Delaware, 1978) (twenty-one lashes or three pounds, at the election of the fornicator); 1 *The Earliest Printed Laws of South Carolina: 1692-1734* at p. 164 (Wilmington, Delaware, 1977) (fornicator to pay a 5 to 10 pounds fine, and if not paid within 20 days after judgment of conviction, then thirty-one lashes on the bare back); and *Acts and Laws of His Majesty's Province of New Hampshire in New England with Sundry Acts of Parliament* 12 (Portsmouth, 1761).

5    See 1 *Records of Rhode Island and Providence Plantations in New England: 1636-1663* 158-160 (Providence, R.I., 1856); and Wm. R. Staples, *The Proceedings of the First General Assembly of the Incorporation of Providence Plantations and the Code of Laws Adopted by that Assembly in 1647* p. V (of *Preface*) & 50 (Providence, R.I., 1847).

6    See 1 *Records of Rhode Island and Providence Plantations, supra* note 5 at 163-64.

High walk in this Colonie without Molestation in the name of Jehovah, their God, for Ever and Ever....[7]

In the absence of evidence to the contrary, it should be presumed that the *Allen* court understood and abided by its own laws. It would seem, then, that the *Allen* charge of attempted abortion was brought on a theory of attempted murder, which at common law was indictable only as a misdemeanor. Such a theory would not necessarily be contrary to the English common law on murder, because at the common law an aborted child was considered a victim of murder, provided the child had died in connection with being aborted after the child had been born alive. Hence, at least when such a child had survived being aborted, then the attempted destruction of the child in the womb could be considered as attempted murder.[8]

Allen undoubtedly gave birth to the child she had attempted to abort before she was sentenced. This is because (and as is demonstrated by the Dalton's foregoing *Countrey Justice* observation), if Allen was pregnant when she was sentenced to be whipped, then the sentencing order would have recited that the whipping be stayed until after Allen gave birth and was restored to full strength.

Nevertheless, it cannot be stated positively that Allen's child was born alive. In Maryland in 1652, and evidently on a Maryland-received common-law theory, one Mitchell, a militia captain, was charged with, and was convicted of the attempted (abortion) murder of an unborn child that had been born dead. Evidently, the only reason why the *Mitchell* prosecutor did not file a murder charge against Mitchell was because the prosecutor formed the opinion that he could not sufficiently prove that

---

7    *Ibid.* at 190.

8    *See* (1^st) *Rafferty, supra* note 15 (of *Side B*) at text (of *Part IV*) accompanying notes 32 & 37, as well as the authorities, etc., cited in those notes. *See also, e.g., Q. v, West* (1848), *infra,* in *Appendix 4.*

the stillborn child had died in connection with the attempted abortion.[9]

It may be argued that Allen's relatively light sentence tends to prove that the *Allen* judge did not equate Allen's act of attempted abortion with the common law misdemeanor offense of attempted murder. The argument is fatally flawed. It will be seen, for example, that in England in 1592, Richard George, on being convicted of the attempted murders by poisoning of a mother and two of her children, received a sentence to be whipped. In 1670 in Essex County, Massachusetts, John Clearke was ordered to be whipped for his conviction of attempted murder by stabbing. In New London, Connecticut in 1712, Daniel Gard, on being convicted of manslaughter (a reprievable, capital felony), was sentenced to be whipped (thirty-nine stripes), to stand for one hour on the gallows with a halter about his neck, and to remain in prison until he paid the costs of his prosecution. Gard had challenged a man to fight; and then had killed the man in the fight.[10]

---

9    *See supra* note 15 (of *Side B*), and (1ˢᵗ) *Rafferty, supra* note 15 (of *Side B*) at text (of *Case No. 1* of *Appendix 2* – p. 483), accompanying note 6, as well as the commentary accompanying that case.

10    *R v. George* (1592) is reproduced in abstracted form in J.S. Cockburn, (*Kent Indictments, Elizabeth I*) 342 (No. 2058) (Lon., 1979). Clearke is in 4 *Records and Files of the Quarterly Courts of Essex County Massachusetts, 1667-1671*, p. 271 (1914). *Gard* is discussed in 5 *The Public Records of the Colony of Connecticut from October, 1706 to October, 1716*, pp. 350-351 (including footnote \*) (1870).

# APPENDIX 3

## REPRODUCTION (WITH ACA) OF

## REGINA V. THOMAS ADKYNS (ESSEX, 1600)[1]

An indented inquest taken at the town of Maldon in the
county of Essex before Thomas Wells and Henry Harte
coroners of the lady the queen within the aforesaid town
according to the liberties and privileges of the same town,
on Saturday 5 July 42 Eliz. [1600], upon the view of the
body of a certain Ann Webb then and there lying dead, by
the oath of … [names of coroner's jurors omitted], good and
lawful men of the aforesaid town: who say upon their oath
that Thomas Adkyns of Maldon aforesaid in the county afsd,
tailor, on 30 March in the above mentioned 42nd year [1600]
about the hour of 8 p.m. of the same day, with force and
arms etc. at the town of Maldon afsd. In the county afsd.
And within the liberties and jurisdiction of the same town,
of his malice aforethought feloniously assaulted the selfsame
Ann Webbe, then and there in the peace of God and of the
said lady the queen, and being *gravida cum quodam fetu* [in
English: "to make the said childe to be untymelie borne"],
then and there feloniously pressed (*contrusit*) the front part
of the belly of the same Ann with his knees and then and
there knelt upon the chest of the said Ann and then and
there with his feet feloniously did spurne [kick] the afsd.

1    ASS. 35/43/1. m.1 (Translation from the Latin supplied by Professor Sir
     J.H. Baker. An abstract of this case will be found in J.S. Cockburn, *Calendar
     of Assize Records Essex Indictments Elizabeth 1* 510 (no. 3054) (London,
     1978) (my initial source).

Ann, and then and there so seriously did crush and bruise the body of...Ann that [she]...from the crushing and bruising, languished from the...30th day of March [1600]...until the 4th day of July [1600]...at Maldon..., and then and there ...died. And so the jurors...say that...Thomas Adkyns... feloniously and willfully and of her [sic: his] malice aforethought... murdered... Ann Webb against the peace... In witness whereof both the coroner and the jurors have...set their seals to this inquisition...[*Annotated in margin*:] cul. ca. null. S' [i.e., guilty — no chattels — to be hanged:] Thomas Adkins.

Hale, in his *Historia Placitorum pp. 429-430* (London, 1736), helps to explain the *Adkyns* murder prosecution:

> But if a woman be with child, and any gives her a potion to destroy the child within her, and she take it, and it works so strongly, that it kills her, this is murder, for it was not given to cure her of a disease, but unlawfully to destroy the child within her, and therefore he, that gives a potion to this end, must take the hazard, and if it kill the mother, it is murder, and so ruled before me at the [Suffolk] assizes at Bury in the year 1670.[2]

Sir Michael Foster (1689-1763), in his *Crown Cases* p. 258 (c.1,sec.1)(1762), gives a more detailed explanation of *Adkyns*:

> In order to bring the case within this description [i.e., within the case of accidental homicide involving neither an act of negligence nor an act constituting an indictable offence], the act upon which death ensues must be lawful. For if the act be unlawful, I mean if it be *malum in se*, the case will amount to felony, either murder or manslaughter, as circumstances may vary the nature of it. If it be done in prosecution of a felonious intention [such as to rob or rape, or alternatively, with a wicked, murderous or mischievous motive] it will be murder;

2    pp. 429-430.

but if the intent went no further than to commit a bare trespass [it will be] manslaughter.

None of the foregoing, however, explains the outcome in Lord Protector v Damarice Baker (London, 1655). Damarice was tried on a murder indictment for killing Elianor Pooley (she being "great with child") in the course of performing a botched abortion on Pooley. The defendant inserted a 2-pronged fire-fork in the birth canal of Pooley resulting in a mortal wound four inches long and two inches wide. Damarice was found not guilty of murder, and guilty of manslaughter (almost certainly because the trial judge, in some manner, erroneously told the jury that such a finding would be permissible under certain circumstances). Damarice was sentenced to hang, reprieved temporarily because of pregnancy, then pardoned by Richard Cromwell, and released from Newgate Prison in late 1659 after having resided there continuously for approximately five years.[3]

---

3    See: MJ/SR/1142/2 (grand jury murder indictment with notation of pardon written on the top right hand corner of the indictment; kindly supplied by LMA); TNA/PRO, C231/6, p.429 (record of the pardon); LMA/MSR, MJ/SR/1142 (Session Roll), Item 26: entry of murder indictment: the top of the entry reads "Not guilty of the murder but guilty of manslaughter...[illegible] goods and [illegible]"; MJ/GB/R (Newgate Prison Delivery Sessions), MJ/GB/R/005 (register of prisoners delivered for trial, Apr. 1644-Feb 1656, October 1655 folio 270d: "Indicted: Damaris Baker, Mur[der]; guilty of [unlawful] homicide, not guilty of murder." References and research supplied and performed by Susan T. Moore, M.A. My original source for Damarice's Case: E.J. Burford, et al, *Private Vices – Public Virtues* 70-72 (1955).

# R V. ANONYMOUS (CIRCA, 1750?)[1]

The most fatal method [of causing abortion] is by punctures of the uterus, with a pointed instrument for the purpose; too often used among us [in England], and not unknown to the ancients. Patin [a leading, 18th-century, French physician] mentions a midwife hanged at Paris, for killing a foetus in the womb [*sic*: for killing the pregnant woman?], by running a stiletto or kind of bodkin up the vagina through the orifices of the uterus by which a miscarriage was procured, but with such ill success that the mother was seized with convulsions, and died miserably [*Patin*, T. 1. Lett. 191, An. 1660). The criminal confessed she had treated many before in the same manner, with good effect. Our own age and country [England] afford a parallel instance, a woman having been a few years ago executed among us for the like fact.[2]

---

1 1 G.L. Scott & Dr. Hill, *A Supplement to Mr. Chamber's Cyclopaedia: Or a Universal Dictionary of Arts and Sciences sub tit. Abortion* (London, 1753).

2 Scott and Hill (*see supra*, note 1) did not give a citation to this *Anonymous* abortion case, and I have been unable to locate it, although I did not engage in a systematic search for it. This *Anonymous* abortion case is not mentioned in the 1728-1750 editions of Chamber's *Cyclopaedia*. However, this does not mean that this case did not take place during the period 1728-1750. Hill, who was an attorney, was not connected with the editions of Chamber's *Cyclopaedia* that were published during the period 1728-1750.

# REPRODUCTION (WITH ACA) OF R V. WINSHIP (DURHAM, 1785) RICHARDSON'S TABLE BOOK ENTRY[1]

July 25 [1785]. John Winship, a farmer, in the neighbourhood of Monkweasmouth, was executed at Durham, having been convicted of poisoning his maid-servant by administering certain drugs to produce abortion. His body was given to the surgeons for dissecttion, and was opened by Mr. Wilkinson, of Sunderland, who in the presence of many gentlemen of the faculty, delivered a lecture on the contents of the cranium, thorax and abdomen. *Local Papers.*

# INDICTMENT[2]

Durham, to wit. The jurors for our lord the King upon their oath present that John Winship late of the parish of Bishop Wearmouth in the County of Durham, yeoman, not having the fear of God before his eyes but being moved and seduced by the instigation of the Devil, and of his malice aforethought, contriving and intending one Grace Smith with poison feloniously to kill and murder, on the twelfth day of March in the twenty-fifth [1785] year of the reign of our sovereign lord George the third

---

1  Reproduced from 2 M.A. Richardson, *The Local Historian's Table Book: Historical Division* 299 (Newcasthe-on-Tyne, 1841-43). This case is mentioned in John Smith, *The Punishment of Capital Felonies in County Durham 1707-1819*, 20 Dur. Co. Loc. Hs. Soc. 18,22 (including n.20) (Oct. 1977) (my initial source).

2  DUR. 17/25. This reproduction of the original *Winship* indictment was supplied by (Professor) Sir John H. Baker. Professor Baker informed me that there is on file here a *Winship* indictment by a Coroner's jury that does not appear to have been proceeded upon. He indicated that these two *Winship* murder indictments are identical in substance, but very slightly in their respective wording. Professor Baker in a letter to Philip A. Rafferty (March 14, 1985).

now King of Great Britain and so forth, with force and arms at the parish aforesaid in the county aforesaid, willfully, wickedly, knowingly and feloniously did mix a deadly poison, to wit, corrosive mercury sublimate, with water and the said water so mixed with the same poison as aforesaid afterwards, to wit the same day and year above mentioned, with force and arms at the parish aforesaid in the county aforesaid, unlawfully, willfully, knowingly and feloniously did give to the said Grace Smith to drink, and the said Grace Smith not knowing the said water to have been mixed with the said poison as aforesaid she the said Grace Smith did then and there drink and swallow the said water so mixed with the said poison as aforesaid, by means whereof the said Grace Smith of the poison aforesaid then and there became sick and distempered in her body, and of such sickness and distemper occasioned by the poison aforesaid from the said twelfth day of March in the year aforesaid until the sixteenth day of March in the same year at the parish of Bishop Wearmouth aforesaid in the county aforesaid did languish and languishing did live, on which said sixteenth day of March in the year aforesaid the said Grace Smith at the parish of Bishop Wearmouth aforesaid in the county aforesaid of the poison aforesaid and of the sickness and distemper thereby occasioned died. And so the jurors aforesaid upon their oath aforesaid do say that the said John Winship the said Grace Smith in manner and by the means aforesaid feloniously, willfully and of his malice aforethought did poison, kill and murder, against the peace of our said lord the King, his crown and dignity.

Radcliffe.[3]

[annotated in left margin:] A True Bill.

[annotated at head:] po: se: Guilty. To be hanged on Monday the 25th July instant and his body to be anatomized.

[endorsed:] Witnesses:[4]

Isabella Smith. sworne.

3    Clerk of assize.

4    "No depositions found on file." Professor Sir John H. Baker in a letter to Philip A. Rafferty (March 14, 1985).

John Smith. sworne.
John Harvey. sworne.
Robert Cheesment. sworne.

## THE GAOL DELIVERY BOOK (FIRST ENTRY)[5]

Friday morning 7 o'clock — Present Mr. Justice Nares. Same jury.

John Winship for feloniously mixing and administering a deadly poison, to wit, corrosive mercury sublimate, with water and giving to one Grace Smith to drink and swallow the 12th March 1785 at the parish of Bishop Wearmouth in the County of Durham, of which poison the said Grace Smith did die on the 16th of the same month of March at the parish aforesaid.

[annotated:] puts — Guilty. To be executed on Monday the 25th instant and his body to be delivered to the surgeons to be anatomized.

## THE GAOL DELIVERY BOOK (SECOND ENTRY)[6]

sentences passed on Saturday morning by Nares J. and the unnamed prosecutor allowed 13.16s. for expenses.

---

5    DUR 16/2, unfoliated (Assize beginning Tuesday, 19 July 1785 at Durham). Reference supplied by Sir John H. Baker.

6    *Ibid.* (at proceeding fo.).

# NEWCASTLE COURANT, 30 JULY 1785[7]

Yesterday ... the Assizes ended at Durham, when John Winship, for murder, ... [names of several other condemned felons omitted] received sentence of death....

Monday, John Winship was executed at Durham, pursuant to his sentence at the last assizes, for the willful murder of Grace Smith, his servant maid. He died a sincere penitent, acknowledging the justness of his sentence. His body was afterwards opened by Mr. Wilkinson, of Sunderland, who, in the presence of many Gentlemen of the Faculty, delivered a lecture on the contents of the *Cranium*, *Thorax* and *Abdomen*; on which occasion two worms were extracted from the Intestines, and the doctrine of the late Mr. Hewson, F.R.S. was demonstrated, that, in executions of this kind, death is not produced, as has been generally supposed, by an extravasation of blood, occasioned by the rupture of the vessels of the brain, but by suffocation: as in the case of drowning, etc. The whole of the internal parts were found in a very sound state, and exhibited great marks of longevity.

Given the validity of Richardson's *Table Book* version of the facts in *Winship*, (specifically, that Winship did not harbor the intent to kill his maid-servant when he gave her water secretly mixed with corrosive mercury sublimate,[8] but rather harbored only the intent to cause her to miscarry), then the *Winship* case can be reasonably said to stand for the proposition that at com-

---

7   P.4.

8   *See R v. Charles Angus* (2 September 1808, at the assizes in Lancaster, Lancashire), as reviewed in Thomas R. Forbes, *Early Forensic Medicine in England: The Angus Murder Trial*, 36 J. Hs. Med. & Allied Scs. 296, 298-99 (1981) ("The coroner's jury indicted him [Angus] for murder: At the subsequent trial the prosecution charged that he had given Miss Burns [the alleged murder victim] a substance ["arsenic ... [and] corrosive sublimate, bichloride of mercury"] to procure an abortion, and that she died as a result". Corrosive sublimate was also used in the abortion-murder-of-a-pregnant-woman case of *R v. Fretwell*, 9 Cox C.C. 152, 152 (1862).

mon law it is murder for a person to kill a woman in connection with an attempt to make her miscarry, irrespective of actual pregnancy. To put this another way, an unintentional killing coupled with an intent to cause an abortion will not negate malice. To put this still another way, if, in the course of a prosecution on a general, common law murder indictment, it is specially proved that the victim died in connection with the defendant's attempt to only make her safely abort, then proof of such a fact suffices to establish the element of malice as generally alleged in the indictment. By way of analogy here, in *Mackalley's Case* (1611) the following appears:

> I moved all the judges and barons, if in this case of killing a minister of justice in the execution of his office the indictment might have been general, without alleging any special matter, and I conceived that it might well be, for the evidence would well maintain the indictment forasmuch as in this case the law implies malice prepense. As if a thief, who offers to rob a true man, kills him in resisting the thief, it is murder of malice prepense, or if one kills another without provocation and without any malice prepense which can be proved, the law adjudges it murder and implies malice, for by the law of God everyone ought to be in love and charity with all men and, therefore, when he kills one without provocation the law implies malice. In both these cases they may be indicted generally, that they killed of malice prepense, for malice implied by law, given in evidence, is sufficient to maintain the general indictment. So in the case at Bar, in this case of the serjeant, the indictment might have been general, that the defendant feloniously and of his malice prepense killed the said Fells, and the special matter might well have been given in evidence, *quod fuit concessum* by all the other judges and barons of the Exchequer.[9]

---

9    [1558-1774] *All E.R. Rep.* 542, 545.

# R V. JOHN GOULD (STAFFORD, 1811)

# AS RELATED IN PARIS & FONBLANQUE MEDICAL JURISPRUDENCE (1823)[1]

A case illustrative of this law [i.e., illustrative of *quick with child*, deliberated abortion as being a criminal offence at common law] occurred at Stafford in the year 1811, when a man was executed for the murder of his wife, whose death he occasioned by inducing abortion, through extreme violence, as by elbowing her in bed, rolling over her, etc.

Here are Professor Sir J.H. Baker's comments on this case:

> The case referred to in Paris & Fonblanque, *Medical Jurisprudence* (1823) as having "occurred at Stafford in the year 1811" is to be identified as *R v. John Gould*, tried at the Lent assizes at Stafford in 1811. The records of Stafford assizes for Lent 1811 are preserved in the Public Record Office, ASSI 5/131, box IV.
>
> There are four depositions from women friends of the deceased (Mrs. Elizabeth Gould), all much to the same effect. One night she had told her husband that she was pregnant, and he had angrily asked her "Where hast been, for it is not my child?" He had thereafter nightly elbowed and struck her in bed, bringing on (within a fortnight) a miscarriage which the deponents considered to be the cause of her death soon afterwards. One deponent added that he had also denied her sufficient food and drink.
>
> The coroner's inquest sealed a presentment for murder, in which the deceased is stated to have been big with child, and particulars are given of the offence, including the starvation.
>
> However, the indictment on which Gould was tried is considerably simplified. It contains no mention of the pregnant condition of the deceased, and lays no specific intent.

---

1    3 Paris & Fonblanque, *Medical Jurisprudence* 84 n.c. (1823).

It charges that the accused feloniously, willfully and of his malice aforethought with both hands and elbows did strike and beat Elizabeth his wife in and upon the sides, belly and groin giving her mortal bruises whereof she died....[2]

---

2    Professor Sir John H. Baker in a letter to the author (May 6, 1989).

# R v. MARY IPSLEY AND ELIZABETH RICKETS (LONDON, 1718)[1]

The defendants in this case were acquitted of the murder of an unknown woman ("X"). Neither the indictment (to the extent it is legible: it is in Latin and is illegible in spots in the first part of the text and is completely illegible towards the end of the text) nor the report of this case mentions the words abortion or miscarriage. Nevertheless, the case was prosecuted almost certainly on a theory of death caused by criminal abortion. Ipsley called many witnesses in her defense.

Ipsley ran a lodging house. Rickets was a nurse, or at least Ipsley called her Nurse. "X" had been a lodger at Ipsley's house for a day or so, before her death. Elizabeth Stephens deposed that she was a servant to Ipsley and that one night she heard "X" cry out for help. Stephens proceeded to go upstairs to see "X" but was stopped by Ipsley who told Stephens that she would "knock out her brains" if she tried to see "X". Stephens deposed further that she did not see "X" until four days later when she saw "X" lying on a bed in Ipsley's house. (It is unclear here if Stephens thought that "X" was then dead). On the fifth day she saw X's naked body, along with a full-term dead infant, in a coffin in Ipsley's house. Ipsley hired some persons to take the closed coffin to a cemetery for burial. Ipsley accompanied the coffin to the cemetery. The Curate of the cemetery testified that he quizzed Ipsley on the contents of the closed coffin and that he caught her in numerous lies as to its contents and to the causes of the deaths. The Curate testified further that she lied in telling him that she had informed the Church Warden or Overseer of the deaths. Another witness testified that the damage to "X"'s vagina area was more than is usually caused in giving birth, that it was not ragged but appeared "to have been cut for the length of an inch or more." A midwife testified that there was a "vacancy" in X's vaginal area "that no

1    1984 Harvester Press Microform Collection of *Old Bailey Session Papers*, April, 1718 at p. 5.

child ever made in a woman by its birth;" and that the nose of the full-term infant had been cut or torn off. She testified further that "upon the whole she did not believe the Life of the Woman and Child went out by the Common Course of Nature." Another witness testified that in her opinion "X" had been cut, for ... no Woman ever received so much damage, or could, by the Birth of a Child; and that the Child had no Nose, only Nostrils, and was [i.e., its face was] as flat as the back of the Hand." Another witness related the following: "I told her [Ipsley] I did believe that somebody deserved to be hang'd [for committing such a barbarity on "X"] ... She [Ipsley] made answer, she knew nothing of the matter; that there being a Woman ... at some distance from her, whom she called Nurse, she said what was done she [Nurse, i.e., Elizabeth Rickets] did. The Woman [Nurse] made answer: 'Ay, Landlady, but you said I should come to no Trouble.' To that Mary Ipsley replied, 'Ay, Girl, so I did; no more shall you.'"

The free-lance reporter in this case ended his report with the following: "Upon the whole, there being no Evidence that attached Eliz. Rickets, and the Evidence against Mary Ipsley, though strong, being but presumptive [i.e., circumstantial], they were both acquitted."[2]

---

2    *Id.* at p. 6.

# APPENDIX 4: MORE SAMPLINGS OF ENGLISH

# COMMON LAW ABORTION PROSECUTIONS (WITH ACA)

## GUNDEWINE V. WARNER, ET AL (1247)[1]

Amice, who was the wife of Ralph Gundewine, appeals Adam Warner, William Warner and Henry Warner that they came to the house of her the said Amice and broke her house, and took her the said Amice and beat her severely (*male*) so that, by reason of that beating, she the said Amice lost her child which was then in her belly. And that they did this to her wickedly and feloniously against the peace etc., she offers etc.

And the aforesaid Adam and others come and deny the [breach of the peace], the beating, and the whole etc. and put themselves upon a jury of the township. And they offer the lord king 50 pounds for having the jury therein, by pledge of [twelve names].

And the jurors say upon their oath that in truth the aforesaid Adam and others beat the aforesaid Amice; but they say that she immediately went off, and walked about hither

---

1 JUST 1/274, m.14d. Translation from the Latin supplied by Professor Sir J.H. Baker. On criminal prosecution by "appeal", *see Baker, infra* note 1 of *Taillour's Case* (reproduced in this *Appendix 4*) at pp. 511-14.

and thither, and afterwards when eight days had elapsed she aborted a certain child having the form of a male (*puerum habentem forman hominis masculi*) five inches long; but they believe that this was rather due to the labour and foolish behaviour (*stultum cestum*) of the selfsame Amice than to the aforesaid beating.

# PREST V. CODE, ET AL (HAMPSHIRE, 1281)[1]

Alice, the wife of Adam Prest, coming from the city of Winchester out of the vill of Upham, met Walter Code, Richard the Potter and Stephen his brother, and Herbert the Carpenter, who knocked her over and beat her and would have lain with her by force, so that by the violence which they committed against her she gave birth to a certain abortive child as if [*quasi*] of the age of one month [*quasi statis unius mensis*]. Therefore let them be taken. William de Stratton, the coroner, did not [come?], therefore to judgment of him. Afterwards the aforesaid Walter and the others come and deny the death, the felony and all ... [and thereof] they put themselves upon the country. And twelve jurors say upon their oath that the aforesaid Walter, Richard and Stephen with force knocked over and beat the aforesaid Alice, as a result of which she gave birth to a certain abortive child of such an age that it was unknown whether it was male or female; which child was eight inches long. And they say that the aforesaid Herbert is not guilty thereof. Therefore [let him be] quit thereof. And the aforesaid Walter, Richard and Stephen are committed to prison.[2]

There can be no real doubt here that the *Code* jurors were aware that a pregnant woman does not have her "quickening" as early as one month into her pregnancy.

---

1    Just 1/789, m.1. Translation from the Latin by Professor Sir J.H. Baker.

2    The three men were pardoned ("de perdon, mortis hominis"), almost certainly because the killing was unintended or non-malicious. *See* Naomi D. Hurnard, *The King's Pardon for Homicide Before A.D. 1307* 106-107 (including note 1 at p. 107) (1969).

# REX V. HAULE (LONDON, 1321)[1]

In the twelfth year (1318) of the aforesaid reign of King
Edward [II] John of Gisors being coroner, Stephen of
Cornhill and Robert de Rokesle then being sheriffs, a certain Maud de Haule [Matillis de Haule] and Agnes the
Convert were fighting together in this ward [Queenhithe],
and a certain Joan of Hallynghurst came along and sepa-
rated them from each other, by reason of which the aforesaid Maud threw the aforesaid Joan out of the house where
she dwelt and she fell on the step of a solarium of the same
house so that on the fourth day following she gave birth to
a certain child of the female sex ten weeks before the due
time [*per decem septimanas ante tempus pariendi*], which same
child died immediately after birth. And the aforesaid Maud
was taken immediately after the deed and led to Newgate
prison in the time of the aforesaid sheriffs. Therefore [let
them answer for what happened].[2] And Robert Gobba, John
Braaz and Richard atte Vyngne, three neighbours, did not
come; but they are not suspected of wrong. The aforesaid
Robert was attached by Walter le Kent; therefore [he is] in
mercy. The other mainpernor has died. The aforesaid John
was attached by Hugh Trigge and John de Haleford; therefore [they are] in mercy. The aforesaid Richard was attached
by John Bardewyne and John le Kent; therefore [they are] in
mercy. Afterwards William le Leyre and Henry ate More,
tenants of part of the lands which were the aforesaid sheriffs', come and fully admit that the aforesaid Maud de Haule
was in the aforesaid prison in the time of the aforesaid sheriffs; and they say that the aforesaid Maud was hanged before
Hamon Hauteyn and his fellows, justices assigned to deliver

---

1    JUST 1/547A, m. 20d. Translation from the Latin supplied by Professor
Sir Baker. My initial source: Harold N. Schneebeck, Jr., *The Law of Felony
in Medieval England from the Accession of Edward I Until the Mid-Fourteenth
Century* 241 (including note 59) (Ph.D dissertation, U. of Iowa, 1973) (pub.
by UMI, Ann Arbor, MI).

2    "Translation uncertain" per Professor Baker.

the gaol aforesaid etc. And that appears from the rolls of the same Jamon etc. She had no chattels etc.[3]

This case is extremely important in relating a true history of the English common law on abortion or unborn-child killing. It occurred, as did the *Kyltavenan* (1311), *Hansard* (1329), *Skotard* (1330), and *Mandson* (1361) cases (and which are the next four cases that are reproduced, respectively, in this *Appendix 4*), very near the time (1327-1328) that *Rex v. Richard de Bourton* (aka., *The Twins-Slayer's Case*) occurred and, therefore, tends to corroborate my opinion that, contrary to a near unanimous opinion among English common law legal commentators (such as Staunford, Coke, Hawkins, and Blackstone), *Bourton's Case* does indeed stand for the proposition that unborn-child killing is a capital felony at common law.

Staunford, Coke, Hawkins, and Blackstone, writing hundreds of years after *Bourton's Case* (Staunford's *Les Plees del Coron* commentary on *The Twins-Slayer Case*: 1557, Coke's *Institutes III* commentary on the same: 1641, Hawkins' *History of the Pleas of the Crown* commentary on the same: 1716, *Blackstone's 1 & 4* commentaries on the same: 1765 & 1770), and relying on a very incomplete report of *Bourton's Case*, misinterpreted the word "felony" in the *Bourton* judicial phrase *the child-killing was not felony* to mean that unborn-child killing was not a capital offence (or homicide) at common law. In point of fact, all that the *Bourton* justices were relating here was that it did not appear that Bourton killed the twins "in felony" (i.e., "with malice or felony aforethought"), and therefore *Bourton* could be admitted to bail on the discretion of the sheriff. (The *Bourton* facts do indeed infer only accidental killings.) This misinterpretation is *wholly* responsible for a reversal in the common law on unborn-child killing: What was murder, ceased to be so (unless the aborted fetus died after first being expelled alive).[4]

---

3    *See Mondson's Case*, reproduced *infra*, in this *Appendix 4*

4    *See, e.g., Q v. West* (1848), abstracted, in pertinent part, *infra*, in *Appendix 4*. Bourton, in the course of forcibly entering into the home of the woman

One does not have to be an expert on the common law to see how the foregoing change in the common law of murder could have come about "only" through (accidental) judicial misinterpretation. He or she need be aware, here, of only three (3) facts: 1) In England, before and at the time of *Bourton's Case*, in-womb child killing constituted unlawful homicide at common law; 2) then-existing English judges lacked the jurisdiction to alter the common law of crimes; and 3) such a change here greatly increased the danger posed to the pregnant woman bent on having an abortion: To make sure her unborn child was expelled dead, the abortionist would be encouraged to use a stronger (or a larger amount of) poison, or a more pointed or sharper instrument, *etc.*

A question of whether in-womb child killing is a (capital) felony at common law was not even put in issue in *Bourton's Case*.

who he caused to miscarry of twins, evidently knocked her down and then stepped on her. Bourton's *Case* is reproduced and discussed in great depth *infra*, in this *Appendix 4*. Here is a case that is somewhat factually similar to *Bourton's Case*:

*R v. Cokkes* (Somerset, c. 1415):

Commission to … sheriff … to inquire concerning all matters contained in certain petitions severally exhibited to the king in Chancery … which the king sends … under the foot of his seal. Westminster.II May 3 Henry V [1415].

Inquisition before the said … sheriff: … Cokkes is guilty of all the matters contained in the said petitions … except that the jurors in no wise know whether or not he beat and wounded the said Elizabeth and ill-treated her by her legs so that she was delivered of 2 children then in her womb 5 weeks before her time, to the great despair of her life, by which assault the back of one child and the legs or limbs of the other were broken — so that they died immediately after their birth.

Reproduced from 7 *Calendar of Inquisitions Miscellaneous (Chancery) Preserved in the Public Record Office 1399-1422* 296 (no. 523) (London, 1968). The outcome of *Cokkes' Case* is unknown. My guess, here, is that he received a pardon.

And in the Anglo-American legal tradition cases can never be said to stand for propositions not considered there.

# R V. JOHN KYLTAVENAN
# (CORK, IRELAND, 1311)[1]

[Against] John Kyltavenan [it is] charged that he burglariously entered the house of Maurice Tancard and robbed him of divers goods to the value of 4s., and that he beat Johanna de Rupe, Maurice's wife, who was with child and maltreated her, whereby he killed a boy in the womb of the said Johanna. [John Kyltavenan] comes and defends, etc....[names of jurors omitted]. [The] jurors say that John Kyltevenan is guilty of the said charges and of several other misdeeds. Therefore let him be hanged. Chattels, none; he has no free land.

The English common law was in effect in Ireland in the fourteenth century.[2] However, and as the following case (*R v. Richard Stakepoll* (1311)) would seem to indicate, Kyltavenan's burglary conviction did not carry a mandatory sentence of death:

[Against] Richard Stakepoll [it is] charged that he burglariously by night entered the house of John Seys and robbed there from four hams worth 4s. [Richard Stakepoll comes and defends, etc.... [names of jurors omitted]. [The] jurors say that Richard is guilty of the charges, and that he stole the hams from excessive want and poverty, and they do not suspect him of any other misdeeds. Therefore, of grace, Richard is admitted to make fine, etc., by 20s., by pledge of John Stakepoll, so that he stand, etc. And John Stakepoll mainprised for Richard that he would for the future always bear himself well and faithfully to the King's peace, and if he do not, he will restore him to the King's prison dead or alive within fifteen days of notice of the repetition of his misdeeds, and also make good their losses to those that suffer by Richard....[3]

---

1 Reproduced from *Calendar of the Justiciary Rolls or Proceedings in the Court of the Justiciary of Ireland I to VII Years of Edward II* 193 (Dublin, Stationary Office, n.d.).

2 *See* G.J. Hand, *English Law in Ireland, 1290-1324* (1967).

3 Reproduced from *Calendar of the Justiciary Rolls, supra,* note 1 at 193.

# R V. HANSARD (EYRE OF LONDON, 1329)[1]

Robert Hansard was attached to answer the lord king as to why he, together with other wrongdoers who were bound to him by an oath [*vinculo sacri confederate*] in the…year of the reign of the present king after his coronation, with force and arms and against the peace etc., came to the house of Henry le Pulter in London and beat Agnes his wife, who was then pregnant, so that she aborted a dead child [*mortuum fecit abortum*) and by threats of death and by other oppressive means took from the aforesaid Henry ten shillings. He comes and says that he is not guilty thereof, and of this puts himself upon the country etc. Robert by threats and oppressive means took ten shillings from the aforesaid Henry as it above charged against him. Therefore let the aforesaid Robert be committed to the gaol etc.

Evidently, the jurors implicitly acquitted Hansard of the alleged homicide.

---

1   JUST 1/548, m.4. Translation from the Latin supplied by professor Sir John Baker. My initial source: *Schneebeck, supra,* note 1 (of *Haule's Case* (in this *Appendix 4*) at p. 238 (including note 50).

# R V. SKOTARD
# (EYRE OF DERBYSHIRE, 1330)[1]

Item, in the 30th year [1301] of the same king grandfather [Edward I], a certain Alan Skotard of Chesterfield beat Eudusa his wife with a stick, whereby she gave birth to a certain dead male child, and the self-same Eudusa afterwards thereof died confessed. And he was arrested and delivered to Nottingham gaol, and from that gaol he was delivered and acquitted of that death. And afterwards he was slain on Whittington Moor by unknown thieves.

---

1    JUST 1/169, m.25. Translation from the Latin supplied by Sir John Baker. My initial source: *Schneebeck, supra* note 1 of *Haule's Case* (in this *Appendix 4*) at p. 239 (n.54).

# R V. MONDSON (LINCOLNSHIRE GAOL DELIVERY, 1361-1362)[1]

Lincolnshire. The jurors…present that William…feloniously stole…from Joan de Scotter twelve silver spoons…They [also] present that John Mondson of Alkborough in the twenty-sixth year [1352] of the reign of the present king [Edward III], at 'Gerlethorp' Marah feloniously raped a certain Elizabeth de Alkborough of 'Gerlethorp' and lay with her and committed such violence against her that the quick child (*infans vivus*) in her womb died; and she herself within half a year died on account of the aforesaid violence. Therefore the sheriff was commanded to take them etc. And now, before the said justices here, come the aforesaid William and John, led by the keeper of the gaol; and, being severally asked by the justices how they would acquit themselves of the aforesaid felonies, they put themselves upon the country on this for good and ill. The jurors, being chosen, tried and sworn for this purpose, say upon their oath that the aforesaid William and John are in no way guilty of the aforesaid felonies, and never ran away for the aforesaid causes. Therefore let them go quit.

---

1    JUST 1/527, m.11d. Translation from the Latin supplied by professor Sir John H. Baker. My initial source: *Schneebeck*, *supra* note 1 of *Haule's Case* (in this *Appendix 4*) at pp. 240-41 (including note 57).

# Q V. WEBB (SOUTHWARD ASSIZES, 1602)[1]

Surrey. The Jurors for our lady the Queen present that Margaret Webb, late of Godalming in the county aforesaid, spinster, on the tenth day of August in the forty-first year (1599) of the reign of our lady Elizabeth, by the grace of faith, with force and arms at Godalming aforesaid in the county aforesaid, not having the fear of God before her eyes but being seduced by the instigation of the devil, ate a certain[2] poison called *ratsbane* with the intention of getting rid of[3] and destroying the child in the womb of her the said Margaret: and thus the aforesaid Margaret, by reason of eating the poison aforesaid, then and there got rid of and destroyed the same child[4] in her womb, to the most pernicious example of all other wrongdoers offending in similar cases, against the peace of the said lady the Queen, her crown and dignity.

Church[5]

Pardoned by the general pardon.

---

1    Assi. 34/44/7 m.18 (Reproduced from J. Keown, *Abortion, Doctors and the Law: Some Aspects of the Legal Regulation of Abortion in England from 1803–1982* 173.m.22 (1988)). Translation from the Latin supplied by Professor Sir John H. Baker. *See also* Keown, *supra* this note at 7-8. My initial sources: J.S. Cockburn, *Surrey Indictments, Elizabeth 1* 512 (n.3146) 1980.

2    "Reading *Quendam*: it actually looks like quondam (once), and Keown so takes it, but this is a scribal error." Professor Baker in a letter to Philip A. Rafferty (April 22, 1989).

3    "This seems to be the sense of spoliare here. Keown plays safe with 'spoil'". *Ibid.*

4    "The adjective *eandem* is female, indicating a female child, though the sex is not expressed directly." *Ibid.*

5    "Clerk of assize". *Ibid.*

This indictment, as it clearly does not allege a felony, must be taken to be charging a misdemeanor.

Keown has reported that Dr. Hunnisett and J.S. Cockburn are of the opinion that *Webb* was pardoned after conviction. What is really frustrating is that Keown did not set forth Hunnisett's and Cockburn's reason or reasons for arriving at this opinion.[6] In my opinion, the presumption should be that *Webb* was never convicted, and probably was never even tried. One basis for this presumption is that the clerk for the *Webb* trial court would have had a duty to enter on the *Webb* record any verdict a *Webb* jury would have returned. But no verdict is entered on the *Webb* record. Since it is fair to presume that the *Webb* clerk properly performed his duties, then it seems fair to conclude that no verdict was recorded for the simple reason there was no verdict to record. Furthermore, *sec. V* of the statute under which Webb was pardoned expressly forbade the clerk of any court to issue, "after the last daie (i.e., after December 19, 1601) of this present Session of Parliament", an order for a defendant to appear in Court on an offence made pardonable by the statute.[7]

I asked Professor James Cockburn to comment on my opinion that Webb was never convicted on the abortion indictment. Here are his comments:

> *Margaret Webb.* In general, your assessment of the evidence for/ against conviction seems to be judicious, and in the light of it I would be inclined to reverse what was apparently my original position (I do not recall the conversation or correspondence with Keown) and say, guardedly, that Webb probably was pardoned *before* conviction. I say "guardedly" because (1) most assize pardons were granted after conviction, and (2) it is by no means unusual for assize clerks to omit details of a conviction &/or sentence. In the light of that fact, you might wish to amend your account to read: "The basis for this presumption is that the clerk of the court

6   *See Keown, supra* note 1 (above) at 7 & 173 n.23.

7   *See* 4 *The Statutes of the Realm (Part. 2)* 1010-1011 (*sec.* 5) (London, 1819); and *id.* at 958.

normally entered details of the verdict and sentence on an indictment tried at assizes. No such details are entered on the indictment of Margaret Webb. Although the evidence is not conclusive, it is probably fair to conclude that no verdict was recorded for the simple reason that Webb was not tried". You might also add that there is no trace of a jury empanelled to try the case. That too is suggestive though, again, not conclusive. I should also make it clear that these are my own thoughts, and do not necessarily concur with those of Dr. Roy Hunnisett.

One detail slightly troubles me. Why, I wonder, was there a two-year delay between the (alleged) date of the offence and the drafting, or at least the entering, of an indictment? Such a delay normally occurred when the suspect had evaded apprehension, but there is no suggestion of that here. It is just possible, therefore, that the charge was malicious and that that was a factor in the decision to include her in the pardon. In any event, the circumstances are clearly too unusual to sustain any general thesis.[8]

After I received the above response from Dr. Cockburn, I discovered two Star Chamber cases that apparently held that a person, who is indicted for an offence that is pardonable under the general pardoning statute that was invoked in the *Webb* case, cannot be saved from trial and possible conviction (and judgment?) unless he or she pleads the pardoning statute before trial.[9] I mentioned this to Professor Cockburn in a telephone conversation, and he stated that if I have correctly interpreted those two Star Chamber cases, then those two cases constitute additional support on the opinion that *Webb* was never tried on the abortion indictment.

The general pardon referred to in *Webb* represents an application of *43 Eliz., c.19*, enacted near the end of 1601, and entitled

---

8    Professor Cockburn in a letter to Philip A. Rafferty (U. of Maryland at College Park (May 18, 1990)).

9    *See* W.P. Baildon (ed.), *Les Reportes del Cases in Camera Stellata 1593-1609* 118 & 334 (1894).

"An Acte for the Queenes Majesties moste gracious generall and free Pardon". The pardon extended to offences (with certain exceptions, such as *murder*)[10] committed before August 7, 1601. The act was enacted during a parliamentary session that began on October 27, 1601. The act states that it shall extend to offences committed "before and unto [up to] the seaventh Daie of August last past."[11]

---

10   4 *Statutes, supra* note 7 at *sec.* 6.

11   *Ibid.* (at *sec.* 1). *See also id.* at *sec.* 2; and *id.* at 958.

# R V. M. C. OF E (1672)[1]

The jurors for the lord king, upon their oath, present that, whereas a certain A. wife of a certain R.P. of E. ... on May 4,... [1672] ... at E. ... in the ... county of G., was then and there pregnant ...; nevertheless, a certain M.C. Of E .... in the ... county of G., knowing the aforesaid A. to be then and there great with child (*gravida*), afterwards, namely the above mentioned day and year, at E. ... assaulted [A.], and then and there against her will so improperly 'examined' (*enormiter lustravit*) ... A., and ill treated her ... in order to have carnal knowledge of her, that he then and there slew a certain male child which the same A. ... carried alive (vivum) in her womb, by reason whereof ... A. Afterwards, namely the above mentioned day and year, at E....in...the...county of G., aborted the same male child, so that...M. in manner and form aforesaid feloniously slew the...male child.

Here are some of Baker's comments on this indictment:

"This indictment was first printed in *Officium Clerici Pacis* (1675), pp. 240-241, and reprinted in the second edition (1686), p. 240, and in the third edition (1726), p. 281... In the third edition the date of the offence has been updated to 10 of the present king (i.e., 1724); but the wording is otherwise the same as the earlier editions, in which the date is 4 May 24 Car. II (i.e., 1672)....

The author, J.W., says in the preface that most of the contents are extracted from the Sessions Records (remaining with the Clerks of the Peace of several counties) which have been extant since the year 1662. The likelihood is, therefore, that this was a case in the Gloucestershire Quarter Sessions records.

I have consulted I.E. Gray and A.T. *Gaydon, Gloucestershire Quarter Sessions Archives* 1689- 1889 (1958), from which it seems that no files or rolls survive....So there seems, alas, no prospect of finding the original case.

---

1    Reproduced (as translated from the Latin by Sir John H. Baker) from J.W. *Officium Clerici Pacis* 240-241 (1675).

Perhaps more significant than any decision by the Gloucestershire justices is the fact the precedent was printed in three successive editions of the standard precedent book of indictments for use at sessions.

I am puzzled by the exact means whereby the abortion was produced; the coy language indicates some kind of unwanted sexual attentions short of intercourse. Was it thought that this could bring about an abortion? The indictment is for manslaughter, not murder, because no intention to kill the child is laid [and perhaps also because defendant's acts did not amount to an independent felony, and were not such as ordinarily would result in death or serious injury to another]. Presumably, if the causation was proved, the impropriety of the activity (an assault) was enough to make this manslaughter.

The indictment is clearly for *feloniously* killing the child, not simply for assaulting the mother. It would surely follow that, had there been malice in the form of an intention to kill the child, it would have been murder.[2]

I would respectively disagree with Baker on his last point (unless, of course, the fetal-human being is initially brought forth alive), and also on his point that precedes it. On his former (or last) point, see e.g. R. v. Evans (London, 1734), *reproduced, supra* (*Unraveling*) at page 77. On the "preceding point," manslaughter would be unavailable because of the "born-alive rule"; and the crime of abortion would be unavailable because "intent" to cause an abortion is lacking. That leaves only the misdemeanor offence of (aggravated) assault. See, e.g. J.S. Cockburn (ed.) *Kent Indictments* (1997) p. 141, item 727: In July of 1681, Henry Holden was indicted, and convicted of the misdemeanor offence of assulting Anne W. so that she miscarried.

---

2    Professor Baker in a letter to Philip A. Rafferty (August 8, 1988).

# R V. TURNER
# (NOTTINGHAMSHIRE, 1755)[1]

Against Thomas Turner of Warsop, weaver, for a misdemeanour in persuading and procuring Elizabeth Mason to take and swallow a certain quantity of arsenick mix'd with treacle in order to kill and destroy a male bastard child by him begotten on her body and which she was then quick with[2] To which indictment he appear'd and pleaded Not Guilty, and upon his trial was acquitted by the jury and discharged.[3]

---

1 Notts. Archives Office, QSM 1/27, Quarter Sessions Order Book. Transcription supplied by Professor Baker. This case is reproduced also in *Keown, supra* note 1 (of Reproduction of *Webb's Case*) at 9-10 (my initial source).

2 As to the probable reason why E. Mason was not prosecuted (if in fact she was not prosecuted), *see supra*, text (of *Appendix 1*) accompanying note 10.

3 "Note: this appears to be the entire record. It speaks for itself. The indictment as paraphrased here does not appear to be specific as to whether the foetus was born alive or dead, and so it may be permissible to regard this as simply abetting an attempt to kill an unborn child." (Professor Baker in a letter to Philip A. Rafferty (May 6, 1989).)

# R V. EDWARD FRY (1801)[1]

## FIRST COUNT

That E.F....being a wicked, malicious, and evil disposed person, and not having the fear of God before his eyes but being moved and seduced by the instigation of the devil, on the twenty-eighth day of February, in the thirty-ninth year [1799] of the reign of our sovereign lord George the third, then king of Great Britain, at the time of taking this inquisition, by the grace of God of the united kingdom of Great Britain and Ireland, king, defender of the faith, with force and arms, at, &c. aforesaid, in and upon one A.E. the wife of F.E. in the peace of God and our said lord the king, then and there being big and pregnant with child, did make a violent assault, and that he the said E.F., then and on divers other days and times, between that day and the day of the taking of this inquisition, with force and arms, at, &c. aforesaid, knowingly, unlawfully, willfully, wickedly, maliciously, and injuriously, did give and administer, and cause and procure to be given and administered to the said A.E., so being big and pregnant with child as aforesaid, divers deadly, dangerous, unwholesome, and pernicious pills, herbs, drugs, potions, and mixtures, with intent feloniously, willfully, and of his the said E.F.'s malice aforethought, to kill and murder the said child, with which the said A.E. was so then big and pregnant as aforesaid, by reason and means whereof, not only the said child, whereof she the said A.E., was afterwards delivered, and which by the providence of God was born alive, became and was rendered weak, sick, diseased, and distempered in body, but also the said A.E. as well before as at the time of her said delivery, and for a long time, (to wit,) for the space of six months then next following, became and was rendered weak, sick, diseased, and distempered in body, and during all that time, underwent and suffered great and excruciating pains, anguish and torture both of body and mind, and other

---

1    Reproduced from 3 Joseph Chitty, *A Practical Treatise On The Criminal Law Containing Precedents of Indictments* 798-801 (London, 1816).

wrongs to the said Anne, he the said E.F. then and there unlawfully, willfully, wickedly, maliciously, and injuriously did, to the grievous damage of the said A.E., and against the peace of, &c.

## SECOND COUNT

And the jurors, &c. do further present that the said E.F. afterwards, (to wit,) on the said, &c. with force and arms at, &c. aforesaid, in and upon the said A.E. in the peace of God and our said lord the king then and there being, and also then and there being big and pregnant with a certain other child, did make another violent assault, and that he the said E.F. then and on divers other days and times, between that day and the day of the taking of this inquisition, with force and arms, at, &c. aforesaid, knowingly, unlawfully, willfully, wickedly, maliciously, and injuriously, did give and administer, and cause and procure to be given and administered to the said A.E., so being big and pregnant with child as last aforesaid, divers other deadly, dangerous, unwholesome, and pernicious pills, herbs, drugs, potions, and mixtures, by reason and means whereof, &c. (as before).

## THIRD COUNT

And the jurors, &c. do further present that the said E.F. afterwards, (to wit,) on the said, &c. with force and arms at, &c. aforesaid, in and upon the said A.E. in the peace of God and our said lord the king then and there being, and also then and there being big and pregnant with a certain other child did make another violent assault; and that he the said E.F. then and on divers other days and times between that day and the day of the taking of this inquisition, with force and arms, at &c. aforesaid, knowingly, unlawfully, willfully, wickedly, maliciously, and injuriously, did give and administer, and cause and procure to be given and administered to the said A.E. so being big and pregnant with child as last aforesaid, divers other deadly, dangerous, unwholesome, and pernicious pills, herbs, drugs, potions, and mixtures with a wicked intent to cause and procure the said A.E. to mis-carry and to bring forth the said last mentioned child, with which she was so big and pregnant as last aforesaid, dead, by reason and means whereof, she the said A.E. became and was rendered weak, sick, diseased, and distempered in body, and remained and continued so weak, sick, diseased, and distempered in body for a long time, (to wit) for the space of six months then next following, and during all the time last mentioned underwent and suffered great and excruciat-ing pains, anguish and torture, both of body and mind, and other wrongs to the said A.E., he the said E.F. then and there unlawfully, willfully, wickedly, maliciously, and inju-riously did, to the grievous damage of the said A.E., and against the peace, &c.

## FOURTH COUNT

And the jurors, &c. do further present that the said E.F. afterwards, (to wit,) on, &c. at, &c. in and upon the said A.E. in the peace of God and our said lord the king, then and there being, and also then and there being big and preg-nant with a certain other child, did make another violent assault, and her the said A.E. then and there did violently beat, bruise, wound, and ill treat, so that her life was thereby greatly despaired of, and then and there violently, wickedly, and inhumanly, pinched and bruised the belly and private parts of the said A.E., and a certain instrument called a rule, which he the said E.F. in his right hand then and there had and held, up and into the womb and body of the said Anne, then and there violently, wickedly, and inhumanly, did force and thrust with a wicked intent to cause and procure the said A.E. to miscarry and to bring forth the said child, of which she was so big and pregnant, as last aforesaid, dead, by reason and means of which last mentioned premises, she the said Anne became and was rendered weak, sick, sore, lame, diseased and disordered in body, and remained and contin-ued so weak, sick, sore, lame, diseased, and disordered in body, as last aforesaid, for a long time, (to wit,) for the space of six months then next following, and during all the time last aforesaid, underwent and suffered great and excruciating pains, anguish, and torture, both of body and mind, and other wrongs to the said A.E. he the said E.F. then and there unlawfully, willfully, wickedly, maliciously, and injuriously did, to the grievous damage of the said Anne, and against the peace of, &c.

Count 1, and perhaps Count 2 of the *Fry* indictment, each allege the attempted abortion-murder on an unborn child who was born alive. It is unclear (at least in *Chitty*) whether these counts involve separate pregnancies or one pregnancy involving twins. Counts 3 and 4 each allege an attempted abortion on a woman who was then pregnant with an existing child. It is unclear (at least in *Chitty*) if Counts 2, 3 & 4 involve 1, 2 or 3 child-victims. If Count 2 did not in fact allege that the child was born alive, then it may be the case that Counts 2-4 involved the same unborn child.

I have not seen the *Fry* indictments. But they are in existence, as Sir John H. Baker makes clear in the following statement:

> The principal record [of *Fry's Case* 1801] is on the Crown Roll of the King's Bench for the Michaelmas term of 1801 (KB 28/399. m.18). It occupies five skins of parchment…The text in *Chitty* is perfectly accurate. I can add that the defendant was Edward Fry of the parish of St. Luke, Middlesex, yeoman, and the woman concerned was Ann, wife of Francis Edwin. The indictment was found at the Middlesex sessions on 29 June 41 Geo. III [1801], but was removed into the King's Bench. The King's Bench record shows that on Friday [July 3] after the morrow of All Souls, Fry came and pleaded Not guilty. A jury was summoned for later in the term, but did not come, and another *venire facias* issued for a trial in the vacation. The case came on for trial before Kenyon C.J., but after proclamation made the defendant was discharged "without day". This "discharge by proclamation" meant that no one came forward to give evidence for the Crown. The validity of the indictment was therefore not judicially considered. Nevertheless, it is clear

that Fry was arraigned on the indictment without any challenge being taken to its legal validity.

There is also a record of the case in the Controlment Roll (KB 29/461, London & Middlesex, no. 13). This notes the *venire facias* only, to answer "for certain misdemeanours". Later in the roll (unnumbered membranes) there is a note of the entry of appearance and the plea of Not guilty "to an indictment for misdemeanour".[2]

---

2    Professor Baker in a letter to Philip A. Rafferty (December 12, 1986).

# Q V. WEST (1848)

The *West* trial court judge, in the course of charging the jury in this abortion-murder-of-a-live-born-child case, related the following:

> The prisoner is charged with murder: and the means stated are that the prisoner caused the premature delivery of the witness Henson, by using some instrument for the purpose of procuring abortion: and that the child so prematurely born was, in consequence of its premature birth, so weak that it died. This, no doubt, is an unusual mode of committing murder: and some doubt has been suggested by the prisoner's counsel whether the prisoner's conduct amounts to that offence: but I am of opinion (and I direct you in point of law), that if a person intending to procure abortion does an act which causes a child to be born so much earlier than the natural time, that it is born in a state such less capable of living, and afterwards dies in consequence of its exposure to the external world, the person who by her misconduct so brings the child into the world, and puts it thereby in a situation in which it cannot live, is guilty of murder. The evidence seems to show clearly that the death of the child was occasioned by its premature birth: and if that premature delivery was brought on by the felonious act of the prisoner, then the offence is complete....If the child, by the felonious act of the prisoner, was brought into the world in a state in which it was more likely to die than it would have been if born in due time, and did die in consequence, the offence is murder: and the mere existence of a possibility that something might have been done to prevent the death, would not render it less murder. If therefore, you are satisfied, to the exclusion of any reasonable doubt, that the prisoner, by a felonious attempt to procure abortion, caused the child to be brought into the world, for which it was not then fitted, and that the child did die in consequence of its exposure to the external world, you will find her guilty; if you entertain a reasonable doubt as to the facts you will, of course, find her not guilty.[1]

---

1    Cox's C.C. 500, 503; 2 Car & K 784; 175 Eng. Rpt. 329. West was found not guilty.

# REX V. RICHARD DE BOURTON, A.K.A. THE TWINS-SLAYER'S CASE (1327-1328)[1]

## CASE SUMMARY

Bourton was indicted on two counts of felonious or capital homicide: the felonious destruction of an unborn child and the felonious destruction of a live born child, who died almost immediately after birth from prenatal injuries. Bourton was arraigned on, and pleaded not guilty to, these two counts of felonious homicide. The matter was set for trial, but Bourton failed to show, so the *Bourton* court issued a writ for his arrest. Some time after his arraignment, Bourton successfully applied for release on mainprise (a form of bail or bond). Prior to the commencement of his jury trial Bourton presented to the trial Court "a charter of the present lord king for ... pardon" which discharged Bourton from being prosecuted, and so his case was dismissed.

The *Bourton* indictment remains undiscovered. However, the indictment, as summarized by then Chief Justice Geoffrey le Scrop[e], alleged the following:

[Bourton] entered the house of William Carles, tailor, at Bristol, and assaulted Alice, wife of the same William, being there greatly pregnant with two children (*grossam doubus pueris pregnantem*), and with his hands beat and ill treated her, and violently knocked her to the ground, and with his feet so trampled upon the ground [sic] that he feloniously killed one of the aforesaid children in the belly of the same Alice its mother, and broke the head and arm of the other of the same children so that it was forthwith

---

1    I earnestly recommend to the reader that he or she study or read again my commentary on *Haule's Case* (*supra*, this *Appendix 4*) before beginning a reading of *Bourton's Case*.

born and baptized by the name of Joan, and immediately after receiving her baptism died from the injury (*de malo*) aforesaid.

## UNCORRECTED, INCOMPLETE YEARBOOK REPORT OF RICHARD DE BOURTON²

A writ issued to the sheriff of Gloucestershire to apprehend one D. who, according to the testimony of Sir G[eoffrey] Scrop[e], is supposed to have beaten a woman in an advanced stage of pregnancy who was carrying twins, whereupon directly afterwards one twin died, and she was delivered of the other, who was baptized John by name, and two days afterwards, through the injury he had sustained, the child died: and the indictment was returned before Sir G. Scrop[e], and D. came, and pled Not guilty, and for the reason that the Justices were unwilling to adjudge this thing as felony [*i.e.*, as being committed with premeditation or with "felony aforethought", and not as: not "a" felony or capital offence], the accused was released [by the sheriff, and not by an order of the *Bourton* Court, although that Court may have recommended release to mainpernors] to mainpernors [a secured form of pre-trial release]³, and then the argument

2    Y.B. Mich. 1 Edw. 3, fol. 23, pl. 18 (1327) (bracketed insertions in the text are the author's).

3    *See* W.A. Morris, *The Medieval English Sheriff* 232-233 (1927); and *R. v. Richard Abbot of Pisford* (1329) 97 Selden Society 181, 218. In *R v. Richard Pisford* the defendant was indicted for felonious homicide. One justice was of the opinion that the deceased was the cause of his own death. Justice Scrope, felt the case was one of self-defense. *Pisford* contains also this entry: [Scrope] told the prisoner to have the record sent to Chancery, for in such a case the Chancellor could grant a charter of pardon without consulting the king. Later a friend of the prisoner's appeared and asked that he might be released by mainprise. Scrope, C.J.: "We cannot do that. But ask the sheriff to do it." He did so, and obtained his release. 97 Selden Society 181 (1997). *And see, e.g.*, *R v. Brente* (1281), reproduced, *infra*, in note 14.

was adjourned *sine die* [i.e., the case remained unresolved]. [T]hus the writ issued, as before stated, and Sir G. Scrop[e] rehearsed the entire case, and how he [D.] came and pled.

Herle: to the sheriff: Produce the body, etc. And the sheriff returned the writ to the bailiff of the franchise of such place, who said, that the same fellow was taken by the mayor of Bristol, but of the cause of this arrest we are wholly ignorant.

The yearbook report of *Bourton's Case* represents the form in which this case was known to such common law commentators as Staunford, Coke, Hale, Blackstone, Hawkins, as well as by all modern commentators on the prosecution of unborn-child killing at the English common law. Evidently, none of these persons knew of the existence of other unborn-child homicide prosecutions. And all of these persons apparently have assumed or formed the opinion that *Bourton's Case* (which they knew only as *The Twins-Slayer Case*) stands for essentially the following: Since the *Bourton* justices expressly held that the facts as alleged in the *Bourton* indictment do not constitute felonies at common law, and since at common law all unlawful homicides constituted felonies, it follows that an unborn child (including one that is born alive and then dies in connection with being aborted or injured while in the mother's womb) is not recognized as a potential victim of unlawful homicide at common law.

I hope to demonstrate conclusively that the use of the term "felony" here (*i.e.*, in the *Bourton* yearbook-report phrase "and for the reason that the justices were unwilling to adjudge this thing as felony") means no more than the following: It appeared to the *Bourton* justices (from a relation or examination of the facts or circumstances of the two homicides) that they were not committed "feloniously", *i.e.*, they were not committed with "felony or malice aforethought" and therefore the defendant would almost certainly be pardoned and, in the meantime, he can be recommended for release on bail.

# CORRECTED, INCOMPLETE YEARBOOK REPORT OF R V. RICHARD DE BOURTON[4]

A writ issued to the sheriff of Glouscestershire to take one D., who, by the testimony of Sir Geoffrey Scrop[e], is supposed to have beaten a woman great with two children, so that immediately afterwards one of the children died, and she was delivered of the other, which was baptized by the name of Joan[5], but died two days later from the injury which the child had; and the indictment was returned before Sir Geoffrey Scrop[e]; and D. came and pleaded Not guilty; and because the justices were not minded to treat[6] this thing as felony, the indictee was released on mainprise and then the matter remained without day, and so the writ was issued as above, and it said that [by testimony of] Sir Geoffrey Scrop[e] [etc., and] recited the whole case [as above], and how he came and pleaded etc., [and that the sheriff should have caused his body to come etc.][7] And the sheriff returned the writ to the bailiffs of the franchise of such and such a

---

4   Notes and corrected translation from the French supplied by Professor Sir John H. Baker (hereinafter: *Baker*). Baker remarked:
I was greatly puzzled by the appearance of Herle C.J. (of the Common Pleas) in this text, and by some of the wording, and so I compared the printed text with four MSS. These all agree with each other and make better sense, especially in omitting the name of Herle (which must have resulted from some misreading). [This corrected] … translation is from the MS. Text, indicating the chief variations from the printed editions: Lincoln's Inn MS. Hale 72, at fo.86v; Lincoln's Inn MS. Hale 116, at fo.3; Lincoln's Inn MS. Hale 137(2), at fo.11; Bodleian Library Oxford MS. Bodl. 363, at fo.9v.
Baker, in a letter to Philip A. Rafferty (December 12, 1985) (on file with the author).

5   John in print, and some MSS. The record shows Joan to be correct.

6   *d'agarder* (i.e., to award) in MSS. *adjudge* only in print.

7   Garbled in print, with mention of Herle C.J.

place, who said that the person in question had been taken by the mayor of Bristol, but they were wholly unaware of the reason for the taking etc. [Therefore, a writ issued to the mayor of Bristol to cause the body to come, together with the cause etc.]

# TRANSLATION OF THE PLEA ROLL RECORD FOR MICH. (1327)[8]

Gloucestershire. The lord king has sent his writ to the sheriff of Gloucestershire in these words: Edward by the grace of God king of England, lord of Ireland and duke of Acquitaine, to the sheriff of Gloucestershire, greeting! Because we have learned by the certificate of our beloved and faithful Geoffrey le Scrop[e], our chief justice, that Richard de Bourton has been indicted for that he entered the house of William Carles, tailor, at Bristol, and assaulted Alice, wife of the same William, being there greatly pregnant with two children (*grossam doubus pueris pregnantem*), and with his hands beat and ill treated her, and violently knocked her to the ground, and with his feet so trampled upon the ground [sic] that he feloniously killed one of the aforesaid children in the belly of the same Alice its mother, and broke the head and arm of the other of the same children so that it was forthwith born and baptized by the name of Joan, and immediately after receiving her baptism died from the injury (*de malo*) aforesaid; and that the foregoing matters still remain undetermined before ourself; and that this Richard had a day before us at a certain day now past for hearing the jury of the country on which, for good and ill, he put himself concerning the felony aforesaid, by mainprise of John le Taverner of Bristol and others named in the said certificate, who mainprised to have him before us at the said term; and on behalf of the selfsame Richard we are given to understand that by reason of the foregoing he has been taken, since that mainprise, and detained in our prison of Bristol, on account of which he could not come

8   KB 27/270, Rex m.9 (Mich. Term 1327). Reference and translation from the Latin supplied by Baker.

before us on the aforesaid day to stand to right upon the foregoing according to the law and custom of our realm: We, willing what is just to be done upon the foregoing, command you (as we commanded before) that if the same Richard is detained in the aforesaid prison by reason of the foregoing and not otherwise, and if he finds you sufficient mainpernors who mainprise to have him before us in a fortnight from Michaelmas day wheresoever we should then be in England, to do and receive what our court should decide in the foregoing, then cause the selfsame Richard to be meanwhile delivered from prison by the mainprise aforesaid. And have you there the names of those mainpernors, and this writ. And if the same Richard is indicted for any other felonies or trespasses in your county, then without delay send us distinctly and openly under your seal the tenor of the aforesaid indictment at the aforesaid day, that we may do further therein what by the law and custom aforesaid should be done, or else signify unto us the reason why you will not or cannot carry out our command heretofore directed unto you. Witness my self at Northallerton, the 14$^{th}$ day of July in the first year of our reign [1327].

By virtue of which writ, the sheriff (namely, Thomas de Rodbergh) returns that he commanded Everand Fraunceys and Robert Grene, bailiffs of the liberty of the vill of Bristol, who answered him that Richard de Bourton, lately indicted for the death of Joan, daughter of William Carles, tailor, at Bristol, as is contained in the writ, has not been taken by them the said bailiffs nor is for that reason detained in prison, but that he has been taken and detained by Roger Rurtele the mayor of the aforesaid vill for certain reasons which are unknown to them the said bailiffs etc. And after inspection of the aforesaid writ and return etc., the mayor and bailiffs of the vill of Bristol are commanded that if the same Richard finds sufficient mainpernors to be before the king in a fortnight from St. Hilary wheresoever etc. to hear the aforesaid jury and to do further and receive what the king's court should decide for him, then they should cause the selfsame Richard to be meanwhile delivered from the aforesaid prison by the above-mentioned mainprise. And if he is indicted for any other felonies or trespasses before them in the vill aforesaid, then they should distinctly and openly under their seals send that indictment (if any there be) or else the cause for which he was taken, to the king at the day aforesaid upon the incumbent peril, so that the lord king further etc. what is to be done etc.

At which day the mayor and bailiffs of the vill of Bristol return that the aforesaid Richard de Bourton did not or would not find sufficient mainpernors for being before the lord king at this day, namely in the quindene of St. Hilary etc., and to do and receive what is commanded in the writ, as a result of which they did nothing further in executing the writ etc. And because the same mayor and bailiffs have not returned here before the king the names of themselves according to the form of the statute etc., and also have not answered etc. for what reason the aforesaid Richard de Bourton has been taken, as in the lord king's writ directed to them therein was commanded, nor whether or not the aforesaid Richard is indicted for any other felonies or trespasses before them in the vill aforesaid, the same mayor and bailiffs (namely, John de Romeseie, mayor, and Hugh de Langebrigge and Stephan Lespicer, bailiffs etc.) are in mercy. And they are assessed by the justices at 40s. And the sheriff is commanded that he should not omit by reason of the liberty of the aforesaid vill to enter the same etc., and if the same Richard should find him sufficient mainpernors to mainprise to have him before the king in a fortnight from Easter day wheresoever etc. to hear the jury aforesaid etc. and further to do etc., then he should cause the selfsame Richard to be meanwhile delivered from the aforesaid prison by the mainprise aforesaid etc. The sheriff is also commanded that he should not omit on account of the liberty to cause the aforesaid mayor and bailiffs to come before the king at the said term to answer the king for the return etc. Also, the mayor and bailiffs are commanded that if the aforesaid Richard is indicted for any felonies and trespasses before them in the aforesaid vill, then they should distinctly and openly under their seals send that indictment (if any there be) or else the cause for which he was taken, to the king at the day aforesaid etc. so that further etc.

## TRANSLATION OF THE RECORD FOR EASTER TERM, 1328[9]

Gloucestershire. The jury at the suit of the lord king to make recognition etc. whether Richard de Bourton of Bristol is guilty of the death of Joan, daughter of William Carles, tailor of Bristol, feloniously slain in the suburbs of Bristol, whereof he has been indicted (as appears to the king by a certain indictment lately made thereof before the coroners of the vill of Bristol, and which the king caused to come before him [in connection with Bourton's petition for a pardon?; insertion mine]) is put in respite until the octaves of St. John the Baptist wheresoever etc., for want of jurors, because none [came] etc. Therefore, let the sheriff have the bodies of all the jurors before the king at the said term, etc. And let the aforesaid Richard meanwhile be released by the mainprise which he heretofore found, from day to day until etc. And the sheriff is commanded that except for them etc., he should put in as many and such etc. and have them before the king at the said term etc.

## TRANSLATION OF THE RECORD OF OCTAVE OF ST. JOHN, 1328[10]

Gloucestershire. The jury at the suit of the lord king to make recognition whether or not Richard de Bourton of Bristol is guilty of the death of Joan, daughter of William Carles, tailor of Bristol, feloniously slain in the suburbs of Bristol, whereof he is indicted — as appears to the king by a certain indictment lately made thereof before the coroners of the vill of Bristol, and which the king has caused to come before [himself] etc. — is put in respite until one month from Michaelmas day, wheresoever etc., for want of jurors, because

9    KB 27/242, Rex m.9 (Easter term, 1328). Reference and translation from the Latin supplied by Baker.

10   KB 27/273, Rex m.12d (Octave of St. John, 2 Edw.III). Reference and translation from the Latin supplied by Baker.

none [came] etc. Therefore let the sheriff have the bodies of all the jurors before the king at the said date etc. And let the aforesaid Richard meanwhile be released by the mainprise which he previously found, from day to day etc. Afterwards, the same term, the aforesaid Richard came and proffered a charter of the present lord king for pardon of the aforesaid felony, which is enrolled in Hilary term in the first year of the reign of the present king. Therefore, he [is to go] thereof without day etc [i.e., the indictment against Bourton is dismissed, and the defendant is discharged. Insertions mine]

## COMMENTS BY PROFESSOR SIR JOHN H. BAKER ON THE BOURTON CASE:"

[I]t appears from the patent roll (Cal. Patent Rolls 1327-30, p.113; Pat. 1 Edw. III, pt. 2, m. 17) that Bourton was included in the general pardon of 29 May 1327, but with the special proviso that, unlike the other persons pardoned with him, he was to be excused from serving against the Scots. The others were evidently ordinary felons conscripted into the army.

The pardon is not to be found in the roll for Hil. I Edw. III, which is defective. The following fragmentary entry alone remains, 'verba. Edwardus dei gracia rex Anglie dominus ... is justic' ad placita coram nobis tenenda assign ... Glouc' de Richardo de Burton et Lucia ... nuper rex Anglie pater noster per breve sum ... -nto predicto ulterius inde quod justum ... —M....'[12]

---

11    Letter from Professor Sir John Baker to Philip A. Rafferty (on file with the author).

12    *Id.* (citing KB 27/267, m.4a (or perhaps 4d.)).
      There was a chance that the *Bourton* indictment could be in surviving Chancery files. Part of the procedure for applying for a pardon involved sending the court record into Chancery. On my behalf, Ella Bubb kindly searched the Chancery files, and certain other files, for the *Bourton* indictment, petition for pardon, and

This looks more like a writ for removing the indictment than a preliminary to entering a pardon, though perhaps the pardon was tacked on (the lower two-thirds or so of the roll is missing).

Richard de Bourton was indicted before the coroners of Bristol (1) for feloniously killing a child which died in the womb, [and] (2) for causing the death of the other (christened Joan). We do not...have the indictment, though as summarized...[in the yearbook report and in the plea roll record for Mich., 1327] it does seem that the words of felony applied to both children. In [some of] the later [plea roll] entries, the offence is described only as the killing of Joan, but that may have been clerical shorthand.

The indictment was removed into the King's Bench some time in the reign of Edward II. The indictment files do not survive. I discovered that the King's Bench held two gaol deliveries in Gloucestershire in the 1320s, but the indictment is not recorded there (KB 27/247, Rex m. KB 27/255, Rex m.24).

Bourton pleaded not guilty, and was released on mainprise to appear at some time before Michaelmas term 1327, but before his appearance he was arrested by the mayor and bailiffs of Bristol for some undisclosed cause. Apparently [Bourton was released on mainprise] because, according to the year book, the judges were not minded to treat it as felony. It seems to me that this was not a final determination of that question — indeed the record says that the issue of felony was still pending in 1328 — but related only to the bail application.[13]

---

possible writ for special inquisition. She was unable to locate any of those items. Letter from Ella Bubb to Philip A. Rafferty (Nov. 15, 1991) (on file with the author).

13 It certainly was not a final determination. *See* Naomi D. Hurnard, *The King's Pardon for Homicide Before A.D. 1307* 110 (1965). Thomas Green observed, "Because of the infrequency of the eyres...homicide defendants frequently obtained orders for special inquisitions into the circumstances of the alleged slaying. Upon a finding of excusable [or non-felonious] homicide, the defendant might be either pardoned or bailed until the next eyre."

Scrop[e] C.J. reopened the case in the time of Edward III, and the new king sent a writ on 14 July 1327 to the sheriff of Gloucestershire to take mainprise from Bourton to appear in the quindene of Michaelmas (October next). At that day the sheriff returned that the bailiffs of Bristol informed him that B. had been arrested by the mayor. So the King's Bench sent a writ to the mayor, to take mainprise & c. to appear in the quindene of Hilary [1328]. At that day the mayor returned that B. would not find mainprise and so they had done nothing. He was amerced 40s. for not returning the cause of B.'s detention in Bristol etc., and the sheriff was now ordered to enter the liberty and take the mainprise himself, for an appearance in the quindene of Easter. The next plea roll shows that in Easter term (April 1328) the jury was respited till the octave of St. John (July) because no jurors showed up, the defendant being released on the same mainprise....

I have searched for [the *Bourton* indictment]...without success. In the King's Bench rolls for Michaelmas term 1326 (KB 27/266), Trinity term 1326 (KB 27/265), Easter term 1326 (KB 27/264), Hilary term 1326 (KB 27/263),...Michaelmas term 1325 (KB 27/262), [and Easter term 1324 (KB 27256). There is no obvious stopping point, since we do not know the date of the offence]. I am not sure how much further it is worth going, though it would indeed be helpful to find the indictment....

As I now see the case, the record shows that Bourton was indicted for feloniously killing a child which died in the womb and another (Joan) which died after birth and baptism; that he pleaded not guilty, but was never tried; and that in Trinity term 1328 he was discharged on the strength of a pardon granted a year earlier. There is therefore nothing of record to show whether the court considered the facts alleged to amount to felony or not, except insofar as the case was continued through several terms on the basis that it *was* felony....

---

Thomas Green, *Verdict According to Conscience: Perspectives on the English Criminal Jury 1200-1800* 422, n.34 (1985) (citing *Hurnard, supra* this note 13 at 37-42, 50).

It is therefore the yearbook report which remains crucial, and this appears to say (in the middle) that Bourton was granted bail because the judges were not minded to treat it as felony. The status and meaning of this pronouncement still seem to me less than clear. For one thing, it seems contrary to the [plea roll] record, which shows that the case was continued on the basis that a jury had been summoned to try whether Bourton was guilty of felonious killing....That issue arose from Bourton's plea of not guilty, which the court had recorded. [T]here is therefore no question of the indictment having been quashed on the ground that it did not disclose a felony. Secondly, although it is probable that Bail was not thought to be grantable for [a charge of] murder [or felonious homicide] in medieval times (YB 25 Edw.III, fo.85; Edward Coke, *Treatise on Bail & Mainprise*; Staunford *P.C.* 72a), it seems to have been allowable for felony. It could hardly be argued that the release of Bourton on bail shows that if the facts were true he would not have been guilty of felony, because that again would be contrary to the [plea roll] record. I therefore do not really understand the yearbook in this respect, and suspect it may be a defective report.

I do not suspect that this "no felony" entry in the year book report of *Bourton's Case* is defective. More to the point, it can be, and will be demonstrated that this *Bourton* year book entry is not at all in conflict with the following three *Bourton* plea roll entries: (1) "the foregoing matters [i.e., the alleged felonious homicides] still remain undetermined before ourself; and ... [Bourton] had ... [an assigned] day before us ... for hearing the jury of the country ... on the felony aforesaid [but he failed to appear"]; (2) "The jury ... to make recognition ... whether ... Bourton ... is guilty of the death of Joan ... feloniously slain ... whereof he has been indicted"; and (3) "Richard [Bourton] came and proffered a ... pardon of the aforesaid felony."

The then-existing English laws and legal customs concerning bail authorized bail in nearly all felonies or capital offences. The major exceptions were "felonious house-burning," "counterfeiting the King's seal," "making counterfeit money," "Treason touching the King," and unlawful homicide — except when preliminarily judged to be based on "light suspicion" or as "nonfelonious" or through misadventure (i.e., excusable, accidental, non-malicious, in self-defence, or not done in the course of committing a serious or dangerous felony).[14] Now the foregoing *Bourton* yearbook entry

14  See 15 *Statute of Westminster* 1 (3 Edw.I) (1275), in 1 *Statutes of the Realm* pt.
1, 26, 30 (1810); *Hurnard, supra,* note 13 at 78-79, & 281, n.2; *Green, supra,*
note 13 at 425, n.50; and 57 Selden Society LXXXIII (1938) (ordinarily
no bail in an appeal of homicide). *See also, e.g., R v. Brente (Eyre of Devon,
1281)*:
Richard de Brente, clerk, struck Ellen his wife, being pregnant, on the ribs with a certain staff whereby she gave birth to a dead female child before her time, as a result of which the aforesaid Ellen languished from the same wound and died from it a month later. And Richard was heretofore taken and imprisoned in Exeter castle, and was afterwards bailed by the lord king's writ, namely to … [names of twelve (12) mainpernors omitted], to have him here on the first day [of the eyre]. And they did not have him: therefore in mercy. And Richard remains in the countryside. Afterwards the sheriff testifies that he ran away. And he is suspected of wrong [*malecredere*]; therefore let him be exacted and outlawed. His chattels [are valued at] 4s. 4d., for which the sheriff shall answer. The same [Richard] had land, whereof the year and waste [is valued at] 13d., for which the same sheriff shall answer.
Just 1/186, m.30 (translation from the Latin supplied by Professor Sir John Baker). My initial source: *Schneebeck, supra,* note 1 of *Haule's Case* (in this *Appendix 4*) at p.239. *And see also, e.g., R v. Scharp (Eyre of London, 1276)*:
Richard Scharp, wool-merchant, beat his wife, Emma, so that she gave birth to a stillborn boy. Because Richard has died, nothing from the outlawry. The mayor and aldermen testify that Richard was arrested and handed over to Richard de Ewell, sheriff, who released him on the pledges of six men. Because according to the law of the City no one accused of a man's death should be released on bail except on the pledges of twelve men,

clearly implies that the *Bourton* justices would "not" have allowed Bourton to be bailed if they had found "felony," which they did not find. So, if the absence of "felony" means here the absence of a capital offence or the absence of a form of common law criminal homicide, then the *Bourton* justices betrayed a fundamental misunderstanding of then-existing English laws and customs on bail in felony cases. The misunderstanding would be the notion that such laws and customs forbid bail in homicide cases.

Furthermore, if the "absence of felony" means here the absence of a capital offence or the absence of a form of common law criminal homicide, then the *Bourton* justices also betrayed a misunderstanding of the then-existing common law on criminal homicide. There exists many cases which clearly show that there is no question that for well over a hundred years before, and for at least some two hundred or so years after *Bourton's Case*, human fetal victims were recognized by the English judiciary as victims of common law criminal homicide.[15] Here is an excellent example of just such a case:

# REX V. SCOT
# (EYRE OF LONDON, 1321)[16]

In the 19th year (1299) of the aforesaid reign of King Edward [I], John de Vinite, clerk, then being coroner, and Thomas

---

any of whom should be able to answer to the king for 100s. as amercement [pecuniary penalty] if he should fail, *to judgment* on Richard de Ewelle.

Reproduced from *The London Eyre of 1276* 23 (London Rec. Soc., 1976).

15   *See* the cases reproduced in (1st) *Rafferty, supra* note 15 (of *Side B*); and *Rex v. Taillour* (Norfolk, 1532) and *R v. Wodlake* (Middlesex, 1530), reproduced *infra* in this *Appendix 4*.

16   Just 1/547A, m.22. Trans. From the Latin supplied by *Baker*. My initial source Harold N. Schneebeck, Jr., *The Law of Felony in Medieval England from the Accession of Edward I Until the Mid-Fourteenth Century*, 238 (unpub. Ph.D dissertation, U. of Iowa, 1973; and pub. by UMI, Ann Arbor, Michigan).

Romayn and William de Layre then being sheriffs, Alice the wife of Roger the Spicer, perceiving a certain John the Scot to be pursuing the aforesaid Roger her husband with a certain stick in order to beat him, wanted to close the door of her house so that the same John should not get in, and she went so quickly to close the said door and closed it, and the aforesaid John pushed the said door with such force that the aforesaid Alice fell on a certain mortar, with the result that she gave birth to Margery and Emma, certain daughters of hers, before the [due] time of birth [*Tempus pariendi*], who immediately after birth and baptism died. And the aforesaid John fled immediately after the deed; he is suspected of wrong. Therefore let him be exacted and outlawed.[17] He had no chattels, and was not in any ward because he was a vagrant. The four neighbours have died.

So, a person who would continue to maintain that the *Bourton Case* stands for the proposition that the fetal victims described in the *Bourton* indictment are not potential or recognized victims of common law criminal homicide, must implicitly adopt each of the following three premises: (1) The three foregoing *Bourton* "felony" plea roll entries represent defective entries; (2) The *Bourton* justices did not understand the then-existing common law on bail in felony cases; (3) The *Bourton* justices did not understand, or what is far more reprehensible, simply refused to apply the then-existing (and factually applicable) common law

17  *Black's Law Dictionary* 904 (Bryan A. Garner ed., 7th abridged ed. 1999), gives this definition of "outlawry": "*Hist.*: The act or process of depriving someone of the benefit and protection of the law." This means, in effect, that an outlawed person could be killed on sight. In outlawry the defendant or appellee had to be exacted or solemnly called to come forth at separate sessions of the County Court, and was only outlawed after four failures. Outlawry applied only to felony or capital offences. *See* 5 *Selden Society, Year Books of Edward II The Eyre of Kent 6 & 7 Edward II A.D 1313-1314* 94 (1910) ("If one be indicted of some matter too small to bring him in danger of judgment of life and limb, even though he come not, yet shall he not be outlawed.").

rule that the unborn child in the womb of its mother is a recognized victim of criminal homicide at common law.

It is virtually certain that the *Bourton* justices, in relating that they "were unwilling [*i.e.*, not minded] to adjudge [or treat] this thing as felony", were relating no more than the following: a preliminary review of the facts surrounding these two homicides indicates that the killings were committed non-maliciously or without malice or felony aforethought (and therefore are pardonable). Also, I maintain that it was the sheriff, and not the *Bourton* justices, who was "unwilling to adjudge this thing as felony".

In *Pernel Clerk's Appeal of Nicholas Cheney* (Eyre of Herfordshire, 1278), the jury found Cheney not guilty because, although he killed Clerk's unborn child, he "did not do this by felony aforethought":

> It is found by the jury on which Nicholas de Cheney and Pernel, the wife of Peter le Clerk, put themselves that the aforesaid Nicholas [coming] to take a certain [court?] at Wye found the aforesaid Pernel standing in the middle of the gateway of the same [court?] of the same vill and trampled her beneath the feet of his horse, whereby the next day she gave birth to a certain male son, which was baptized and called John and died on the third day. And because it is found that the aforesaid Nicholas did not do this by felony aforethought, therefore [let him go] quit with respect to life and limb; but let him be in mercy for the trespass.[18]

Bracton (1210-1268), in the course of describing unlawful homicide, stated: it is committed "in premeditated assault and felony."[19] Pollack and Maitland observed: "in the thirteenth century the chancery is beginning to contrast a homicide by misadventure, which deserves a pardon, with homicide which

18  Just 1/323, m.47d. Trans. From the Latin supplied by Sir John H. Baker. My initial source *Schneebeck, supra* n.16 at 234 (including n.1).

19  *Bracton De Legibus et Consuetudinibus Angliae* 438, n.155 (6 Woodbine, ed., S. Thorne trans. 1986).

has been committed *in felonia et per malitiam praecogitatam.*[20] And Hurnard observed that the term "felony" was used so in deciding whether defendants, who were indicted for felonious homicide, should be granted mainprise (a secured form of pretrial release) pending trial or the outcome of a petition for pardon. Evidently, the application for mainprise was brought by means of a writ for a special or preliminary inquisition.[21]

The *Bourton Case*, when correctly interpreted, actually supports the proposition that both of the fetal victims described in the *Bourton* indictment are recognized victims of common law criminal homicide. *Bourton* has been accepted as the leading case in support of the proposition that at common law a child that is destroyed inside the womb of its mother is not considered a victim of criminal homicide (unless the unborn child is born alive and then dies from its prenatal injuries or from being prematurely expelled).[22] Hence, but for the fact that *Bourton* was so fundamentally misinterpreted, there is every reason to believe that at the English common law such a child would have continued to be recognized as a victim of criminal homicide.

---

20   Sir Frederick Pollack & Frederic Maitland, 2 *The History of English Law Before the Time of Edward I* 468 (2d ed., 1968).

21   *Hurnard, supra* 13 at 281 n.2.

22   *See, e.g., Q v. West, supra Appendix 4. And see* the commentary on *Haule's Case, supra* this *Appendix 4.*

# R V. ANONYMOUS (AKA, THE ABORTIONIST'S CASE) (1348)[1]

One was indicted for that he killed a child in its mother's belly, and the opinion [was] that he shall not be arraigned (*arraigne*) on this since no name of baptism was in the indictment, and also it is hard to know whether he killed it or not etc.

This report of *R v. Anonymous*, as translated from the French by Professor Baker, is taken from Fitzherbert's *Abridgment* (1514/1516), where the case is dated Mich. *22 (1348) Edw. III.* According to Baker, this case is not to be found in the vulgate edition of the year book *22 (1348) Edw. III*, and there do not appear to be any surviving manuscript texts of this year. This "text is, therefore, probably the best we shall ever have."[2] Baker added that the source of Fitzherbert's *Abridgment* report of *R v. Anonymous* is Statham's *Abridgment* (c.1490).[3]

Arguably, the source of Statham's report of *R v. Anonymous* (1348) is the underscored portion of the following passage in 22 (1348) *Liber Assisarus* (*Book of Assizes*):

---

1    Fitzherbert, *Abridgment, Corone* (1514/16) pl. 263 ("Un fuit endit de ceo que il tuo enfant en le venter sa mere, et lopinion que il ne sacre arraigne sur ceo eo que nul nosme de baptisme fuit en lenditement, et auxi est dure de conustre sil luy occist ou non etc."). Translation supplied by Professor Sir John H. Baker (hereinafter, *Baker*). Per Baker in a letter to Philip A. Rafferty (December 12, 1985): "Fitzherbert's source was Statham's *Abridgment* fo. [58v], *Corona* case [91] (printed without title c. 1490): "Un fuist endite de ceo qil tue une enfaunt deinz le ventre sa mier. Et loppinoin qil ne sera arraigne surceo eo que nulle noune de baptisme fuist en lenditement, et auxint il est dure de conustre sil le occist etc.' (same translation)."

2    Baker, *supra* note 1.

3    *See supra*, note 1.

Note that no one is bound to answer to an appeal of felony where the plaintiff does not mention the name of the dead man, though a man shall answer an indictment for the death of an unknown man (as happened concerning W. Chamble, [and] K. Burgeis, who were indicted for the death of an unknown man killed at "Lok", for which they were arraigned in the King's Bench and put to answer and found not guilty etc). *Query, if a man kills a child in its mother's belly, whether he shall suffer death for this? I believe not, because the deceased is not named and was never "in rerum natura"* (literally: in existence; but here: born alive or brought forth alive into the world.[4]

The underscored portion of the above quote is obviously a commentary on a legal point or issue, and is not a report of an actual case. Could it be, however, that it is a commentary on an actual English abortion case that occurred in 1348? It seems doubtful. Professor Baker noted that no abortion case is contained in either the vulgate edition of the year book *22 (1348) Edw. III* or the surviving manuscript texts of the year book *22 (1348) Edw. III*.[5] He noted also the following:

In 1348 the King's Bench held a very thorough session of gaol delivery at York. Most of the indictments are in a very short form, some even in French. I have been through the surviving indictment file (KB 9/156) and the entries on the *Rex roll* (KB 27/354), and found only two possibly relevant cases, neither of them exactly in point:

---

4    22 *Lib. Ass.* pl. 94 (1348). Reference and translation from the French supplied by Baker. There follows in the 1679 edition of the 22 *Lib. Ass.* at p.4 & 106, respectively, a reference to the *Twin-Slayer's Case* (1327/28) (reproduced *supra*, in this *Appendix 4*), and a reference to *R v. Anonymous* as it is set forth in *Fitzherbert's Abridgment*. The same conclusion and rationale (no legal name and not *in rerum natura*) will be found in Robert Brooke *Abridgment, Corone* pl. 91 (1568).

5    *See supra*, text accompanying note 2, and *infra*, text accompanying note 6. On the yearbooks, *see* J.H. Baker (ed.), *Judicial Records, Law Reports, and the Growth of Case Law* 17-42 (1989).

KB 27/354, Rex m. 3d: William, son of Thomas de Byndalle, chaplain, indicted before the said sheriff for that he feloniously killed a certain unknown boy *puerum igneum*) at Tunstall, on the Sunday next before the feast of St. Bartholomew the Apostle in the 18<sup>th</sup> year [1324] of the reign of King Edward [II], father of the present lord king and the aforesaid William after the felony was committed buried the aforesaid boy at the Grenedyk ende next Sonnyngcros ... [Found not guilty and discharged.]

KB 27/354, Rex m. 66: William de Carton of Newsham in Rydal indicted before the lord king in Michaelmas term in the 22<sup>nd</sup> year (1348) of the present king of England for that he on the Tuesday next after the feast of St. George in the 22<sup>nd</sup> year of the reign of the present lord king of England feloniously killed Ellen his wife with the quick child (*cum infante vivo*) in her belly, at Newsham ... [Found not guilty and discharged.]

[Cf. also KB 9/156/79, a woman indicted for feloniously killing her (unnamed) boy aged one month. Outcome not recorded on the file.)[6]

A person may want to argue that the fact, that the second rationale ("it is hard to know whether he killed it or not") in *R v. Anonymous* is different from the second rationale (the child "was never *in rerum natura* [born alive]") in the 22 (1348) *Liber Assisarum* abortion passage, supports the proposition that *R v. Anonymous* is not a confused version of the 22 *Liber Assisarum* abortion passage. However, the precise rationale behind the supposed requirement that the unborn child must be born alive (in order to be recognized as a potential victim of homicide) was that when the child was born dead it was considered too hard to determine whether or not the defendant killed the child. John Baldwin in approximately 1460, observed:

It is also a good indictment before the coroner, if the dead person cannot be identified, to say 'he killed a certain unknown person'; and for this he shall suffer death. It is otherwise if a

---

6    *Baker, supra* note 1.

man strikes a pregnant woman, and then she is delivered of one who is dead; there it is not felony, for it cannot be known (*en notice*) whether it was through the striking or for another cause, because it was not at such time *in rerum natura* etc., and so it cannot be tried.[7]

The rationale in *R v. Anonymous* and the 22 *Liber Assisarum* abortion passages are, then, virtually identical. That, of course, supports the proposition that *R v. Anonymous* (1348) is but a confused version of the 22 (1348) *Liber Assisarum* abortion passage. Also, in addition to the fact that *R v. Anonymous* and the 22 *Liber Assisarum* abortion passage have the same date (1348), is the fact that they are equally brief or short.

A person may want to argue that it cannot be reasonably argued that the real source of Statham's report of *R v. Anonymous* is the 22 *Liber Assisarum* abortion passage, inasmuch as the former purports to recite a ruling or decision on an actual abortion indictment, whereas the latter simply recites a commentator's or recorder's "opinion" on a hypothetical abortion case. Such an argument might prove too much. The report of *R v. Anonymous* recites an answer to the question ("query") posed in the 22 *Liber Assisarum* abortion passage. Yet this same report (of *R v. Anonymous*), does not recite that this same question was posed in *R v. Anonymous*. And note the *R v. Anonymous* phrasing "and the opinion was …". Such a phrasing correctly describes what was done in the 22 *Liber Assisarum* abortion passage. However, and technically speaking, it would incorrectly describe what was supposedly done in *R v. Anonymous*. When a Court rules on a legal question, the Court is rendering a "decision", and not an opinion, although the latter serves as the basis of the former.[8]

---

7   John Baldwin, *Reading (Lecture) in Gray's Inn. C. 1460. on the Statute of Marlborough. Cap. 25 (Murdrum)*, Cambridge Univ. Lib. MS. Hh. 2. 6, fo. 92v. (Reference and translation from the French supplied by Baker.)

8   *See* Peter Goodrich, *Language of Law: From Logics of Memory to Nomadic Masks* 227 n.2 (London, 1990) (quoting *J.H. Baker*: "'In those cases where judges were declaring law, it was a transient, oral, informal process, and

Statham was certainly aware of the fact that a *Liber Assisarum* consists largely of reports of cases or reports of debates or arguments on legal issues in actual cases. That awareness may have caused Statham to represent *R v. Anonymous* as an actual case instead of as a hypothetical case.

Perhaps the greatest reason for concluding that *R v. Anonymous* was not an actual case is that its supposed holding would have been contrary to then-existing law. The cases set forth in *Appendix 4* clearly demonstrate that at the 14th century common law, a child killed in the mother's womb was indeed recognized as a victim of criminal homicide. Judges are, of course, presumed to know, and to abide by, applicable law.[9]

Furthermore, neither of the rationales set forth in *R v. Anonymous* found their way into the received common law. The first rationale would dictate that infanticide would not have been governed by the common law rules on homicide.[10] The second rationale, if carried out to its logical extensions, would mandate that it would not be even a common law misdemeanor or misprision to commit such a killing because, in the context of such a misdemeanor prosecution, the fact would remain that it cannot be legally proved that the abortional act brought about the death of the child in the womb. However, and as has been shown already, it was indeed an indictable misdemeanor to slay the unborn child in the womb.

Finally, so far as is known, at the fourteenth century common law there was not available to a defendant a procedural tool for presenting a pre- (or at) arraignment, evidentiary challenge to an indictment for felony.[11]

only those present at the arguments could hope to achieve a wholly accurate impression of what had been decided, and then only when the judges spoke loudly enough.'").

9   *See, e.g., People v. Lewis* (1987), 191 C.A.3d 1288, 1296.

10   *See infra*, text (of *Epilogue to the Appendices*), accompanying notes 10-11.

11   *See, e.g.,* John March, *Some New Cases of the Years and Time of King Hen. 8 and Queen; Mary; Written out of the Great Abridgment, Composed by Sir Robert Brook* ... 15 (1615); and 2 *Hale, Historia Placitorum Corone* 258 (1736).

Some readers may want to argue that, for all it may be known, the defendant in *R v. Anonymous* challenged the indictment on the grounds that at common law an unborn child is not recognized as a victim of criminal homicide because it is settled law or a universal rule that it never can be sufficiently proved that an unborn child died in connection with a defendant's abortional act or battery on the child's mother. The problem with such an argument is that it seems highly doubtful that at this period in the development of the common law (or for that matter, at any subsequent period of the common law) there existed such a settled rule. There is no known "accretion of cases" that would support such a rule. Available case evidence indicates that at the then-existing common law, it was indeed recognized that it can be legally proved (or is a question of fact) whether a particular abortional act brought about the in-womb destruction of a child. And the test or criterion, here, appears to not have been such relatively modern legal concepts such as proximate cause, or foreseeability, or substantial factor, but rather, whether the defendant's act or acts "hastened" the decedent's death. Or, putting this another way, whether, by defendant's act or acts, the deceased "became nearer to death or further from life". For example, here, in *R v. Boleye* (Shropshire, 1292), the jurors, upon their oath, decided that the defendants "never beat ... Alice [who was pregnant with twins, and who, along with her twins died or were killed]...whereby she or her...children became nearer to death or further from life".[12]

Even assuming that the report of *R v. Anonymous* represents an actual case, still, there is nothing in the very brief report of that case that relates that the clause "and also it is hard to know whether he killed it or not" reflected the thinking of the trial judge in *Anonymous*. It may be that the foregoing clause is but a commentary on *R v. Anonymous* by some unknown lawyer.

---

12    Just. 1/303, m.69d. Just. 1/303, m.69d. *Boleye* is reproduced in (1ˢᵗ) Rafferty, supra, *note 15 (of* Side B*) at pp. 542-543.*

# R. V. NICHOLAS ATTE WELL (GLOUCESTER, 1409)

Inquistion taken...April 17, 1409 before...sheriff [and 12 jurors omitted], who say upon their oath that Nicholas... on...February 16, 1403,...[at] the house of...and Sybil his wife, has beaten, [and] wounded [Sybil], and feloniously destroyed one boy in the belly of Sybil, herself then pregnant. (Mueller has it: "Nicholas...beat Sybilla. In doing so [he] caused injury [to Sybil], and feloniously killed a boy in the womb of Sybilla). (The Latin: "eius verberavit vulneravit et felonice unum puerum in ventre ipsius Sibille tunc pregnantis interfecit.")[1]

On a calendar of gaol prisoners, the *Nicholas* court clerk wrote the following above the name Nicholas atte Well: "released from jail by way of pardoning and because the indictment is insufficient." ("deliberatus quia perdonatur et indictamentum insufficiens:" membrane 45: see fn.1 below.) Mueller maintains 1), that this clerk's notation can mean "only" that the *Nicholas* justice(s) decided as a matter of law that an unborn child does not qualify as a victim of criminal homicide; 2), that this *Nicholas* ruling is the "only" evidence known to exist that bears on the issue of how the King's justices dealt with abortion and unborn child-killing at common law; and 3), the Nicholas ruling confirms his theory that in England abortion and unborn child-killing ceased being prosecuted as a felony (or even as a lesser crime) after the mid-15th century.[2]

One huge problem with Mueller's analysis of *Nicholas* is that no such judicial ruling could have been made for the simple reason that the pardon terminated completely judicial jurisdiction over Nicholas other than to order that he be released pursuant to the pardon. This means that even if the *Nicholas* justice(s)

1    TNA: Just 3/30/4 membrane 44 (reference from Susan T. Moore, M.A; translation from Latin by Duncan Harrington, F.S.A., F.S.G, L.H.G). Wolfgang P. Mueller, *The Criminalization of Abortion in the West* (2012), p 143

2    *Mueller, supra, note 1 at pp.141-147.*

purported to rule as Mueller claims, the fact remains, the ruling would not qualify even as "obiter dictum." Another problem is that such a ruling would have qualified as an act of "high treason" against the crown. The king's justices lacked the authority to alter the common or king's law on felony. And the evidence is overwhelming that for nearly 200 years before and after *Nicholas Case*, abortion and unborn child-killing were prosecuted as felonies. (See the three (3) *Rafferty* citations, *infra* (*Unraveling*) at p. 233.)

It is easy to see the fatal defect in the *Nicholas Indictment*: it failed to allege facts which, if proved, prove that the killing was done <u>feloniously</u>. Putting this another way, the Nicholas indictment failed to tie the beating and wounding of Sybil as being the cause of the death of Sybil's child. A proper tie-in would have alleged: Nicholas so beat and wounded Sybil that he thereby caused a boy then in her belly to die, and that Nicholas did all this feloniously, i.e., "with felony or malice aforethought". (*See, e.g. Taillour's Case* (1532), and *Cheney's Case* (1278), *infra (Unraveling)* at p. 154., and *supra* p. 141, respectively.) A final observation is in order: was this omission of "a proper tie-in" due to inadvertance, or was it done intentionally because insufficient facts existed to allege this "tie-in"? *See, e.g., R. v Cokkes* (Somerset, c. 1415), *supra (Unraveling)* at p. 107.

The pardoning of Nicholas probably was given  because the killing of Sybil's unborn child was done unintentionally,<u> i.e.</u> Nicholas did not kill the boy with "malice or felony aforethought" (which mental state is inherent in the crime of procured abortion almost by definition). For hundreds of years before and after *Nicholas Case*, the only form of criminal homicide known to the common law was murder (the crime of manslaughter was unknown), and a guilty verdict on a murder charge required a jury finding that the defendant killed "with felony or malice aforethought" (*See, e.g. Cheney's Case, Bracton*, and *Maitland* (all) *supra (Unraveling)* at p. 141.) This explains also why, during, before, and after *Nicholas'* day, in England, one finds so many-many "not guilty" verdicts (and pardons) on criminal homicide prosecutions.

# R V. WODLAKE (MIDDLESEX, 1530)[1]

Middlesex. The jurors present that William Wodlake of the parish of St. Clement Danes in the county of Middlesex, net-maker, on the twentieth day of May in the seventeenth year [1525] of the reign of King Henry VIII, with force and arms (namely knives etc.) at the aforesaid parish of St. Clement, assaulted Katherine Alaund, then a girl of fourteen years of age, and then and there violently and against her will feloniously raped her and carnally knew her, against the peace of the lord king etc.

Middlesex. The jurors present that William Wodlake of the parish of St. Clement Danes in the county of Middlesex, net-maker, on the tenth day of November in the eighteenth year [1526] of the reign of King Henry VIII, by the instigation of the devil, knowing that a certain Katharine Alaund was pregnant with a child [*cum puero esse pregnatam (sic)*], with dissembling words gave the same Katharine to drink a certain drink in order to destroy the child then being in the said Katharine's body [*dictum puerum in corpore dicte Katerine existentum*], and desired and caused her the said Katharine to drink the self-same drink, by reason of which drink the same Katharine was afterwards delivered of that child [*puero*] dead: so that the same William Wodlake feloniously killed and murdered the child [*puerum*] with the drink in manner and form aforesaid, against the peace of the lord king etc.

## ENDORSEMENT OF THE INDICTMENT[2]

TRUE BILL taken at St. John's Street in the county of Middlesex before Sir John More, knight, Robert Wroth, Robert Cheseman, John Brown, Richard Hawkes and John Palmer, keepers of the peace of the lord king and the same king's justices assigned to hear and determine various felo-

---

1  KB 9/513/m.23. Translation from the Latin supplied by Professor Sir J.H. Baker.

2  KB 9/513/m.23d.

nies, trespasses and misdeeds in the county of Middlesex, on the Thursday next after the feast of the Conception of the Blessed Virgin Mary [December 9] in the twenty-first year [1529] of the reign of King Henry VIII, by the oath etc. of … jurors [of the grand jury] delivered before the lord king on the Saturday [July 9, 1530] next after the quindene of St. John this same term, by the hand of the aforesaid John More, one of the aforesaid justices, in order to be determined.

## MANDAMUS FOR REMOVAL INTO THE KING'S BENCH

[Sewn to the bill, in the King's Bench file, is a writ dated 29 April 22 Hen. VIII [1530], ordering the justices of the peace for Middlesex to send before the lord king in the octave of Trinity all indictments concerning William Wodlake. The writ, tested by Chief Justice FitzJames, is endorsed by Sir John More to the effect that he has sent in all the indictments wherein William Wodelake is indicted, according to the tenor of the writ.[3]

---

3    Per Professor Baker in a letter to Philip A. Rafferty (24 Apr. 1984). In this same letter, Professor Baker remarked that it is unclear why the writ was issued to remove the Wodlake indictments from Middlesex to the King's Bench in Westminster. He suggested that one possible reason is that the *Wodlake* abortion indictment may have been technically defective for failing to state the place of the murder. However, he added: "that would not explain the removal of the rape indictment". Professor Baker also stated that the reason may have been simply routine: "many Middlesex cases were tried at bar in Westminster Hall".

# RECORD IS THE CONTROLMENT ROLL OF THE CLERK OF THE CROWN[4]

Middlesex. William Wodlake (dead) of the parish of St. Clement Danes in the county aforesaid, net-maker, is to be taken [and brought here] in the octave of Michaelmas [to answer] for various felonies, murders and misdemeanours of which he is indicted, [as appears] by the Baga de Secretis. Afterwards, in Hilary term 22 Hen. VIII [1531] he is to be taken [and brought here] in the quindene of Easter: at which day [the sheriff returns that] he is dead. Therefore let the process against him here totally cease.[5]

The *Wodlake* chronology is as follows: (1) the indictments were found true on December 9, 1529; (2) on April 29, 1530 the King's Bench issued a writ to remove the Wodlake indictments from the Middlesex Justices to the King's Bench in Westminster; (3) on July 9, 1530, the indictments were delivered to the King's Bench. The Controlment Roll remembrance indicates that Wodlake died before the end of April, 1531.

---

4   KB 29/162/m.11d. (Trin. 22 Hen. VIII).

5   Per Professor Baker in a letter to Philip A. Rafferty (April 24, 1984): [This roll] is not strictly a record, but rather a remembrance made by the clerk of the Crown. This explains the note form, which is extended here to give the sense. The "Baga" is the file in which the indictment still remains (KB 9/513). The remembrance indicates that a capias was issued for Wodlake's arrest in Trinity term, and another was issued in Hilary term 1531, but that Wodlake died before Easter term 1531 (which began at the end of April) and before his appearance in the King's Bench.

# R. V. TAILLOUR (NORFOLK, 1532)[1]

Let inquiry be made for the lord king whether Robert
Taillour of Tibenham near New Buckenham in the county
of Norfolk, labourer, on the first day of February [1532] in
the 23rd year of the reign of King Henry VIII, by the grace of
God king of England and France, defender of the Faith, and
lord of Ireland, with force and arms, namely with swords,
staves and knives,[2] at Tibenham aforesaid in the county
aforesaid, made assault upon Anne Sutton of Tibenham
aforesaid, and then and there beat and ill-treated her to such
an extent that he then and there feloniously killed and murdered two live children (*infants habentes vitas*) then and there
being in the womb of the selfsame Anne, against the peace
of the lord king etc.

*Endorsed:* True bill.[3]

---

1    Norwich Record Office, C/[item:] 53/1,45c. Reference and translation
     from the Latin supplied by professor, Sir John H. Baker. This case is cited
     in Sir John Baker, *The Oxford History of the Laws of England: Volume VI:
     1483-1558* (2003), p. 555 n. 22.

2    Per Baker: a "Common-form fiction".

3    "Note that item 56 [, here,] is an indictment of Robert Taillour of Tibenham
     for burglary and raping Anne Sutton, but with no mention of the children.
     This is also found to be a true bill. So far as I know, there are no surviving
     records to indicate whether these cases were tried." (Sir Baker, in an email
     to the author (7-22-09).)

# APPENDIX 5

## R V. PHILLIPS (MONMOUTH SUMMER ASSIZES, 1811)[1]

In the case of *R v. Phillips* (1811), which involved abortion pros-ecutions under *sections 1* and *2* of England's original criminal abortion statute (1803),[2] the trial court erroneously equated the terms *quickening* and *quick with child*:

> The prisoner had been previously tried [and acquitted] on the *first* section of the statute for the capital charge, in adminis-tering savin to Miss Goldsmith to procure abortion, she being [allegedly] "then quick with child." In point of fact, she was in the fourth month of her pregnancy. She swore, however, that she had not felt the child move within her before taking the medicine, and that she was not then quick with child [*i.e.,* pregnant with a live child]. The medical men in their exami-nations, differed as to the time when the foetus may be stated to be quick [living], and to have a distinct existence, [referring to precisely what (irrelevant) fact or concept: to viability?] but they all agreed that in common understanding, a woman is not considered to be quick with child [*i.e.,* pregnant with a live child] till she has herself felt the child alive and quick within her, which happens with different women in different stages of pregnancy, although most usually about the fifteenth or sixteenth week after conception.

---

1   *R v. Phillips* (Monmouth Summer Assi., cor. Lawrence, J.), 170 Eng. Rpts. 1310; 3 Camp.73.

2   Reproduced in 44 *Statutes at Large* 203-205 (1804). 43 Geo.3 c.58, secs. 1 & 2 are reproduced also in (1st) *Rafferty, supra* note 15 (of *Side B*) in *Statute No. 1* (of *Appendix 1*).

Lawrence, J. said this was the interpretation that must be put upon the words *quick with child* in the statute [The phrase in the statute in which these words are found reads: "then being quick with child."]; and as the woman in this case had not felt the child alive within her before taking the medicine, he directed an acquittal.[3]

The *Phillips* trial judge did not interpret the term *quick with child*. What he actually interpreted were the words "then being" in the statutory phrase "then being quick with child". To identify "when" an occurrence or event comes about obviously does not define and, therefore, is not an interpretation of, what that occurrence is or means. If the term *quick with child* means or refers to *quickening*, and not to "pregnant with a live child," then the foregoing statement, "a woman is not considered to be *quick with child* till she has herself felt the child alive ... [or] quick within her," does not make sense; for it would really read: A woman is not considered to have felt the child alive or quick within her until she has felt the child alive or quick within her. Consider how much better that same statement reads if the term *quick with child* is given to mean simply "pregnant with a live child": A woman is not considered to be pregnant with a live child until she has felt the child alive (quick) within her.

The foregoing is one reason why there should be no real doubt that the *Phillips* trial judge knew that the statutory term *quick with child* meant simply pregnant with a live child. (*See e.g.*, 2 W. Forbes, *The Institutes of the Law of Scotland* 99-100 (Edinburgh, 1722-1730): "It is Murder ... to destroy ... a living child in the Mother's Belly ... But the Time when a Child unborn is understood in law to be quick, is determined by the Discretion of the Judge; there being no fixed Rule about it and the Doctors very much divided in their Opinions.) The error the *Phillips* trial judge made was in thinking that "when" a woman becomes *quick with child* is necessarily included in the definition of that term. It is certainly true that it is a rule of statutory construction that

---

3    *R v. Phillips*, 170 Eng. Rpts. at 1311-12.

words or phrases in a statute are ordinarily construed as they are commonly used or understood. However, the issue in *Phillips* did not involve the question of what construction should be put upon the term *quick with child*. The obvious issue was: "When" is a woman considered to be *quick with child* or pregnant with a live child within the meaning of the words "then being" in the *43 Geo. 3 c.58 sec. 1*-statutory phrase "then being quick with child?" The answer to that question in *Phillips* should no more have been resolved by resort to then-popular or vulgar conceptions or notions of when a pregnant woman is considered to be pregnant with a live child than, for example, is the question of whether defendant "X", while driving a vehicle, was then under the influence of alcohol (within the meaning of the "particular" statutory phrase "under the influence of alcohol") should be resolved by resorting to popular notions (*e.g.*, in a drunken state) of when a person is "legally" considered to be under the influence of alcohol. The *Phillips* trial judge, in seeking to resolve the question when is a woman considered to be pregnant with a live child, should have attempted to resolve the following two questions: (1) At common law, when is a pregnant woman considered to be *quick with child?* (*See, e.g., Arkansas v. Pierson* (1884): The common law in force at the time a statute is passed is to be taken into account in construing the statute;[4] and Coke: "'To know what the common law was before the making of the statute is the ... key to set open the windows of the statute.'");[5] and (2): What is the received opinion among the contemporary learned (or among the members of the relevant discipline — and the identification of those disciplines would have been a large question in *Phillips*) on the question: When does the unborn product of human conception begin its existence as a human being. The *Phillips* trial judge should have called in some theologians and philosophers and posed this "non-religious" and non-scientific question: What

---

4    44 Ark. 265, 266.

5    L.H. La Rue, *Statutory Interpretation: Lord Coke Revisited*, 48 U. of Pitt. L. Rev. 733, 745-49 (1987).

is the generally received opinion on when God infuses a human soul into the unborn product of human conception?

Finally, so far as is known, no condemned women, in the history of the English common law, was ever granted a pregnancy reprieve simply by swearing at her sentencing that she was "quick with child".[6]

In such English, criminal abortion cases as *R v. Pizzy and Codd* (1808)[7] and *R v. Russell* (1832),[8] it was not decided, but was simply assumed, that the term *quick with child* was synonymous with *quickening*. This assumption undoubtedly derived from the then-existing fact that the term *quick with child* was a popular or common way of referring to that stage in pregnancy that commences with *quickening*. That fact probably came about because of one or both of the following: (1) In popular or vulgar thinking *quickening* always had been understood to signal the infusion of the human soul into the fetus; (2): *quickening* was the only way the pregnant woman could perceive that her fetus had received its human soul or *had become alive*. It is said that in 1638, the mother of the then-unborn Louis XIV ordered a large fireworks display when she *quickened* with the future king.[9]

---

6     *See supra*, text (of *Side B*) accompanying note 14.

7     J. Bransby (printer & vendor), *The Remarkable Trial at Large of William Pizzy and Mary Codd at Bury St. Edmunds Assizes, August 11, 1808*, (Ipswich, 1808). This case can be viewed online, at *www.parafferty.com* : Download *Roe v. Wade: The Birth of a Constitutional Right*, and go to pp. 735-747.

8     168 Eng. Rpts. 1302; 1 Mood. 356. *Russell's Case* is discussed, *infra*, in *Appendix 6*.

9     *See* Jeremy Baker, *Tolstoy's Bicycle* 4 (paperback ed., 1982).

# APPENDIX 6

## R V. RUSSELL (HUNTINGDON, 1832)[1]

In pertinent part the indictment in this case charged Russell (R) with the capital offence of being an accessory before the fact to Sarah Wormsley's (S.W.) self-murder. The jury returned a verdict of guilty. The trial court imposed a sentence of death on R, and then stayed R's execution in order that an appeal could be taken on certain points of law in the case. The relevant facts, as found by the *Russell* jury, were the following. R. delivered arsenic to S.W., who was then pregnant but not *quick with child* (meaning here: S.W. had not yet experienced *quickening*)[2], so that S.W. would consume it in order to make herself miscarry. S.W., while outside of R's presence, consumed the arsenic with the intent of making herself miscarry. S.W. then died from ingesting the arsenic.[3]

In the course of charging or addressing the jury, the *Russell* trial court stated in effect the following: if you are satisfied that S.W. took the arsenic with the intention of making herself miscarry, she would be, in judgment of the common law, a *felo de se* (i.e., a self-murderer), even though, in taking the arsenic, she did not then harbor the intent to take her own life.[4]

At common law there was no offence of accessory before the fact to the criminal offence of felony-suicide. This was due to the common law rule that an accessory before the fact could not be

---

1    168 Eng. Rpts. 1302; 1 Mood. 356. This case should be compared to *R v. Gaylor* (1857), 169 Eng. Rpts. 1011, 7 Cox C.C. 253, Deare & B.C.C. 288.

2    *See R v. Phillips* (1811) *supra*, at *Appendix 5.*

3    168 Eng. Rpts. At 1304.

4    *Ibid.*

tried and convicted unless the principal felon was first tried and convicted. And this was impossible in the case of a felony-suicide because the principal (the *felo de se*) was dead and, therefore, could not be tried. However, in England at the time of S.W.'s felony-suicide there existed a statute, *7 Geo. IV. C. 64. s. 9* (1826), that enabled an accessory before the fact to be tried and convicted, notwithstanding that the principal had yet to be tried and convicted. This statute read in pertinent part as follows:

> And for the more effectual Prosecution of Accessories before the Fact to Felony; Be it enacted, That if any Person shall counsel, procure or command any other Person to commit any Felony, whether the same be a Felony at Common Law, or by virtue of any Statute or Statutes made or to be made, the Person so counseling, procuring or commanding shall be deemed guilty of Felony, and may be indicted and convicted, either as an Accessory before the Fact to the principal Felony, together with the principal Felon, or after the Conviction of the principal Felon, or may be indicted and convicted of a substantive Felony, whether the principal Felon shall or shall not have been previously convicted, or shall or shall not be amenable to Justice, and may be punished in the same Manner as any Accessory before the Fact to the same Felony, if convicted as an Accessory, may be punished.[5]

The question in *Russell* was whether *7 Geo. IV. C.64. s.9* authorized R. to be prosecuted pursuant to an indictment charging him with the common law, capital offence of being an accessory before the fact to felony-suicide. The appellate court in *Russell* voted eight (8) to four (4) that S.W. was a *felo de se*. They also voted twelve (12) to zero (0) that R. was an accessory before the fact to the felony-suicide. However, by a vote of nine(9) to three (3), they construed *7 Geo. IV. C.64 s.9* to be applicable only to accessories who *could have been* tried at common law "together with or after the principal felon". To put this another

---

5    Reproduced from *The Statutes of the United Kingdom of Great Britain and Ireland 7 Gel. IV 1826* 277 (London, 1826).

way, nine *Russell* justices ruled that the *7 Geo. IV. C.64. s.9* term, "Accessories before the Fact to Felony", does not include an accessory to felony-suicide because at common law it was not an indictable offence to be an accessory to felony-suicide, and the statute was not designed to create any new felonies.[6] To put this still another way, they held that *7 Geo. IV. C.64 s.9* was not intended to apply to cases in which the principal cannot from the nature of the case be tried. Since self-murder is such a case, the *Russell* appellate court set aside R's conviction of accessory before the fact to S.W.'s self-murder. (I would add the following. At common law an accessory before the fact to a felony was liable to the same punishment as the principal felon. But since an accessory before the fact to felony-suicide can still be living after the suicide, it would be impossible for such an accessory to receive the same punishment as the *felo de se*.)[7]

R., at his own request, was transported for fourteen years, instead of being tried on another indictment for the statutory, felony offence of furnishing to a woman, who was not then *quick with child*, a substance in order to cause her to miscarry.[8]

S.W., who was pregnant, but not *quick with child*, when she killed herself in the course of attempting an abortion on herself, could not be considered a *felo de se* at common law unless she killed herself in connection with the commission of a criminal offense that posed more than a remote risk of death.[9] Hence, eight of the *Russell* justices implicitly concluded that S.W.'s act of attempted self-abortion was an indictable offence, notwithstanding that S.W. was not then *quick with child*. This could have been an offence only by virtue of a statute or by virtue of the common law. The *Russell* appellate prosecutor argued both grounds.[10] The only criminal abortion statute in effect in England when S.W.

6    168 Eng. Rpts. at 1306. *See also Reg. v. Ashmall and Tay* (1840), 9 Carr & P. 236.

7    *See Bloch* (*and also Shaffer*), *supra*, note 16 (of *Side B*).

8    158 Eng. Rpts. at 1306. The statute, here, is *9 Geo. 4, c.31, sec. 13* (1828).

9    *See supra*, the commentary on *Adkyns Case* in *Appendix 3*.

10    *See* 168 Eng. Rpts. at 1305.

killed herself was *9 Geo. IV. c.31. s.13* (1828). So far as pertinent here, this statute read as follows: "if any person, with intent to procure the miscarriage of any woman not being, or not being proved to be, then *quick with child*, unlawfully and maliciously shall ... cause to be taken by her, any medicine or other thing ..., every such offender, and every person counseling, aiding, or abetting such offender, shall be guilty of felony, and being convicted thereof, shall be liable ... to be transported ... for any term not exceeding Fourteen years nor less than seven years ..."[11] It seems almost certain, however, that the eight *Russell* justices, who concluded that S.W. was a *felo de se* were of the opinion that the word "person" (as it "initially" appears in the foregoing quoted portion of *9 Geo. IV. c.31. s.13*) does not include the woman who administers to herself a substance in order to induce her own miscarriage. This is so, if only for the reason that the common law rule that criminal statutes are strictly construed in favor of the defendant would have dictated just such an opinion.[12] This rule (and the *Russell* court invoked this rule in the course of construing *7 Geo. IV. c.64. s.9* in Russell's favor)[13] stands for the following rules of statutory construction: if an act does not fall within the express prohibition of the penal statute, then the act is not considered to come within the statute; and if a criminal statute is susceptible of two reasonable interpretations, one of which favors the defendant and the other of which disfavors him or her, then the court should adopt that interpretation which favors the defendant and should reject that interpretation that disfavors him or her.[14] Now, it seems evident that at the very least, it is just

11   *See The Statutes of the United Kingdom of Great Britain and Ireland 9 Geo. IV., 1828* 104 (1828).

12   This would appear not to be the case relative to the word "person" as it appears for the second time in the foregoing quoted portion of *9 Geo. IV. c.31. s.13*. The woman who is plotting to have an abortion might "counsel" or "aid and abet" a *9 Geo. IV. c.31. s.13* offender. *See*, by way of analogy, *R v. Sockett*, 72 J.P. 428 (1909).

13   *See* 168 Eng. Rpts. at 1306.

14   *See, e.g.*, 1 Blackstone's *Commentaries* 87 (1765).

as reasonable to conclude that S.W. is not a person within the meaning of the word "person" (as it initially appears in the foregoing quoted portion of *9 Geo. IV. c.31. s.13*) as it is reasonable to conclude that S.W. is such a person. Furthermore, a strong argument can be made that it would be unreasonable to conclude that S.W. qualified as such a person. The statute, in exempting such a person, lessened the great difficulty in successfully prosecuting criminal abortion cases.[15] Also, it was not until 1861 that the English Parliament made it a "statutory" offence for a woman to attempt self-abortion.[16] Hence, the conclusion seems inescapable that the eight *Russell* justices, who concluded that S.W. was a *felo de se*, based that conclusion on their determination that pre-*quick-with-child*-deliberated abortion (and, or, its attempt) were indictable offenses (misdemeanors) at the English common law. *Russell* was construed so in *Reg. v. Fretwell* (1862).[17]

---

15  *See supra*, text accompanying note 10 of *Beare's Case* (in *Appendix I*), and *infra*, text accompanying note 4 (of *Epilogue*), as well as that note 4.

16  *See* 24 & 25 Vict., c.107, sec. 48 & 59 (1861), in: *The Statutes of the United Kingdom of Great Britain and Ireland* 438-39 (London, 1861).

17  9 Cox C.C. 152, 154; 31 L.J.M.C. 145; 26 J.P. 499, 6 L.T. 333.

# EPILOGUE TO THE APPENDICES:INTRACTABLE PROBLEMS IN RELATING A HISTORY OF ABORTION PROSECUTION AT THE ENGLISH COMMON LAW

This is no easy task. One reason is, beginning in the early 1960s, (and largely in connection with movements to repeal long-standing criminal abortion laws in England and the United States), countless, untrue, misleading, and unresolved-conflicting statements have been made regarding various aspects of this history. These erroneous statements have found their way into all sorts of writings on law, medicine, religion, politics, philosophy, and women rights.

Another reason is that there are so few known criminal abortion prosecutions at the English common law (it seems a virtual certainty here that many criminal abortion acts remain hidden in crimes of assault or poisoning, and murder of pregnant women.) Also, neither these few abortion prosecutions nor the brief passages on abortion in the common law books of authority (more than one of which misstates the status of criminal abortion at common law) are self-explanatory. Professor Sir John Baker has observed:

> The [English] criminal law has hardly received generous attention from the English legal historian.... More records of criminal sessions are ... finding their way to the presses. A certain amount of law is to be learned from [this] ... mate-

rial....[However],...[such] record [material] ... tells little or nothing about the interpretation of the terms used in the indictment, the nature of the evidence given, the rules of evidence (if any), the considerations which weighed with the jury, the influence of the judge, or the extent to which strict law might be softened by discretion. Such questions are notoriously difficult to answer; but until the answers are found there can be no history of English criminal law.[1]

The immediate explanation for this paucity of abortion prosecutions is undoubtedly because the commission of this offense very seldom came to the attention of the secular, English criminal courts. However, the reason why those courts heard so few abortion prosecutions is not, as some persons have erroneously suggested or speculated, because those courts considered the offense to be, for the most part, under the criminal jurisdiction of the pre-Reformation, Catholic Church courts or the post-Reformation, English Church courts.[2] (This is not to say that some — a relative few — abortion cases, if not also some infanticide cases, were not prosecuted in these Church courts at least into the sixteenth century.)[3] Nor is the reason why the common law

---

1    John H. Baker, *The Legal Profession and the Common Law: Historical Essays*, 325 (1986).

2    *See, e.g.*, D.S. Davies, *The Law of Abortion and Necessity*, 2 Mod. L.Rev. 126, 133 (1938) ("It is probably due to the fact that the offence [of abortion] was one of ecclesiastical cognizance which accounts for the extreme paucity of references to abortion in the authorities on English criminal law."); and Agnus McLaren, *Reproductive Rituals: The Perception of Fertility in England from the Sixteenth Century to the Nineteenth Century* 122-128 & 137-138 (1984). On ecclesiastical prosecution, here, *see* R.H. Helmholz, *The Oxford History of the Laws of England: Volume I: The Canon Law and Ecclesiastical Jurisdiction from 597 to the 1640s* (2004) at pp. 599-631.

3    *See* the English ecclesiastical abortion prosecutions set forth in *Rafferty*, *supra* note 15 (of *Side B*) in *Appendix 21*, p.727. For some instances of English ecclesiastical prosecutions for infanticide and negligent child

criminal courts heard so few abortion cases is that abortion was very rarely attempted. There is every reason to believe that more than a few unmarried, pregnant women and their sexual partners or other associates attempted it by one method or another. However, it would be highly unlikely that an attempted abortion which had not brought about the death or near death of the pregnant woman would have come to light. Any such attempted abortion would have been performed in utter secrecy; and the participants in the crime, not to mention the fetal victim, could not have been expected to come forth.[4]

Available evidence indicates that one of the reasons why the English secular courts heard so few abortion cases is that the abortion methods (such as: the ingestion of various obnoxious potions, drugs and herbs, the administration of certain douches, the inser-

---

destruction in the sixteenth century, *see* R. Houlbrooke, *Church Courts and the People During the English Reformation 1520-1570* 78 n.76 (1979): CB3, fo.110r: husband and wife (hereinafter: H.& W.) examined for negligently suffocating (by rolling on top of?) their four-months-old child while the child slept with them (outcome unknown); CB3, fo.123r:H.& W. ordered to prove their infant child was not suffocated (probably acquitted, as they produced a witness who testified that the child did not suffocate); CB3, fo.172r: H.& W. examined for suffocating their child (outcome unknown); CCB3, fo.192r: J.H. examined upon articles for counseling the destruction of two children (outcome unknown); CB4, fo.46v: H.& W. for suffocating their child (both acquitted); CB4, fo.105v: Agnes D. for suspected child destruction, or perhaps for abortion, for while pregnant she went away for two weeks, and then returned not pregnant, and without the child (outcome unknown). *See also* Richard Wunderli, *London Church Courts and Society on the Eve of the Reformation* 78 & 128-29 (1981).

4    *See, e.g., Commonwealth v. Smalansky*, 64 *Dauphin County Reports* 310, 316 (1953) (" 'The act of [inducing abortion], of course, is always shrouded in mystery and consummated in utter secrecy. Again, since a criminal miscarriage and a natural miscarriage are practically synonymous in external appearance and after-effects, it is extremely difficult to distinguish the one from the other.' ")

tion of certain suppositories, the application of severe force to the lower abdomen, the application of certain plasters to the lower abdomen, bloodletting, the employment of one or more of the then-recognized means for initiating or restoring menstruation, and the performance of some form of rough sport or exercise) that were then most utilized, were not — as will be shown — even capable of inducing abortion. Operative or instrumental methods of performing abortion seem to have been very rarely employed. William Defoe, in his satirical attack on the "diabolical practice" of abortion in his *A Treatise Concerning the Use and Abuse of the Marriage Bed* (1727), did not include operative or instrumental abortion in his list of abortion methods used by a suspected female abortionist: "Drugs and Physicians [i.e., "physics" or medicines], whether Astringents, Diureticks, Emeticks, or of whatever kind, nay, even to Purgations, Potions, Poisons, or anything that Apothecaries or Druggists can supply…, [and]…Devil Spells, Filtres, Charms [and] Witchcraft …"[5] One reason why operative or instrumental methods of performing abortion were evidently rarely employed may have been due in part to "the relatively inaccessible position of the uterus", coupled with a general ignorance of the female reproductive anatomy. Another reason may have been the then-common belief that when a woman conceives (i.e., when the male's seed is deposited in, and retained by the womb or "matrix"), the cervix or "mouth of the womb" closes so firmly and tightly that not even the point of a needle can penetrate it without doing much violence.[6]

Several modern writers have concluded that then-existing, covertly popular methods for inducing abortion were often successful.[7] However, old case histories of attempted abortion, mod-

---

5     D. Defoe, *A Treatise Concerning the Use and Abuse of the Marriage Bed: Shewing… the Diabolical Practice of Attempting to Prevent Child-bearing by Physical Preparations* 152 (London, 1727). *And see id.* at 154-55.

6     *See, e.g.,* J. Sharp, *The Midwives Book* 38 (1671).

7     *See, e.g.,* J. Weeks, *Sex, Politics and Society* 72 (1981); and R. Stark, *The Rise of Christianity* 119-121 (paperback ed., 1996).

ern medical science, and a comparative history of abortion and infanticide in pre-20ᵗʰ-century England, contradict this conclusion. The 19ᵗʰ-century, English physician William Cummin observed:

> To what extent, however, personal violence may be employed without procuring abortion, is well exemplified by a case that occurred not long ago … in Dr. Wagner's practice at Berlin. "Among the remarkable cases which came before us", says the Professor, in his half-yearly report, "was one of *Attempted abortion*. A young woman, seven months with child, had employed savine and other drugs, with a view to produce miscarriage. As these had not the desired effect, a strong leather strap (the thong of a skate) was tightly bound round her body. This, too, availing nothing, her paramour (according to his own confession) knelt upon her, and compressed the abdomen with all his strength: yet neither did this effect the desired object. The man now trampled on the Girl's person while she lay on her back; and as this also failed, he took a sharp-pointed pair of scissors and proceeded to perforate the uterus through the vagina. Much pain and hemorrhage ensued, but did not last long. The woman's health did not suffer in the least and pretty much about the regular time a living child was brought into the world without any marks of external injury upon it."[8]

Lester Adelson, in his *The Pathology of Homicide* (1974), observed:

> *External Physical Methods [of Attempting Abortion]*…. include … horseback riding …, and applying direct force to the lower abdomen.

---

8    W. Cummin, *Lectures on Forensic Medicine, in Syllabus of a Course of Lectures on Forensic Medicine*, as reproduced in the *London Medical Gazette*, Saturday, February 4, 1837, pp. 679-80 (lecture no. CIC).

These crude measures are notoriously ineffective in creating the desired result *unless* the mother's visceral injuries are sufficiently severe to endanger her life....

*Drugs and Chemicals*....Even at toxic levels none of these "traditional" drugs is truly abortifacient in the first two trimesters of pregnancy. When administered in amounts far in excess of their therapeutic dosage, they *may* stimulate uterine evacuation. This effect is unpredictable and represents a response to toxic overdosage....

One of the more common fallacious bases for using a specific drug (or combination of drugs) as an abortifacient is the "experience" of some woman who "aborted" successfully and uneventfully after using it. The truth of the matter is that she was not pregnant to begin with but was suffering from a combination of a delayed menstrual period and apprehension about an unwanted pregnancy. Sequence and consequence become confused, and a "new", "safe" and "effective" abortifacient is born.

*Volatile Oils and Cathartics.* On rare occasions, [they] may stimulate the uterus to contract. Included in this group are oil of savin ... and oil of pennyroyal....

*Oxytocic Drugs.* [Practically speaking,] ergot preparations ... can cause premature labor [only] when administered in large doses *near term*....

*Systemic Poisons.* This group of compounds includes ... arsenic and mercury, ... and a host of weird concoctions.... these substances rarely empty a pregnant uterus unless they have been taken in doses so large that the mother's health or life is endangered....

*Intravaginal Introduction of Chemicals.* Intravaginal introduction of chemicals to produce abortion ..., [such as] douches and insertion of suppositories ..., [lack] the capacity to enter the cervical canal whose external is occluded by a plug of tenacious mucus....[9]

---

9    Lester Adelson, *The Pathology of Homicide* 693-95 (1974) (reprinted with permission of Charles C. Thomas, Publisher, Springfield, Illinois). *See also, e.g.,* I. Gordon, *et al* (eds.), *Forensic Medicine: A Guide to Principles* 369-70 (3rd ed., 1988); *Taylor's Principles and Practice of Medical Jurisprudence*

Now, add to the foregoing observations the fact that at the English common law infanticide prosecutions exceeded abortion prosecutions by several hundreds (or thousands) or so to one.[10] By the late sixteenth century, abortion was not a capital offence at common law unless the aborted child was born alive and subsequently died in connection with being aborted.[11] However, infanticide was a capital offense. So, if effective abortion techniques were available in pre-19th- century England, then women (and their abortion aiders, etc.) bent on getting rid of an unwanted child would have employed these techniques, and would not have risked being "launched into eternity" at the end of a rope for having committed infanticide.

David Hume (1737-1838), the nephew of the British empiricist philosopher by the same name, in his *Commentaries on the Law of Scotland Respecting Crimes* (1797-1800), stated that the newborn bastard child is the most common victim of murder.[12] Elizabeth Cellier, in her *A Scheme for the Foundation of a Royal Hospital* (1687), observed: "There are a great number of [newborns] which are overlaid and willfully murdered by their wicked and cruel mothers, for want of fit ways to conceal their shame and provide for their children, as ... [is shown by]

---

328-29 (13th ed., 1984), and *Williams Obstetrics* 505-506 (18th ed., 1989). Contraceptive methods were equally ineffective. *See* C. Given-Wilson & A. Curtis, *The Royal Bastards of Medieval England* 41-42 (Routledge paperback, 1984/88).

10   *See* the citations of infanticide prosecutions in(1st) *Rafferty, supra*, note 15 (of *Side B*) at pp. 359-367 (nn. 17-20).

11   *See Q v. West* (1848), *supra*, in *Appendix 4*.

12   1 D. Hume, *Commentaries on the Law of Scotland, Respecting Crimes* 291 (B.R. Bell, ed., 1844) (1st ed., 1797-1800).

the many executions on their offenders."[13] L.A. Perry, in his *Criminal Abortion* (1932), observed:

> At the commencement of the Stuart period [about 1603], it seems to have been a very usual custom for women who were going to have illegitimate children to wait and allow delivery to take place naturally, rather than to procure abortion. When the child was born it was at once killed, and the mother usually declared that it had been born dead. So frequent was this crime of infanticide of illegitimate children that an Act of Parliament was passed in 1623 (*21 Jas. 1. c.27*) with the object of lessening the evil.[14]

Had the *Roe* Court been aware of this history of widespread infanticide,[15] then the Court probably would have argued that the framers of the Fifth Amendment undoubtedly viewed induced abortion as a worthwhile preventive of infanticide.

I end this book where it began: The early Christian communities viewed abortion and infanticide as being virtually indistinguishable in terms of being anti-human life (and therefore as being also anti-Christ). The women of early Christian communities in Rome gathered the untold number of victims of infan-

---

13   E. Cellier, *A Scheme for the Foundation of a Royal Hospital* 1 (1687). *See also MacLaren, supra* note 2 at 131 ("William Walsh in *A Dialogue Concerning Women* (1699) [in Curil (ed.), *Works* 156 (London, 1736)] had a character declare: "'Go but one Curcuit with the Judges here in England; observe how many women are condemned for killing their Bastard Children'") (quoting J. Addison, *Guardian*, no. 105, July 11, 1713).

14   L.A. Perry, *Criminal Abortion* 95-96 (1932). *21 Jas. 1. c.27 (1623)* is reproduced in *Davies, supra* note 13 (of *Side B*), and also (and with *aca*) in (1st) *Rafferty, supra* note 15 (of *Side B*) at p.475 (*Statute No. 5 of Appendix 1*).

15   *See*, Joseph W. Dellapenna, *Dispelling the Myths of Abortion History* 89-124 (2006).

ticide and took them to the catacombs for burial. [16] Today, no reasonable person (or one who is not a complete moral idiot) would maintain that the outlawing of infanticide reflects what is exclusively a religious belief. That being true, then, for a person to even suggest that the outlawing of abortion, or the belief that abortion is "too close" to infanticide reflect what is exclusively a religious belief, is to advocate in favor of naked anti-religious bigotry. As observed by Christoph Cardinal Schönborn:

> What is there in creation more sublime, more precious, than a new human child? What is in greater danger, nowadays, than an unborn child? ["The painful fact [is] that the animal [rights]...lobby is given a better hearing in politics today than those who [lobby for the]...unborn child."] And] it is hard to understand how one's commitment to environmental protection is not turned as a priority to protecting children. For nothing demands our respect for creation more than care for its more precious possession: the child that has been vouchsafed as a gift to this world in order to know it, respect it, and cultivate it. [17]

---

16  *See, Vidmar, supra* note 39 (of *Side A*) at 29. *See also, supra,* text (of *Side A*) accompanying notes 14-20.

17  C. Cardinal Schönborn, *Chance or Purpose: Creation, Evolution and a Rational Faith* 160 (Ignatius, 2007). The quote in brackets is cited as *id.* at 152. *And see Budziszewski, supra,* 1st *epigraph* page at 66-67: "Not even the greatest of the pagans could admit what was wrong with infanticide, although they knew that the child was of our kind. Neither can we admit what is wrong with abortion."

# ENDNOTES

## NOTE TO THE READER

1 The *Roe* decision was affirmed in *Casey* by a vote of 5 to 4. *See* p. 215 (at note 25), and pp. 55-58, and 65-69

2 *See*, text of *Side B* accompanying nn. 31 & 32 (pp.58-59), and pp. 66 (beginning at last para.) - 68.

3 *See Side B* at pp. 49-54.

## PREFACE

1 *Lawler*, note 27 (of *Side A*) at p.63. See *Van Nostrand's Scientific Encyclopedia*, text (of *Side A*) at pp.39-40 (and p.189 at n.23). *See also* text (of *Epilogue*) accompanying nn.15-16 (pp.171-72); and p.188 (at n.227). See *Hall v Hancock* (1834), note 4 (of *Side B*) p.196.

2 Russell Shaw, *The Cause of Rampant Catholic Moral Immaturity*, in *Our Sunday Visitor*, May 17, 2009, p.5. For a good sampling of early Christian statements against abortion, see David Bercot (ed.), *A Dictionary of Early Christian Beliefs* 2-3 (1998).

3 The "process" of the incarnation (i.e., the process of the "person," God the Son becoming a human being began with his human conception by the Holy Spirit in the womb of the virgin Mary (and which, by the way, might imply that this "person" God the Son, rendered Himself non-cognitive (in his Father's bosom and under his loving eye) while he resided within his mother Mary's womb):

> [a]...statement in the letter of Cyril, which the Council [of Ephesus, 431 C.E] approved, is about the title "Mother of God" 'It was not that an ordinary

man was born first of the holy virgin on whom afterwards the Word descended; what we say is that, being united ["from conception"] with the flesh from the womb, the Word [i.e., the "person" — God the Son] has undergone birth in the flesh.'

*Kereszty, supra* page 17 (of my text) at 240 & 373. (*See also* 1 William E. May, *Catholic Bioethics and the Gift of Human Life* 188 (2nd ed. 2008) citing John Saward, *Redeemer in the Womb: Jesus Living in Mary* (1993), pp. 165-168); Elena Bosetti, *John: The Word of Light* 72-73 (PBN & M, paperback, 2007) (Who better than a mother can exemplify the vocation of giving life, making room within one's own being, generating, and nourishing?); and *Kereszty, ibid* at p.350 (In the Jewish or Old Testament "Yahweh is ...likened to a mother 'pregnant with a child in her womb, crying out in labor, [and] giving birth").

It may be that the truth of the incarnation reveals that a human person does not come into existence "merely" by virtue of the union of his soul and body or flesh (ie., it may be that this "union" is not what generates or gives birth to a human person). The human being, Jesus of Nazareth, came into existence, by virtue of just such a union, and yet he is not now, and was never a human person (because he already was a person, albeit, a Divine one, who originated in his Fathers bosom, which is eternal and outside of created existence). To say that the Father suppressed the would-be human person of Jesus that would have otherwise come forth from the union of his body and human soul is to attribute to God a true act of violence; but that is utterly foreign to His nature. So, I conclude that a human person (say you or me) derives from nothing less than a creative act of God in the very act of loving. I conclude also that a human person (say you or me, but not Jesus of Nazareth) is a composite of body, soul, and "human" person.

4  Marko Ivan Rupnik, S.J., *Discernment: Acquiring the Heart of God* 20 (Pauline Books & Media, 2006: 1st English ed.).

5  *See* the citations *infra*, in note 26 (of *Side A*).

6  *See Forming Consciences for Faithful Citizenship: A Call to Political Responsibility* (online at usccb.org): "A Catholic cannot vote for a [political] candidate who takes a position in favor of an intrinsic evil, such as abortion or racism, *if the voter's intent is to support that position* ... In such cases, a Catholic would be guilty of formal cooperation in grave [intrinsic] evil."

The *Side A* argument is directed at the pro-*Roe* (or pro-choice) position of those Christian persons who (1) profess to be committed, orthodox, Christian believers, but who feel that the lived Christian faith can accommodate abortion, or (2) accept that abortion cannot be accommodated by or reconciled to the lived Christian faith, but nevertheless insist that it be made available in a pluralistic society that is more than willing to accommodate it. This latter group of persons seems to be saying, in effect, that pluralism, secularism, and the principle of separation of church and state dictate that practicing Christians "box up their faith" so that it doesn't give full expression to the gospel of "abundant life". (Paul, of course, would disagree: "Woe to me if I do not preach the gospel [of "abundant life," whether in season or out of season]," *1 Cor. 9:16.*) The former group seems to be saying that the God of "abundant life" approves of abortion.

The *Los Angeles Times* (via the *Washington Post*) reported that President Obama announced that, in speaking with his Supreme Court nominee, Justice Sotomayor, she assured him that she is committed to upholding *Roe* should she, as a Supreme Court justice, be called upon to vote on the issue of whether the Court, in light of certain new medical / scientific developments, or historical facts, should overrule Roe. (*L.A. Times*, Friday, May 29, 2009 at A:17: *Sotomayor in Line on Abortion, White House Says*). The White House made that announcement in response to repeated statements by various pro-*Roe v. Wade* entities and supporters that, in nominating Justice Sotomayor the President may not be adhering to a (several times repeated) campaign promise to nominate a person committed to upholding *Roe v. Wade*. After that White House release, not so much as a peep, here, was heard from the various pro-*Roe* entities — and notwithstanding that in that White House announcement the President specifically related that he did not discuss *Roe* or abortion rights with Sotomayor. The President did, however, relate that the two of them had a very agreeable discussion on the "rights of privacy." The inescapable or obvious inference is that "rights of privacy" is a code phrase for abortion rights.

This White House release should qualify as perhaps the most politically unartful, presidential release in the history of the presidency. Not only does it lend (presidentially-backed) credence to the popular misconception that the constitutional decision-making process is simply a (partisan) political act, but it puts Sotomayor in the "unconstitutional" position of committing in advance to ruling a particular way.

If this White House release would have been put to Sotomayor at her confirmation hearings, and had she, there, been properly cross-examined on it, then she would have had to admit to one of the following: (1) she never implied any such thing to President Obama (which means that the President was being untruthful — and we know that Sotomayor would not imply that the President was being untruthful to the public), or (2) she would have had to admit that she said that, i.e., that she was "in line" on the "rights of privacy". And if she had admitted to having said that, then she would have had to admit also that the Fifth Amendment, due process principle of the impartiality of the adjudicator would dictate that she "must" be disqualified from hearing or ruling on any future case involving the constitutional legitimacy of *Roe v. Wade*. *See*, by way of analogy, *In re Murchison* (1955), 348 U.S. 133 at 136 (due process dictates that a judge be disqualified from hearing the prosecution of a criminal charge involving a defendant when earlier that judge had participated in a hearing to determine whether that defendant should be criminally charged in the first place).

Or, suppose that the issue in *Roe v. Wade* had been whether a Texas "statutory-rape" statute, outlawing consensual sex between an adult male and a female under the age of eighteen, is unconstitutional in that an adult male has a fundamental right (constitutionally speaking) to engage in consensual sex with a (so-called) mature, minor female past the age of fifteen. Suppose also that one of the *Roe* justices (say, Justice X) who joined the *Roe* majority opinion (which held that such older / younger sex does indeed qualify as a fundamental right) had — several years before voting so in *Roe* — committed himself to voting so should that issue ever come before the Court. I maintain that all reasonable authorities on constitutional law would argue that the Fifth Amendment, due process mandate of the "impartiality of the adjudicator" dictates that Justice X(-rated) should have disqualified himself in *Roe*.

So, what does all this mean? It means that political correctness dictates that, in the context of sounding off for abortion rights, Supreme Court justices are not bound by the Fifth Amendment, due process mandate of the "impartiality of the adjudicator" (which is suppose to serve as the very foundation of all of our legal systems (*Gray v. Mississippi* (1987), 481 U.S. 648, 668)). It means that, in the name of political correctness, the constitutional principle of "the rule of law" must fall to the great cause of the moment: the securing of abortion rights at all costs.

It means also that Sotomayor is committed to upholding *Roe* even if legal scholarship has demonstrated (or can demonstrate) conclusively that *Roe's* fundamental premises are "not to be found [neither explicitly nor implicitly] in the Constitution" (*Thornburg v. American Coll. Of OBGYNS* (1986), 476 U.S. 747, 779: Justice Stevens concurring).

7   Those persons who insist on considering such a debate can knock themselves out in Nathan Schlueter and Robert H. Bork, *Constitutional Persons: An Exchange on Abortion* in Robert H. Bork, *A Time to Speak: Selected Writings and Arguments* 349 (2009).

8   *Marshall*: 414 U.S. 417, 427; *Paris*: 413 U.S. 49, at 60 & 63.

9    197 U.S.11, 30-31. *See infra*, the last *para.* of *note* 25 (of *Side B*), and *supra*, text (of *Side B*) accompanying nn. 13 & 14, as well as the 1st *para.* of that n. 14.

10   The *Roe* Court knew that it could not even begin to demonstrate that the practice of abortion represents a "principle of justice [or personal liberty] so rooted in the [legal and cultural] traditions and collective conscience of our people as to be ranked as fundamental" (*Washington v. Glucksberg* (1997), 521 U.S. 702, 710-721), without demonstrating that at the English common law, the practice of abortion was a recognized personal liberty (and not at all a recognized crime). *See infra*, note 19 (of *Side B*). *See also, e.g., McDonald v. Chicago*, 561 U.S.___, 2010, *Montana v. Egelhoff* (1996), 518 U.S. 37, 43-44, and *Dowling v. U.S.* (1990), 493 U.S. 342, 353. For an "in-depth" treatment of fundamental rights analysis within the context of the constitutional decision-making process — as it relates to abortion — *see Rafferty, infra*, note 1 (of *Side A*) at *paras.* 48-71 (including accompanying notes). The truth be known, there is no basis in Court precedent, or in reason or common sense, for the very explicit *Roe* holding that the constitutional right of privacy is limited to protecting only "given" or already - "established" fundamental rights. Justice Blackmun simply made it up so that he could employ "strict or close scrutiny analysis" to constitutionally balance a (now) fundamental right against a conflicting, legitimate state interest. However, the truth be known, a true fundamental right and a true legitimate state interest cannot collide period on our constitutional plane. *See Rafferty, infra*, note 1 (of *Side A*) at note 96 of *para.* 44.

The thought or contention that abortion qualifies as a fundamental right because it is subsumed by the constitutional right of privacy (*see, e.g., San Antonio Indep. Sch. Dist. v. Rodriguez* (1973), 411 U.S. 1, 34 n.76), squarely contradicts *Roe's* express holding that no interest or right period can qualify for protection under the constitutional right of privacy unless initially the asserted interest or right can be "legitimately" deemed as a "fundamental right" independently of any alleged nexus it might have to the right of privacy. (*See Roe v. Wade*, 410 U.S. 113, 152.) This holding has been affirmed in a host of cases. *See, e.g., Paul v. Davis*, 424 U.S.

693, 713 (1976): "[o]ur...'right of privacy' cases...deal...with the substantive aspects of the Fourteenth Amendment. In *Roe*, the Court pointed out that the...rights found in the guarantee of...privacy must be limited to those which are "fundamental" or "implicit in the concept of ordered liberty". See *Rafferty*, *infra* note 1 (of *Side A*) at *para.* 43 (including its accompanying footnote 95). What is downright hilarious is that *Roe*, in expressly qualifying the constitutional right of privacy to protecting or including "only" "given fundamental rights", unwittingly qualified this so-called right of privacy right out of constitutional existence. See *Rafferty*, *id.* at *paras.* 42-47, and *supra*, text accompanying note 16 (of *A Long Conclusion to Side B*), as well as that note 16.

Michael Dorf and Laurence Tribe, in their *On Reading the Constitution* 72-73 (1991), stated: "whether to designate a [supposed] right as "fundamental" poses perhaps the central substantive question of modern constitutional law." There is not a person under the sun who can identify or articulate (with any thing even approaching reasonable certainty) the criterion of fundamental rights employed by the *Roe* Court in deeming as a fundamental right a woman's interest in having an abortion. The *Roe* opinion has made "fundamental rights determination" utterly incomprehensible to reasonably thinking persons. The truth be known, the *Roe* Court simply created, from judicial predilection, a fundamental right to an abortion. And I defy absolutely any constitutional scholar or lawyer to demonstrate otherwise.

11   *Thornburg v. American Coll. of OBGYNS* (1986), 476 U.S. 747, 779 (concurring opinion). *See also, e.g.., Smith v. Allwright* (1944), 321 U.S. 649, 665. The Court has stood the doctrine or principle of *stare decisis* on its head. There are probably a thousand or so Court decisions overruling prior Court decisions (precedents). Hence, there are a thousand or so precedents overruling prior precedents. (*See, e.g., infra*, text (of *Side B*) accompanying note 29). Hence, the principle of *stare decisis*, itself, demands that the principle not be accepted or followed (because there is precedent for rejecting or overruling precedent). Or, consider the following proposition: Notwithstanding — and contrary to *Roe* and *Casey*, that in truth

the human fetus, alive in the womb of his or her mother, is a
5th and 14th Amendment, due process clause person, the fact
remains, generations of pregnant, American women have been
led to believe that their unborn constitutional persons can be disposed of at will. Therefore, the principle of *stare decisis* dictates
that American women be allowed to continue disposing so.

12    521 U.S. 702, 736.


## SIDE A

1    The quote is from James V. Schall, S.J., *The Order of Things* 152 (2007)
(quoting Yves Simon, *General Theory of Authority* 90-91 (1980)).
*And see*, Peter S. Williamson, *Catholic Principles for Interpreting
Scripture* 45-47 (Editrice Pontificio Instituto Biblica, Roma, 2001)
(Truth is objective, is discoverable, and is one-meaning: "there can
be no contradiction between truths acquired through human scientific research, *i.e.*, through reason, and the truths received through
divine revelation. Christian faith has nothing to fear from science.")
    To view online a complete, detailed dismantling of the utterly
contrived opinion in *Roe v. Wade*, including a complete, piece-
by-piece dismembering of *Roe's* patently false and, indeed, absurd
contention that abortion was recognized as a right (and not at all
as a crime) at the English common law, *see* the author's online
article, *Roe v. Wade: A Scandal Upon the Court*, 7 *Rutgers J. of Law
& Religion*. No. 7.1.1 (2006), *paras.* 12-27. Justice Blackmun's
rewrite (in his *Roe* opinion) of the common law on abortion is one
more confirmation of this observation of Hannah Arendt: ' "the
power of the modern state makes it possible for it to turn lies into
truth by destroying the facts which existed before and by making
new realities to conform to what until then had been ideological
fiction".' (Quoted in W. Pfaff, *Refugees: The Beast of Unreason Stirs
Again*, *L.A. Times*, July 8, 1979, Pt. V (*Opinion Sec.*), p.3). On *Roe's*
creation, here, of "new realities", *see Rafferty*, *id.* at paras. 60-67.

2    *Healy*, *supra* text accompanying note 27 (of *Side A*) at p.38. *See also*
*O'Collins*, *supra* (page 11) at p.354 (in *Matt.* 10:34-5 Jesus "presents

his mission in combative and divisive terms"). That Jesus is a human being — but not a human person, *see Kereszty, supra,* page 17 at 358-377.

3   *Apostles,* p.96, OSV Publishing Division, 2007. *See also* Luke T. Johnson, *The Living Gospel* 176 (paperback, 2004): "Knowing *persons* is not the same thing as knowing facts or learning theories. This is the sort of knowledge ... that ... persons experience when they give themselves to each other in trust and loyalty over time." *And see,* Gerald O'Collins, SJ, *Jesus: A Portrait* (Orbis Books paperback ed., 2008) XIV-XV: "knowledge of persons ... always [includes] ... *knowing someone,* not simply our *knowing about* him or her.... [¶] Really knowing another person in depth ... always demands that we relate to and participate in another personal mystery;" and *id,* at 225 (paraphrasing Augustine: " 'you need to be a friend of someone before you truly know him' ").

4   Henry Wansbrough, OSB, *The Story of the Bible: How It Came to Us* 117-118 (The Word Among Us Press, paperback, 2006). *See also* Sandra M. Schneiders, *The Resurrection of the Body in the Fourth Gospel: A Key to Johannine Spirituality,* in John R. Donahue, ed., *Life in Abundance: Studies of John's Gospel in Tribute to Raymond E. Brown* (Liturgical Press, 2005) 168 at 170-71:

> "Eternal life" is a technical theological term in *John* meaning God's own life lived by Jesus as the ... [Word] incarnate, and participated in, before as well as after death, by those who, born of God through the Spirit, are now ... children of God....The term refers not to some quality or even power possessed by the human being, but to the whole person as divinely alive.

5   So far as is known, man, before the fall, did not have an ability (or capacity) to receive the "beatific vision".
    *See* Pope Benedict XVI, *Credo for Today: What Christians Believe* 93 (2009): " Heaven is to be defined as the contact of the being man with the being God". The resurrected human being is

incorporated into the active life of a creator — God who is other-oriented. So, for all we know, God will bestow on the resurrected human being the privilege of watching God in the very act of creating. We cannot put limits on God's infinitely creative love.

6    It is inconceivable that Peter, James ("the brother of the Lord"), and John, and the rest of the apostles, would have accepted Paul as one of them, had they not been somehow convinced that Paul had seen the risen Lord just as they had seen the risen Lord.

See Ez. 36:26: "I will give you a new heart and place a new spirit within you." And see, e.g., Rt. Rev. Alexi Smith, Participation in the Pascal Mystery, The Tidings, March 14, 2008, p.14: by virtue of the Resurrection "'[w]e are given a new being, a new ontological existence which comes from God.'" See also Johnson, supra, note 3 at 170: "that Jesus' [human] body is glorified means that Jesus is now more than human, indeed shares God's own power and life. He is no longer confined to the empirical, historical body that was his before his death". And see Schneider, supra note 4 at 184: The post-crucified Jesus "standing in their midst is not simply resuscitated. He is alive with a new life that is bodily but no longer subject to death or to the laws of historical space, time, and causality. He is the same person Jesus, but in a new mode of being and presence." See also 1 Jn. 31-2: "Beloved, we are God's children now; what we shall be has not yet been revealed. We do know that when it is revealed we shall be like him, for we shall see him as he is."; and 1 Cor 15:42-44, Phil 2-21, and Matt. 23:30. And see "particularly", Gerald O'Collins, Jesus Our Redeemer: A Christian Approach to Salvation 238-67 (2009).

Pope Benedict XVI (supra, note 5 at 100) has observed: "biblical pronouncements about the resurrection ... aim ... to tell man that they ... live on, not by virtue of their own power, but because they are known and loved by God in such a way that they can no longer perish". What, precisely, does this "in such a way" consist of or include? The answer to such a question cannot, of course, be known by man. However, arguably, it would not be unreasonable to speculate that just as God gives to a man, say, eyes, ears, and legs so that he, himself, can see, hear, and walk, then, so also will God give to or superimpose or graft onto this same man (but now resurrected) a means by which he, himself *(and* the person of Christ living in him), is able to receive his Father, and become impervious to nonexistence (and to any form or degree of loneliness, or boredom, or fear, or regret, or feeling of not measuring up or of being lesser than, or self-seeking, *etc.*). He or she, having been overwhelmed with joy in experiencing Divine Life, will be "other-directed", in the image of his Creator.

The incarnate person of Jesus Christ is not a humanly conceived human being. So, it cannot be said that his bodily resurrection is necessarily the measure of our bodily resurrection. But it may be said that ours is analogous to his. *See Kereszty, supra*, page 17 at 479.

7   *Schall, supra,* note 1 at 188. *And see* Craig R. Koester, *The Death of Jesus and the Human Condition: Exploring the Theology of John's Gospel,* in *Donahue (supra*, note 4) 141 at 151: "This theological world recognizes that people were created to know God." *See also May, infra,* note 22 at 187: "The dignity of the human being is linked not only to its beginning, to the fact that it comes from God, but also to its final end, to its destiny of fellowship with God in knowledge and love of him."

St. Thomas, following Aristotle (*see infra,* text (of *Side B*) accompanying notes 8-10, as well as those notes), thought that the unborn product of human conception becomes an existing human being once it achieves fetal formation. He thought also that human beings "who die in the womb of their mothers ... will rise in conformity of the nature that they have with the nature of Christ" (IV *Sent.*, dist. 43, q.1, a.1, quaest. 2 ad 5.).

8   *See Mt.* 19:14: "Let the children come to me ... and do not prevent them; for the kingdom of heaven belongs to such as these." *See also Is. 55:10-11*: "my word shall not return to me void, but shall do my will, achieving the end for which I sent it." *And see* Johnson, *supra,* note 3 at 57: "the way one receives children [including children-to-be?] is the way one receives the kingdom of God ... [W]elcoming children is the measure of one's reception of God's rule. We can extrapolate: the way one treats children [including children not yet

born?] is a measure of how seriously one lives under the rule of God." *See also* the following from *The Parable of the Vineyard Workers* (*Mt.* 30: 12-15): " 'These last ones worked only one hour, and you have made them equal to us, who bore the day's burden and the heat'. He ... repl[ied]: 'My friend, I am not cheating you. What if I want to give this last one the same as you? Am I not free to do as I wish with my own money? Are you envious because I am generous' "? It may be, that in God's eyes, aborted fetuses and embryos are also "last ones".

9   *See* Raymond E. Brown, *The Birth of the Messiah* 261 (1993, Updated, Paperback Edition). To the argument that it is unscholarly to use Luckan concepts to explain a Johannine concept, I argue the following: Given that Christ inspired both Luke and John, then it is unscholarly to argue that Christ is not authority for Christ.

10  J. Murphy O'Connor, *Jesus and Paul: Parallel Lives* 41 (2007) *See also*, John Vidmar, *The Catholic Church Through the Ages* 66 (paperback, 2005).. *And see Isa.* 49:15-16: "Can a woman forget her nursing child, or show no compassion for the child of her womb: Even these may forget, yet I will not forget you." *See also, infra,* note 16, and this from *A Theologian's Brief, (2001):*

> Often in the Scriptures the forming of the child in the womb is described in ways that echo the formation of Adam from the dust of the earth (Job 10:8-12; Ecclesiastes 11:5; Ezekiel 37:7-10; cf. Wisdom 7:1, 15:10-11). This is why Psalm 1:39 describes the child in the womb as being formed "in the depths of the earth" (139:15). The formation of the human embryo is archetypal of the mysterious works of God (Psalm 139:15; Ecclesiastes 11:5). A passage that is significant for uncovering the connections between Genesis and embryogenesis is found in the deutero - canonical book of 2 *Maccabees* 7:22-23, in a mother's speech to her son:
>
> "I do not know how you came into being in

my womb. It was not I who gave you life and breath, nor I who set in order the elements within each of you. Therefore the Creator of the world, who shaped the beginning of man and devised the origin of all things, will in his mercy give life and breath back to you again."

p.41 of *Christian Reflection's* online republication (in the *Cloning* issue) of *A Theologian's Brief* (2001): *http://www.baylor.edu/ Christianethics/Cloningarticle_TheologiansBrief.pdf.* See also, John Paul II, *The Gospel of Life* [44-45] 73-75 & *Pope Benedict XVI supra*, note 5 at 69:

The Hebrew text of the Old Testament does not draw on psychology to speak about God's compassionate suffering with man. Rather, in accordance with the concreteness of Semitic thought, it designates it with a word whose basic meaning refers to a bodily organ, namely, ... the mother's womb. ... [T]he womb becomes the term for being with another; it becomes the deepest reference to man's capacity to stand for another, to take the other into himself, to suffer him ..., and in this long-suffering to give him life. The Old Testament, with a word taken from the language of the body, tells us how God shelters us in himself, how he bears us in himself with compassionate love.

11  *Ephesians 1:4, Living Bible. And see* Pope Benedict XVI, *Questions and Answers* 147 (OSV Publishing Division, 2008): "we are truly the reflection of creative reason. We were thought of and desired, thus, there is an idea [of me] that preceded me". To maintain otherwise is (or so it seems to me) to reject the belief that "each of us is a mystery of God's creative love and his omniscient action" (Mother Mary Francis, P.C.C., *But I Have Called You Friends: Reflections on the Art of Christian Friendship*, 80, Ignatius Press, paperback ed., 2006). *And see Rupnik, supra*, note 4 (of *Preface*) at 126: "Life flows through rela-

tionships, and faith is an affirmation of the primacy of relationship and communion on both a divine and human level."

12  *Johnson, supra,* note 3 at pp. 44 & 45. *See also* Rev. James Socias (ed.), *Daily Roman Missal* 1246 (Midwest Theological Forum, Inc., 6th ed., 2004): "'The truth that God is at work in all the actions of his creatures is inseparable from faith in God the Creator'". *And see* Gerald O'Collins, *Jesus Our Redeemer* 231 (2007): Our Creator's love for each and every human being (beginning from the pre-history commencement of the human race to ever forward), discloses its presence in an endless variety of choices, ways, degrees, and intensities. Love constitutes … the heart of redemption. "Active presence", which assumes endlessly different forms, is its mode; and *Kereszty,supra,* page 17 at 70 ("God's creative intervention enables the parents to transcend themselves. The parents, by themselves, are capable providing only the biological realities of sperm and ovum, but only God can create a new spiritual soul"). *See also* Thomas Dubay, S.M., *Deep Conversion Deep Prayer* 21 (Ignatius Press paperback ed., 2006): "God does nothing by happenstance. For him everything has point and purpose….He is fully aware of what he is about and he intends it with complete thoroughness".

13  Raniero Cantalamessa, *Remember Jesus Christ: Responding to the Challenges of Faith in Our Time* 30 (2007).

14  *See Gorman, infra* text accompanying note 20 at 49-50, and A. Milavec, *The Didache: Text, Translation, Analysis, and Commentary* 5 (at 2:2 A8-A9) (2003). *See also id.* at ix & x, respectively (The "*Didache* reveals more about how [the earliest] Christians saw themselves and how they lived their everyday lives than any book in the Christian Scriptures," and it "represents the first concerted attempt by [Christian] householders … to adapt the way of Jesus to the exigencies of family, occupation, [and] home").

15  *See* Dominique Barthelemy, O.P., *God and His Image: An Outline of Biblical Theology* 91 (revised ed. paperback, Ignatius Press, 2007).

*See also* M.H. Heim, *Joseph Ratzinger: Life in the Church and Living Theology* 368 (2007) ("there is only one will of God for men, only one historical activity of God with and for man").

16  *See supra,* text accompanying note 12; and possibly *Jn. 5:17*: "My Father is at work until now, so I am at work." *See also Ps. 139:13-15*: "You formed my inmost being. You knit me in my mother's womb.... My very self you knew...when I was being made [by You] in secret."

17  *See,* by way of analogy, *Barthelemy, supra,* note 15 at 49: and so "Abraham learned that he was the boy's (Isaac's) father in God's name, not in his own, so that he must not appropriate to himself even his own son." *See also* Michael Casey, *Fully Human, Fully Divine: An Interactive Christology* 45 (paperback, 2004): "An action becomes a sin [which always causes a three-fold degree of alienation: from self, from others — both living and dead — and from God] when it is a means of claiming an inappropriate autonomy."

18  *The Septuagint Version of the Old Testament and Apocrypha* 98 (Zondervan Publishing House Ed., Grand Rapids, Michigan, 1972). The *Septuagint* was the *Bible* used by early Christians. *See* Henry Wansbrough, OSB, *The Story of the Bible* 6 (the Word among us Press, paperwork ed., 2006), and *Juan Alfaro, supra* page 9 at 61 ("the Greek text of the Bible...was used widely in the time of Jesus").

English laws prohibiting unborn-child destruction predate the initial development of the English common law under Henry II (1154-1189). It is probably certain that these early laws derived from the *Septuagint* version of *Ex. 21:22-23*. For example here, the *Leges Henrici Primi* (compiled probably between 1100 and 1118), and which consists of a compilation of various legal sources on Anglo-Saxon law as modified by Henry I the Fowler (c.919-936) and William I the Conqueror (1066-87), contains the following :

If a pregnant woman (*pregnans*) is slain, and the child is living, each shall be compensated for by the full wergild. If the child is not yet living [i.e., if the fetus is not yet formed and ensouled?], half the wergild shall be paid to the relatives [on the father's side]. With regard to the *manbot* [a fine payable to the lord for the death of one of his men] of both, or either one, the amount shall lawfully be determined by the standing of the lord.

1 B. Thorp (ed.), *Ancient Laws and Institutes of England* 573 (c.LXX.14 [:*Ex.* 21:22-23?]) (1840). *See also* Harold D. Kletchka, *A Treatise on Human Life: An Unalienable Right* II-5 — II-42 (Alethos Press LLC, paperback 2002-2003).

19 *Of Plymouth Plantation 1620-1647, by William Bradford Sometime Governor Thereof: A New Edition: the Complete Text, with Notes and an Introduction by Samuel Eliot Mouson* 411 (N.Y., 1952). *And see John Paul II, supra,* note 10 at [61] 98-99: "The texts of *Sacred Scripture* ... show such great respect for the human being in the mother's womb that they require, as a logical consequence, that God's commandment 'You shall not kill' be extended to the unborn child as well."

20 p. 124 (1st paperback ed., 1997). *See also John Paul II, supra* note 10 at [61-63] 99-102.

21 *Los Angeles Daily Journal,* Weds., February 28, 2007, p.6. Although professor Einhorn ranks high in delivering anti-religious smack, top prize, here, has to go to Thomas Cahill. In the course of delivering a *Dantesque* criticism of the U.S. Catholic Church's sex scandal (and its cover-up by several bishops), he writes:

the twelve-year-old Christ ... is made to give blow jobs and [is] rammed up the ass the whole day long by the doctors of the law of New Jerusalem while the high priests of the Temple stand guard at the entrances lest any uninitiated outsiders should discover what is going on.

Thomas Cahill, *Mysteries of the Middle Ages and the Beginning of the Modern World* 315-316 (2008).

22 P.848. *And see particularly, Rafferty, supra,* note 1 at para. 80. According to the Court's own decisions, the Court "must" accept as true the

implied statement of the Roman Catholic Church to the effect that it has never decreed as a matter of faith or morals that a new human being comes into existence at conception, or fetal formation, or at any other point during the gestation process. The Constitution rightly holds that the Church is the ultimate or final interpreter of its own moral law and faith. *See, e.g., Serbian Orthodox Diocese v. Milivojevich* (1976), 426 U.S. 696. And so, the following observation of the *Roe* Court (410 U.S. at 161) is in error: the belief or opinion that a human being begins his or her existence as the same at conception is now "the official belief of the Catholic Church."

The Church does, however, hold as doctrine that the human embryo or fetus is to be treated as though it is a human being in all cases for its benefit. *See John Paul II, supra* note 10 at [60] 97-98, and William E. May, *Catholic Bioethics and the Gift of Human Life* 41-42 (2nd ed., 2008). The English common law does the same. *See infra,* note 4 (of *Side B*).

23  P.4 (5th  ed., 1976). *See also id.* at *Preface* ("The editors...have attempted to stress the proven, generally accepted description of both new and old...concepts. In soundly controversial areas, however, where two, well-grounded schools of thought may be arguing while awaiting the results of further investigations and experimentation, both sides of such questions are given.") *See also May, supra* note 22 at 176 ("A human embryo has the active potentiality or radical capacity to develop from within its own resources all it needs to exercise the property or set of characteristics of adult members of the species.") *See also Van Nostrand's Scientific Encyclopedia* 1056 (7th ed., 1989) ("At the moment the sperm cell of the human male meets the ovum of the female and the union results in a fertilized ovum (zygote), a new [human] life has begun."). Since only God can create a human soul, then the Church will never concede to science a monopoly on the question of what makes a human being a human being. *See Kereszty, supra* page 17 at p. 70.

24  *Los Angeles Times,* Thurs., Oct. 4, 2008 at p. A19.

25  Quoted in *The Tidings,* Feb. 22, 2008 at p.5. *See also* Pope Benedict XVI, *Saint Paul* 40 (Ignatius Press, 2009): "the Church ..., by her

nature, is opposed to any separation between worship and life, between faith and works, [and] between prayer and charity."

26 Pontifical Council for Justice and Peace, *Compendium of the Social Doctrine of the Church* 247 (No. 570) (Libreria Editrice Vaticana, 2004). *See also May, supra* note 22 at 31 (citing John Paul II: The Magisterium teaches that "civil laws legalizing ... abortion and euthanasia are totally opposed to the inviolable right to Life ... Since no human law can [legitimately] authorize such evils, there is a grave obligation in conscience to oppose them; it is never right to ... take part in ... campaigns in favor of them or to vote for them.") *And see, Text of the Dogmatic Constitution "Dei Filius" of Vatican Council I,* Chapter 4, Canons DS 3044 & 3045; James T. O'Connor (translator) *The Gift of Infallibility: The Official Relatio on Infallibility of Bishop Vincent Ferrer Gasier at Vatican Council 1* 116-17 (2nd ed., updated); and C. Kalzor & Th. Sherman, *Thomas Aquinas on the Cardinal Virtues: Edited and Explained for Everyone* 113-114 (n.20) 2009. *And see Healy, infra* at text accompanying next note (27) at 242: "Our obligation to the state ... is subsumed under our obligation to God, which is absolute. Jesus is ... warning his listeners: Do not give to Caesar (, to the state ..., or to any human institution [or human beings, such as pregnant women]) what belongs to God alone and to his son."

27 P.20 (Baker Academic paperback ed.). *See also* Philip E. Lawler, *The Faithful Departed* (2008), *infra*, note 31 (laments the failure of the Church hierarchy to discipline Catholic politicians who intentionally support access to abortion). On the continuous condemnation of abortion by the Church, *see Stark, supra* text accompanying note 20, *John Paul II, supra* note 20, and John Connery, *Abortion: The Development of the Roman Catholic Perspective* (1977). *And see* Archbishop Raymond Burke, *Reflections on the Struggle to Advance the Culture of Life* (in a speech the Archbishop gave on September 26, 2009, he observed: "One of the ironies of the present situation is that the person, who experiences scandal at the gravely sinful public actions of a fellow Catholic, is accused of a lack of charity, and of causing division within the unity of the Church").

28  495 U.S. 226, 249. If the statute serves a "secular" purpose, then the fact that this purpose coincides with or serves also a religious purpose does not make the statute unconstitutional by virtue of the 1st Amendment. *See, e.g., McGowan v. Maryland* (1961), 366 U.S. 420, 442, and *Bowen v. Hendrick* (1988), 487 U.S. 589, 605, & 612-613.

29  Paul Kengor, *God and Hillary Clinton: A Spiritual Life* (Harper Collins Publishers, 2007), p.125 (citing a report titled *The Clinton RU-486 Files* as reproduced on the website of *Judicial Watch. See Kengor id.* at p.300 (n.9)).

And then there is this statement made by President Clinton appointee, Justice Ginsburg, a former abortion-access advocate and former counsel to such abortion-rights organizations as the ACLU and to N.O.W., at Atlanta's Ahavath Achim synagogue: while the overruling of *Roe v. Wade* would not hurt women of means who could then simply temporarily cross state lines to obtain an abortion, it would "have a devastating impact on poor women". (*Los Angeles Times*, Monday, Oct. 22, 2007 at p. A19.)

Who appointed Ginsburg as a spokesperson for poor, pregnant women? I doubt that even so much as one such woman was then present at the Ahavath Achim synagogue. Her statement simply, conveniently assumes that poor, pregnant women feel that, when Jesus' solidarity with them, and when moral considerations are thrown out of the equation, then the non-worsening of poverty (as in one less mouth to feed) is more to be desired than the birth and raising (in poverty) of an unborn child.

It is simply too much for Ginsburg to accuse such women as thinking as callously as did Justice Brennan on at least one occasion. (*See Brennan, infra* note 35). Ginsburg would cure the injustice caused by poverty by destroying the would-be victims of such injustice. So, she may very well qualify as a closet Ron Weddington. *See* Jonah Goldberg, *A Case of Judicial Eugenics* (*LA Times*, July 14, 2009, at A19): "Here's what ... Ginsburg said in Sunday's [*i.e.*, the July 12 ed. of the] *New York Times Magazine*: 'Frankly, I had thought that at the time [*Roe v. Wade*] was decided ... there was concern about population growth and particularly growth in populations [*i.e.*, in Ron Weddington's "the barely educated, unhealthy, poor" and other unfortunates(?)] that we [*i.e.*, Justice Ginsburg (?) and other Clinton-liberals, *etc.*, and pro-choice organizations such as Planned Parenthood, NARAL, N.O.W., and the ACLU(?)] don't want to have too many of".

One thing is certainly true: Justice Ginsburg's credibility as an "impartial adjudicator" will be devastated should she not recuse herself from deciding any case involving the constitutional validity or extension of *Roe v. Wade*.

To the extent Ginsburg is intimating that the equal protection clause would demand equal abortion denial (should *Roe* be overruled), she is surely very wrong. Equal protection guarantees equal "governmental" treatment, not equal opportunity or access or denial, *etc.*, unless, of course, the opportunity or access or denial in question, is "governmentally" created or denied. And Ginsburg faces a difficult task, to say the least, in trying to demonstrate objectively that poverty is "governmentally" created. In any event, a state could simply criminally prohibit any resident-woman (whether rich or poor) from leaving the state in order to destroy her fetus. Similarly, the federal government could simply criminalize the crossing of state lines for the purpose of procuring an abortion. The federal government could also make it a crime for a physician, in an abortion-free state, to perform an abortion on a woman who, while living in a state which outlaws abortion, enters an abortion-free state in order to have an abortion.

30   This remains the case even if Atheism cannot be considered a religion. *See, e.g., McCreary County v. ACLU* (2005), 545 U.S. 844, 860 ("'The First Amendment mandates government neutrality … between religion and non-religion'").

31   Reproduced online in the unpaginated *The New York Review of Books, Vol. 31, No. 16,* Oct. 25, 1984. Cuomo did not originate his argument. *See Lawler, supra* note 27 at pp. 80-84.

32   1st quote: *Dred Scott v. Sanford* (1857), 60 U.S. (19 How.), 393, 426; 2nd (or *Addington* quote): 441 U.S. 418, 431.

33    *See Roe* 410 U.S. at 165: we feel that our holding "is consistent with ... the demands of the profound problems of the present day". What drivel. Any person, who is even remotely familiar with human history, knows that the dawn of every single day brings on or continues profound problems for some very large portion of humanity. There is simply no human cure for the "terrible everyday". *See,* Luke T. Johnson, *The Living Gospel* 11 (paperback, 2004): "These who are in pain — most of the world's population at any given moment — do not do a lot of thinking, speaking or writing about suffering. All their energy goes into surviving."

34    *See* Raymond Randolph, *Address: Before Roe v. Wade: Judge Friendly's Draft Abortion Opinion,* 29 *Harvard J. of Law & Public Policy* 1035, 1049-1055 (2006). *See also* J. Budziszewski, *The Line Through the Heart: Natural Law as Fact, Theory, and Sign of Contradiction* chap. 10 (2009) (The author argues that the liberal ideology of "not imposing morality on others" is a smokescreen for a coercive imposition of liberal morality on others).

35    *See Lawrence,* 539 U.S. 558, at 571: "that a governing majority in a state has traditionally viewed a particular practice as immoral is not a sufficient reason for upholding a law prohibiting the practice." Putting this another way, such a prohibition is not "rationally related to furthering a legitimate state interest" (within the meaning of "rational basis, substantive, due process analysis") because the pursuit of an active homosexual life style, which includes engaging in sodomy, while not a "fundamental" liberty, is, nevertheless, a "non-fundamental" liberty, and, therefore, it is immoral for the state to claim a "legitimate" interest in suppressing the homosexual life style." Lovers of sheep (at least when they are loved privately in a private place, such as a barn), adulterers, drug users (when they use in private), purveyors and viewers of pornography, perjurers, and the criminally insane (i.e., those persons "incapable of distinguishing what is morally right from what is morally wrong"), to name just a few moral minorities, arguably now have constitutional license to engage in their unusual practices. And this may mean that the Court is driving our Nation's culture to insanity.

*Lawrence* was authored by Justice Kennedy, the very justice who urged all of our Nation's justices to impose their views of morality on every person under their jurisdiction. (*See infra*, text (of *Conclusion*) accompanying note 19.) How hypocritical! Given the utter incomprehensibility of the *Roe-Casey* opinions (on *Casey*, *see infra*, text (of *Conclusion*) accompanying notes 15-18), then, in light of the foregoing *Lawrence* observation on the unacceptability (because of the 1st Amendment's prohibition of religion in government?) of morality in due process analysis, very arguably the *Roe* decision rests on nothing more than this insane observation of Justice Brennan: " 'Abortion and childbirth, when stripped of the sensitive moral arguments surrounding the abortion controversy, are simply two alternative medical methods of dealing with pregnancy.' " In other words, stripped of morality, which is nothing more than religious belief (disguised as secular morality) — prohibited by the 1st Amendment, the human fetus, alive in the womb of his mother, has no more intrinsic value than "medical waste". Stripped of morality, murder for hire and killing in self-defense are simply two alternative methods of killing. Stripped of morality, working for a living and stealing for a living are simply two different ways of earning a living. Evidently, in the context of sounding off for the constitutional right to choose induced abortion, there can be no such thing as an absurd statement. (The foregoing Brennan observation is cited as follows: *Beal v. Doe* (1977), 432 U.S. 438, 449, dissenting opinion, and quoting *Roe v. Norton* (1975), 408 F. Supp. 660, 663 n.3.) *And see* Robert H. Bork, *Slouching Towards Gomorrah: Modern Liberalism and American Decline* 174 (Harper Collins Rev. paperback ed. 2003): "*Roe* is nothing more than the Supreme Court's imposition on us of the morality of our cultural elites."

To reiterate: Given that legal insanity is defined as the "inability (of a person who has reached the age of reason) to distinguish what is morally right from what is morally wrong, then, arguably, *Roe-Casey* and *Lawrence* are driving our Nation's culture to insanity, and which means necessarily that we, as a nation, are on our way to becoming a nation of moral idiots.

A final observation is in order here. The *Lawrence* majority opinion intimates that in Anglo-American legal history, the law kind of turned a blind eye to homosexual sodomy. The *Lawrence* majority justices, themselves turned a blind eye, here, to the prosecution of sodomy in the Courts of Admiralty.

36  J. Farmer, Jr., *Pope: Confronted by a Cultural Crisis in American Catholicism*, *The Tidings*, p.14 (April 25, 2008).

37  *DT.* 30:19.

38  62-63. *See also* Gerald O'Collins, *Jesus our Redeemer: A Christian Approach to Salvation* 116-118, & 127 (2007). *And see particularly, Kereszty, supra, page 18.*

39  John Vidmar, *The Catholic Church Through the Ages* 320-321 (Paulist Press, paperback ed., 2005).

40  298 (citations omitted).

41  410 U.S. 113, 116 (1973).

42  *Tushnet, infra*, note 23 (of *Side B*).

43  *See infra*, text (of *A Long Conclusion to Side B*) accompanying notes 16-27.


# SIDE B

* The conceived unborn product of human conception reaches fetal formation at about the completion of eight weeks from its conception. *Mosby's Dictionary of Medicine* 720 (2009) defines *fetus* as follows: "The human being in utero after the embryonic [stage] and the beginning of development of the major structural features, from the ninth week after fertilization [at which beginning stage the fetus is approximately one inch in length]".

Nothing argued here should be construed as implicitly conceding that the unborn product of human conception that has yet to develop into a fetus does not qualify as a 5th and 14th Amendment

person.    See Hall v. Hancock, infra, note 4; and Scientific
Encyclopedia, supra at my text pp.39-40. At common law, it was a
criminal offence to abort the pre-human being product of human
conception. See R v. Beare, in Appendix 1, and Russell's Case, in
Appendix 6.

Substantial portions of the thoughts presented here have
appeared previously online in: Philip A. Rafferty, Roe v. Wade: A
Scandal Upon the Court 7 RJLR No. 7.1.1 (2006) [http://www.
lawandreligion.com/vol7.shtml]. I am grateful for RJLR's kindness in permitting the use of this material. (Letter of Permission
on file with author.)

1    *See, e.g., Ingraham v. Wright* (1977), 430 U.S. 651, 672 (5th
Amendment due process dictates have been incorporated into
14th Amendment due process dictates), and *Paul v. Davis* (1976),
424 U.S. 693, 702 n.3 (the 14th Amendment "imposes no more
stringent [or lesser] requirements upon state officials than does
the Fifth upon their federal counterparts"). *And see Morissette v
U.S.* (1952) 342 U.S. 246, 263 (borrowed "terms of art" carry with
them their accumulated judicial interpretations); and *Miles v Apex
Marine Corp* (1990), 498 U.S. 19, 32 (Congress is presumed to be
aware of "legal terms of art" [such as "person" and due process of
law] when incorporating them into new or different legislation)

2    *The Roe Court* acknowledged as much. *See Roe v. Wade* (1973), 410
U.S. 113, 156-57.

3    *Thornburg v. ACOG* (1986), 476 U.S. 747, 779 (including n.8)
(Justice Stevens concurring). Justice Stevens may be thinking
here that "state inaction" — as in the failure of the state to protect human fetuses from being aborted — can, via the doctrine
of *parens patriae*, be deemed "state action," in that the State has
an "affirmative" duty to safeguard those persons who are, by definition, incapable of caring for themselves. *See Palmore v. Sidoti*
(1984), 466 U.S. 429, 433: "The State ...has a duty of the highest
order to protect the interests of minor children".

4    *See, e.g., Hall v. Hancock* (1834), 32 Mass. 255, 257-58: at common
law, the human fetus or unborn child is generally considered to
be "in being ... in all cases where it will be for the benefit of such

child to be so considered". In <u>Roe</u>, the Texas Attorney General, Lloyd Wade, argued on behalf of Texas (and not as attorney for <u>Roe's</u> fetus) that the fetus qualifies as a constitutional person. However, and as specifically noted by the <u>Roe</u> majority justices, Texas had, here, a serious conflict of interest. See <u>Roe v Wade</u>, 410 U.S. at 157, N. 52.

Each and every item which the *Roe* Court cited in support of the holding that the fetus does not qualify as a 14th Amendment, due process person is exploded in *Rafferty, supra* asterisk note at *paras.* 12-29. The whole of the *Roe* Court's stated reasons in support of this holding that the human fetus, alive in the womb of his mother, does not qualify as a <u>14th Amendment</u>, due process clause person is wholly contrived. The Court arrived at that holding independently of — and without reference to — its earlier holding that the mother of an unborn child enjoys a "fundamental" (or inalienable) right to have the child destroyed so that it cannot be brought forth alive into the world. Since, almost by definition, "fundamental rights" are complementary, or, at least, cannot cancel out or contradict each other, then the very fact that a mother's right to destroy her unborn child qualifies as a fundamental right, alone suffices to establish conclusively that her unborn child has no right period not to be aborted. The problem here is that the <u>Roe</u> Court's holding that the right to have an abortion is "fundamental" is even more contrived than the <u>Roe</u> Court's holding that the fetus, alive in the womb of its mother, does not have a right not to be aborted (*i.e.*, does not qualify as a <u>14th Amendment</u>, due process clause person). See *Rafferty, supra,* asterisk note at *paras.* 42-71.

An argument can be made that the Court's decision in *Planned Parenthood (of MO) v. Danforth* (1976), 428 U.S. 52, 70, is also void *ab initio* at least in one essential part. Here the Court held, in effect, that a married woman's abortion decision cannot be conditioned upon her husband's consent (and notwithstanding that her husband enjoys — as his wife also enjoys — a "fundamental", constitutional right to procreate and raise children — which used to be recognized as the primary purpose of marriage in the first place). In so holding, the Court failed to provide the husband with a "procedural due process"-mandated opportunity to be heard on the proposed deprivation of one of his fundamental or inalienable rights. (*See Caban v. Mohammed* (1979), 441 U.S. 380, 389: "an unwed father may have a relationship with his children fully comparable to that of the mother".) The basis of this *Danforth's* holding is the state cannot "'delegate to a spouse a veto power which the state itself [under *Roe v. Wade*] is absolutely and totally prohibited from exercising'" (428 U.S. 52, 70). This basis is nonsense. In the first place, even if the state possessed such a veto power, the fact would remain, the state could not delegate the exercise of that power to a private individual or third party (any more so, for example, than could the state delegate, a decision on a tax hike, or a decision whether to carry out capital punishment, to a private individual or third party). Secondly, the state is not the source of fundamental or inalienable rights. The individual precedes the state, which means that an individual, in deciding to exercise one of his or her fundamental rights (such as the right to procreate and raise children in the context of a valid marriage) does not have to take his cue or seek permission from the state.

Here are some of the constitutional issues the *Danforth* Court was able to duck successfully by unconstitutionally denying the husband a due process-mandated opportunity to be heard: can fundamental or inalienable, constitutional rights ever fatally or irreconcilably collide on a constitutional plane and, if so, then what, specifically, are the recognized or accepted constitutional criteria for deciding which fundamental right shall receive the lone right of passage on the constitutional plane.

5    *See* Peleg Chandler, *American Criminal Trials* (1844), 49-50, 53, & 379-83.

6    Justice Paul Stevens, *Addresses: Construing the Constitution*, 18 U.C. Davis L.R.1, 20 (1985).

7    P.14.

8    p.378.

9    Lib.7, c.3, 4:583

10   P.42, And see infra, note 13.

11   124 U.S. 465, 478 (1888)

12   457 U.S. 202, 212 at n.11 (1982).

13   1 *Blackstone's Commentaries* 125-126 (1765). In 4 *Blackstone's Commentaries* 198 (1769) Blackstone notes that this crime is murder if the aborted child is liveborn and then dies. (*See, e.g., Q v. West* (1848), *supra Appendix 3* at p.125). The quote in parentheses describing *Blackstonian* authority is from *Washington v. Glucksberg* (1997), 521 U.S. 702, 710. *And, consider* this observation of *Roe* author, Justice Blackmun in his concurring opinion in *O'Bannon V. TCNC* (1980), 447 U.S. 773, 803 n.11: "Blackstone, whose vision of liberty unquestionably informed the Framers of the *Bill of Rights*,... wrote [in 1 *Commentaries* *129] that the "right of personal security consists in a person's legal and uninterrupted enjoyment of his life."

No one has produced so much as a single dot of evidence (unproved theories do not qualify as evidence) that "quickening" played any role in abortion prosecution at the "pre-19th" century English common law. I have proved, upon available evidence, that "quickening" never came into play here. until the 19th century (and not intentionally, but only through judicial errors in construing the meaning of "quick with child"). (*See infra*, this note 13.)

Note that *Blackstone* does "not" say that quick-with-child abortion is a serious crime in connection with denying implicitly that pre-quick-with-child also is a serious criminal offence. And so said Joel Pretiss Bishop in his *Commentaries on the Law of Statutory Crimes* 512, sec. 744 (3RD ed., 1901; 1ST ed., 1873; cits. Omitted).

> Some have denied that [induced abortion... is indictable at the common law, unless...[the pregnant woman was then] quick with child. And Hale [and Coke have] on this subject the expression ... "quick with child"; but not in connections denying that the offence

may be committed at an earlier stage of pregnancy.

Chief Justice Mansfield, in the English case of *Jones v.* Randall, 98 *Eng. Rep.* 706, 707 (1774) observed:

> The law would be a strange science if it rested solely upon cases; and if after so large an increase of commerce, arts and circumstances accruing, we must go to the time of Rich. 1 (1189-1199) to find a case, and see what is law. Precedent indeed may serve to fix principles, which for certainty's sake are not suffered to be shaken, whatever might be the weight of the principle, independent of precedent. But precedent, though it be evidence of law, is not law in itself, much less the whole of the law. Whatever is contrary, *bonos mores est decorum* (literally: whatever is against good manners (or customs) and seemliness (or propriety); freely: whatever is against public morals), the principles of our law prohibit, and the King's Court as the general censor and guardian of the public manners, is bound to restrain and punish.

*See also, e.g., R v. Lynn* (1788), 2 *Dunford & Easts' Reports* 733, 734 (4th ed., 1794) (removing a dead body from its grave is an offence "cognizable in a criminal court, as being highly indecent, and *contra bonos mores*, at the bare idea alone of which nature revolted").

On Blackstone's phrase "Life is the immediate gift of God", *see, e.g,* Walter Charleton, *The Natural History of the Passions* 60 (1674): "Nothing can remain to divorce me from that common opinion which holds that she [the human soul] is created immediately by God, and infused into the body of a human Embryon, so soon as that it is organized, formed, and prepared to receive her."

Samuel Johnson, in his *A Dictionary of the English Language* (1755) (*vol. 2, sub. tit.: quick*) defined "quick" (as in "quick with child") as "the child in the womb after it is perfectly formed." George Mason, in his *A Supplement to Johnson's English Dictionary*

(1801) (sub. tit.: *quick*) defined "quick" (as in "with quick child") as "pregnant with a live child." In a 1990 letter (on file with the author), J.A. Simpson, then Co-Editor of the Oxford English Dictionary, corrected (and which correction appears in the 2007 SOED) that dictionary's "quick with child" entry (and I am grateful to Mr. Simpson for his permission to publish this letter):

> From the discussion you present, it would seem reasonable to infer that the ["quickening"] entry in the *Oxford English Dictionary* for "quick with child", while adequately representing the meaning that had come to be current in the 19th century, does not reflect the earlier history of the phrase, and its changing relationship with the term "quickening." A revised entry might read something like:

> Constr. with.
> a. quick with child, orig., pregnant with a live foetus [which is Latin for offspring or young child]; later [i.e., sometime during the course of the 19th century], at the stage of pregnancy at which the motion of the foetus is felt (infl. By QUICKENING vbl. Sb.). Now rare or Obs.

The "only" way for a person to conclude that Blackstone understood the criterion of "when" a woman becomes "quick with child" to be "quickening" (i.e., at the mother's initial perception of the stirrings or movements of her fetus), and not "at the completion of the process of fetal formation", is if this person reads backwards (beginning at the 19th century), the history of the use of the term "quick with child".

The onset of fetal stirring (not to be confused with "quickening" which refers to the pregnant woman's "initial perception" of this fetal stirring) was then understood to coincide with fetal formation. The following is a great example of this understanding. It is taken from Bartholomaeus Anglicus' *De Proprietatibus* (written between 1230 and 1250), which was during the later middle ages and quite possibly into the 17th century, the most-read book after the Bible:

> This child is bred forth…in four degrees. The first is….The last [or 4th] degree is when all the external members are completely shaped. And when the body is thus made and shaped with members and limbs, and disposed to receive the soul, then it receives soul and life, and begins to move itself and sprawl with its feet and hands…In the degree of milk it remains seven (7) days; in the degree of blood it remains nine (9) days; in the degree of a lump of blood or unformed flesh it remains twelve (12) days; and in the fourth degree, when all its members are fully formed, it remains eighteen (18) days…So, from the day of conception to the day of complete disposition or formation and first life of the child is forty-six (46) days.

1 *On the Properties of Things: John Treviso's Translation of "Bartholomaeus Anglicus De Proprietatibus Rerum": A Critical Text* 296-297 (Oxford 1975). Treviso's translation was completed at Berkeley, Gloucestershire, in February, 1398. *Id.* at xi. *See also Batman Upon Bartholome, His Books as Proprietatibus Rerum* 71-72 (Thom, East: 1582). *And see Chambers, supra*, text accompanying note 8 (of *Appendix 1*) (fetal formation and ensoulment occur 42 days after conception).

There is, then, one reason, and "only" one reason why, in the context of in-womb child killing prosecution at the English common law, that some time during the 19th century "quickening" came to replace "fetal formation" as the common law criterion of when a pregnant woman can be said to be "quick with child": a subtle mistake in legal interpretation. In several abortion cases prosecuted during the period 1808-1832, English judges mistook *quickening* for the definition of the term *quick with child* (which in its primary sense, as does the term *with quick child*, means simply "to be pregnant with a live child"). They did this because in England before, during, and after the reign of common law offenses, it was a common expression among pregnant women to refer to themselves as being *with quick child* or *quick with child* (i.e., as being pregnant with a live child) once they had experienced *quickening*. These judges mistook a vulgar opinion on the subject of "when" a pregnant women becomes *quick with child* for the definition of that term. They mistook a "when", and a wrong one at that, for the definition of the "what". *See R v. Phillips, supra*, in *Appendix 5*.

The then-existing opinion that a human being begins its existence as the same at the completion of the process of fetal formation, while virtually unanimous, was not so entirely. For example, Charles Morton, a one-time president of Harvard College, in his *Compendium Physicae* (1680) (the science textbook used by Harvard college students from 1687 to 1728), stated (p. 146):

> Here a question may be moved: at what time the soul is infused? It has been formerly thought not to be till the complete organization of the body....And here the law of England [i.e., 21 Jac. (Jas) 1, c.27 (1623/24, and reproduced online at *www.parafferty.com* : Download *Roe v. Wade: The Birth of a Constitutional Right*, and go to pp. 475-482]...condemns not the whore who destroys her [bastard] child for murther unless it appears that the child was perfectly formed...Upon this supposal: that till then there is no union...of soul and body; but indeed it seems more agreeable to reason that the soul is infused [at]...conception.

14   *Baynton's Case*, 14 <u>Howell St. Trials</u> 598, 634 (1702). On "pleading the belly", *see* the works cited in *Rafferty* (*Birth of a Constitutional Right*), *infra* note 15 at p.442 n.31, and in *Baker, supra* note 1 of *Taillour's Case* (reproduced *supra*, in *Appendix 4* at pp. 551-552).

15  The reporting of the *Beare* trial proceedings is set forth in 2 *Gentlemen's Magazine* 931-932 (August, 1732) (reproduced *infra*, in *Appendix 1*). For additional cases here, *see infra, Appendices 2-4 & 6*; and Philip A. Rafferty, *Roe v. Wade: The Birth of a Constitutional Right* 483-765 (1992) (U.M.I. Dissertation Abstracts No. LD02339) (Library of Congress Call Number: *KF228.R59.R24 1992*). This research paper (774 pp.) can be downloaded free of charge at *www. parafferty.com.*

16  74 KB 9/434/12. This case appears also in R.F. Hunnisett (ed.), *Calendar of Nottinghamshire Coroner's Inquests 1485-1558*, p.8 (no.10) (25 Thornton Soc. Rec. Series, 1966) (my initial source), and in J. Keown, *Abortion, Doctors, and the Law: Some Aspects of the Legal Regulation of Abortion in England from 1803 to 1898* 2 (2002). *See also R v. Russell* (1832), *supra* at *Appendix 6*.

The punishment for felony-suicide ("felo de se") consisted of an "ignominious [non-Christian] burial in the night at a cross-roads with a stake driven through the torso and a stone on the face of the deceased," and forfeiture of all goods and chattels. *See* Kate E. Bloch, *The Role of Law in Suicide Prevention: Beyond Civil Commitment – A Duty to Report Suicide Threats*, 39 Stan. L. Rev. 929, 930-31 (1987). *See also* Catherine D. Shaffer, *Criminal Liability for Assisting Suicide*, 86 Colum. L. Rev. 348, 349 (1986).

If another person had administered the abortion concoction to Wynspere, that person, upon conviction, would have been launched into eternity at the end of a rope. *See* the cases set forth *supra*, in *Appendix 3*.

In 1747, in Windham County, Connecticut, John Hallowell was convicted of the "high handed [common law], misdemeanor offense of attempting to destroy … 'the fruit of … [the] womb' of Sarah Grosvenor." It was not alleged that Grosvenor was then "quick with child" Hallowell fled the Court's jurisdiction before he could be punished. This case is related and discussed in detail in C.H. Dayton, *Taking the Trade: Abortion and Relations in an Eighteenth Century New England Village*, 48 *William & Mary Quarterly*, 19 (1991). In 1683, in the Colony of Rhode Island and

Providence Plantations, Deborah Allen pled guilty to fornication (resulting in the birth of a bastard child) and to attempting to destroy the child in her womb. She was sentenced to be "severly wipped...with fifteen Stripes on the naked back." *Allen's Case* is reproduced *supra*, in *Appendix 2*. In 1652, in the Province of Maryland, William Mitchell, a captain in the militia, pled guilty to a four-count indictment charging him with blasphemy, adultery, the attempted murder (which at common law was only a misdemeanor) of Susan Warren's unborn child, and living "in fornication with his now pretended wife Joane." He received a sentence to pay "five thousand pounds of Tobacco and Cask or the value thereof as a fine to the Lord Proprietary, and to enter into bond for his good behavior." (*Mitchell's Case* is cited as: 10 *Maryland Archives* 182-185 (1891).) It can be viewed online at *www.parafferty.com* : Download *Roe v. Wade: The Birth of a Constitutional Right*, and go to pp. 483-490.

In New York City in 1716, a municipal ordinance was enacted that forbade midwives, among other things, to "'[g]ive any Counsel or Administer any Herb, Medicine or Potion, or any other thing to any Women being with Child whereby She Should Destroy or Miscarry of that she goeth withal before here time'." *See* D. Moran and T. Marsen, *Abortion and Midwifery: A Footnote in Legal History*, in T.W. Hilgers, *et al*, (eds.), *New Perspectives on Human Abortion* 199 (1981) (citing: *Minutes of the Common Council of the City of New York* 3 (1712-1729) at 122. The ordinance (or a variation of it) is reproduced in M.B. Gordon, *Aesculapius Comes to the Colonies: The Story of the Early Days of Medicine in the Thirteen Original Colonies* 174-175 (1949); and in N.W. Haggard, *Devils, Drugs, and Doctors: The Story of the Science of Healing from Medicine-Man to Doctor* 69-70 (1929).

17   *See Roe v. Wade*, 410 U.S. at 158 & 132-141.

18   Quoted in W. Pfaff, *Refugees: The Beast of Unreason Stirs Again*, *L.A. Times*, July 8, 1979, Pt. V (*Opinion Sec.*), p.3.

Putting this more specifically and graphically, agents of the State of the United States, consisting of a majority of Supreme

Court justices led by Justice Blackmun, turned into truth (by virtue of the Court's prestige and by virtue of its express statement in its *Roe* opinion to judge impartially — *see supra*, text of *Conclusion to Side B* accompanying footnote 1) Cyril Means' great lie that in pre-19th century England abortion was not criminally prosecuted as a "barbaric act of savage human nature" — as it most certainly was, there, so prosecuted, but rather was recognized, there, as a right or liberty. (And, therefore, was recognized as so, also (1) throughout Colonial America, and in (2) the states and (3) territories of the United States well into the 19th century since, for the most part, these three adopted as their own law, the then-existing, English common law on crimes.) (*See Roe v. Wade*, 410 U.S. at 132-141 & 165.)

History, having been turned upside down, and inside out, these *Roe* justices then proceeded to create the reality that abortion is necessary to the emancipation of women (from their biology, and from the inconvenience caused by the burden of raising an unwanted child). These justices created this new reality by improperly and covertly "judicially noticing" disputed facts as undisputed facts, such as: being forced to raise an unwanted child may cause a woman far more psychological harm than that which might result from guilt caused by destroying her unborn child. (*See Rafferty, supra* asterisk note at paras. 60-67.)

The *Roe* majority based its conclusion that abortion was a common law liberty on nothing more than its unprofessional and bias-laden decision to adopt "uncritically" (because these provided the <u>*Roe*</u> majority justices with a way to where they were bound and determined to go) certain common law abortion conclusions set forth in two law review articles by Cyril Means, Jr. (since deceased, but then a New York law professor and abortion rights advocate. He served as counsel for *NARAL, etc. See* the references to Means in *Dellapenna, supra* (footnote 15 of *Epilogue*), at the index entry: *Means, Cyril, Jr. See Roe v. Wade*, 410 U.S. at 135-36 (including n.26). (Means' arguments are explained, and then exploded in *Rafferty* (*Birth of a Constitutional Right*), *supra* note 15 at 195-225.) *See also Rafferty, supra* asterisk note (of *Side B*); and

John Keown, *Back to the Future of Abortion Law: Roe's Rejection of America's History and Traditions* in *Issues in Law and Medicine* (Summer, 2006) at pp. 5-6, and *Keown, supra,* note 16 at pp. 3-12. See also, Shelley Gavigan, *The Criminal Sanction as It Relates to Human Reproduction: The Genesis of the Statutory Prohibition of Abortion,* 5 (no.1) J. Legal Hist. 20, 22-23 (1984).

Can the reader imagine what would have happened had a majority of *Roe* justices simply "uncritically" accepted as true the contention put forth in *Roe* briefs filed by Wade and by certain *amici,* that the human embryo or fetus is a human being and, therefore, also is a 14th Amendment, due process clause person? Here's what would have happened: Impeachment proceedings would have been immediately initiated against these *Roe* majority justices.

In the final analysis Means' contention that abortion was a common law liberty rests upon nothing more than the following: (1) his 359-degree misinterpretation of *Bourton's Case* (reproduced *supra,* in *Appendix 4*), (2) his erroneous belief that there exists no known case of abortion prosecution at the English common law, and *R v. Anonymous,* (a.k.a.) *The Abortionist's Case* (1348), which cannot be even reasonably confirmed to ever have been a *case* in the first place. This case is reproduced *supra,* in *Appendix 4.*

Means went so far as to (falsely) accuse Sir Edward Coke (1552-1634), Lord Chief Justice of England, of "deliberately" misstating the status of abortion as a criminal offence at the English Common law. Coke, in his day, "earned a reputation as the most learned, honest, and incorruptible of judges, the 'oracle of the law'." Michael A.S. Newman, *Voice of Legal Scholar Coke, Circa 1600 Applies in 2005, Los Angeles Daily Journal,* Feb. 9, 2005, at 6. Means' absurd accusation should have alerted the *Roe* Court that they may be dealing with a fanatical, pro-abortion-access advocate. Instead, the *Roe* Court went out of its way to note in its opinion that there may even be a real basis for Means' accusation. *See Roe,* 410 U.S. at 136 n.26:

Means "concludes that Coke [1552-1634]...may have [Means stated: "did", and not "may have"] intentionally misstated the [common law on criminal abortion]." The author even suggests a reason: Coke's strong feelings against abortion coupled with his determination to assert common law (secular) jurisdiction to assess penalties for an offence that traditionally had been an exclusively ecclesiastical or canon law crime.

To be sure Coke did misrepresent the common law on criminal abortion. But his (unintentional) misrepresentation (which derived from his misinterpretation of *Bourton's Case*) brought about the virtual opposite of what Means claims it did: far from creating an offence where none existed before, it lessened the reach of the then-existing offence of capital homicide or murder: what was then-existing capital homicide or murder at common law (in this case, in-womb child killing), ceased to be so (unless the fetus was born alive before it died). See *Rex v. Haule*, and *Q v. West, supra, Appendices 4 and 6 respectively*, and the extended discussion of *Bourton's Case* (1327-28) *supra*, in *Appendix 4. See also supra*, note 3 (and accompanying text) of *Appendix 1*.

Under English law, "[p]ersuasive value attaches to decisions of the Supreme Court of the United States." (David M. Walker, *The Oxford Companion to Law* 979 (1980).) In my opinion, because the Supreme Court bestowed its prestige and imprimatur both on Means' attempted vandalization of the English common law on criminal abortion, and his patently false accusation that Coke intentionally misstated the common law on criminal abortion, the English judiciary would not be out of line if it tossed the weight it gives to our Supreme Court's decisions into the deepest part of the River Thames.

Throughout the course of the 19th century, the several states and territories of the United States enacted, amended, and revised literally hundreds of criminal abortion statutes. For the most part, the statutes were obviously enacted, etc., to close ("erroneously") perceived gaps (such as the erroneous perception that pre-quick with child abortion was not a crime) in the English common law on criminal abortion (which virtually all of the states and territories had adopted either by statute or by judicial decision). Here, again, the Roe Court conveniently, uncritically adopted another one of Means' great lies on the history of Anglo-American law on abortion: these 19th-century criminal abortion statutes were designed, not to safeguard the child in the womb of his mother, but rather "solely" to protect women's lives and health from the then-perceived dangers of surgical abortion. See, Rafferty, supra, asterisk note (of Side B) at paras. 52-53, and 85-86 (including n. 160).

The *Roe* Court, in uncritically accepting Means on abortion, elected to play Means' fool. (Means was able to feed successfully — beyond his wildest imagination — the pro-abortion-access prejudices of the *Roe* majority justices.) As one (sympathetic) critic of Means on abortion has noted:

> Means' 'own conclusions sometime strain credibility: in the presence of manifest public outcry over fetal deaths just prior to the passage of New York's 1872 [criminal] abortion statute, Means disclaims any impact upon the legislature of this popular pressure (even though the statute itself copies the language of a pro-fetal group). [Nevertheless], [w]here the important thing is to win the case no matter how … [then], I suppose I agree with Means' technique: begin with a scholarly attempt at historical research; if it doesn't work, fudge it as necessary; write a piece so long that others will read only your introduction and conclusion; then keep citing it until courts begin picking it up. This preserves the guise of impartial scholarship while advancing the proper ideological goals.'

David Tundermann in a report to Roy Lucas, quoted in David J. Garrow, *Liberty and Sexuality: The Right to Privacy and the Making of Roe v. Wade* 891-92 n.41 (paperback ed., 1998).

To view online a complete, piece-by-piece dismembering of *Roe's* patently false contention that abortion was recognized as a right (and not at all as a crime) at the English common law, see Rafferty, supra, asterisk note (of Side B) at paras. 12-27.

19   Thomas E. Woods, Jr., *et al, Who Killed the Constitution?* 199 (2008) (citing John Hart Ely, *The Wages of Crying Wolf: A Comment on "Roe v. Wade"*, 82 Yale Law Journal 920 (1973).)

On *Roe* and the nonexistence of a "right to privacy," see infra, p.220 (at n.16). That the *Roe* opinion unwittingly concedes the "constitutionality" of the very Texas criminal abortion statute which it declares as unconstitutional is demonstrated easily. One item which the *Roe* Court relied on, in holding that the unborn human fetus is not a 14th Amendment, due process clause person, is the Court's *Vuitch* decision (402 U.S. 62 (1971)). *Roe* states: "indeed, our decision in *United States v. Vuitch*, inferentially, is to the same effect, for we would not have indulged in statutory interpretation favorable to abortion in specified circumstances if the necessary consequence was the termination of fetal life entitled to 14th Amendment protection" (410 U.S. At 159). In other words, it is Court policy not to give a statute an interpretation which would save it from being found unconstitutional on specified grounds, if the statute, even as favorably construed so, would still be unconstitutional. Now, the criminal abortion statute in *Vuitch*, even after being favorably construed so as to be upheld against a "vagueness" challenge, clearly, still infringed on a woman's *Roe*-defined right to an abortion: The criminal abortion statute in *Vuitch*, even after being favorably construed, still outlawed what Roe holds to be constitutionally guaranteed: a woman's right to obtain a "pre-fetal viability" abortion not necessary to preserve her life or physical or psychological health. (See *Vuitch*, 402 U.S. at 67-68, & 71-72. ) And consider this observation of the Court in *NFIB v. Sebelius*, 567 U.S. ---, ---(2012): "No court ought, unless the terms of the act [or statute] render it unavoidable, to give a construction to it which should involve a violation, however unintentional, of the Constitution." By parity of reasoning to *Roe's* reasoning from *Vuitch*, had the *Vuitch* Court thought that the criminal abortion statute in question there infringed on any constitutional right of a woman to obtain an abortion, then the *Vuitch* Court would not have indulged in statutory construction favorable to upholding that statute. If the *Vuitch* Court had done so, then such Court action would have had the consequence of leaving on the books a criminal statute that infringes on an individual's fundamental, constitutional right, in this case a woman's *Roe*-defined constitutional right to a physician-induced abortion. Hence, according to *Roe*, the *Vuitch* Court held that a woman does not have a constitutional right to an abortion within the meaning of *Roe*. Chief Justice Warren Burger, who joined in the *Roe* majority opinion, implied as much at oral argument in *Roe*. He asked appellant's counsel, Sarah Weddington, whether the issues in *Roe* had not already been implicitly decided in *Vuitch*. See David M. O'Brien, *Storm Center: The Supreme Court in American Politics* 26 (1986. *See also, Woodward, infra,* note 20 at70: Justice Blackmun, in a pre-*Roe v. Wade* memorandum, stated: "I would dislike to have to undergo another assault on…[a *Vuitch*-type abortion] statute based, this time, on privacy. I am willing to continue the approval of the *Vuitch*-type statute on privacy, as well as on vagueness [grounds]". *See Savage, infra* note 5 (of the *Conclusion*). *See also* B. Schwarz, *The Unpublished Opinions of the Burger Court* 89-90 (1989).

Chief Justice Burger should have asked Weddington if it is fair and just to hold that every human being recognized as the same in late 18th Century United States shall remain recognized as so today, except for formed human fetuses, alive in the wombs of their mothers. To view online a complete dismantling of the *Roe* opinion (particularly its conclusion that, from a constitutional perspective, access to physician-performed abortion qualifies as a "fundamental right", *see Rafferty, supra,* asterisk note (of *Side B*) at paras. 42-71).

So, here is, yet, another reason why the *Roe* Court gave uncritical acceptance to *Means* on abortion: There was no other way to conclude that physician-performed abortion qualifies as a "substantive, due process - fundamental right". *See, e.g., Washington v. Glucksberg* (1997), 521 U.S. 702, 710-721 (no fundamental right to physician-assisted suicide because for over 700 years the Anglo-American common law traditions punished or otherwise disapproved of both suicide and assisting suicide).

There is no male counterpart or equivalent to a woman's right to an abortion. And since, almost by definition, fundamental rights are particular to human beings (and not to particular classes of human beings, such as women), it follows that abortion access cannot logically be considered as a fundamental right.

Undoubtedly, a counter to the foregoing argument will go something like this: Both men and women enjoy a right to do their own thing (except where it would be harmful to another); and abortion is simply a woman's thing. Here is a question: Who, here, gets to decide if the doing of one's thing is harmful to another? The State or the individual? If it is the individual, then anarchy necessarily rules the day.

20  *See* B. Woodward, *The Abortion Papers, Washington Post,* Jan. 22, 1989. *See also,* L. Greenhouse, *Becoming Justice Blackmun* 95 (2005).

*See Planned Parenthood v. Casey* (1992), 505 U.S. 833, 871 ("The woman's right to terminate her pregnancy before viability is the most central principle of *Roe v. Wade*"). *And see particularly, Rafferty, supra,* asterisk note (of *Side B*) at para. 44 n. 96 (a demonstration of the fact that the right to a post-fetal viability abortion is very nearly unbridled under *Roe*).

21  *See* J.M. Balkin, *What Roe v. Wade Should Have Said,* 253 (2005). *And see* David J. Garrow, *When Clerks Rule, L.A. Times* (Sunday, May 29, 2005) at p.M5 (of *Opinion Section*):

The recent release of Justice Harry A. Blackmun's private Supreme Court case files has starkly illuminated an embarrassing problem that previously was discussed only in whispers among court insiders and aficionados: the degree to which young law clerks, most of them just two years out of law school, make extensive, highly substantive and arguably inappropriate contributions to the decisions issued in their bosses' names.

Even *Roe v. Wade*...owed lots of its language... and breadth to...[Roe author, Justice Blackmun's] clerks and the clerks of other justices. A decade later, when Blackmun's defense of abortion rights shifted from an emphasis on doctors' medical pre-rogatives to women's equality [as in his "abortion [or unborn-child killing] is necessary to the eman-cipation of women"], it was his young clerks who were responsible for his increasingly feminist tone.

In his concurring opinion in *Illinois State Bd. Of Elections v. Socialist Workers Party*, 440 U.S. 173, 188-89 (1979) (Blackmun, J. concurring), Justice Blackmun denied ever knowing how to con-stitutionally distinguish a "compelling" state interest from a "non-compelling" state interest: "I have never been able ... to appreci-ate just what a compelling state interest is ... I feel, therefore, and always have felt, that these phrases are ... not ... helpful for constitutional analysis. They are too convenient and result ori-ented." For a criticism of the contrived doctrine of "close scrutiny" or "compelling interest analysis", *see Rafferty, supra*, asterisk note (*of Side B*) at fn. 96 of *para.* 44

22   *Woodward, supra note 20.* See also Jefferies, infra p. 217 (at endnote 6) at 341-343.

23   *See* David S. Savage, *Roe Ruling More than Its Author Intended, L.A. Times*, Wed., Sept. 14, 2005, p. A1 at p. A16 (quoting Mark Tushnet): "All they [the Roe majority justices] wanted was to get... [criminal abortion statutes] off the books". The "wants and private beliefs" of justices are not the measure of what is the Law.

Fifth Amendment due process mandates that a Court opin-ion serves "only" the Constitution (and the *Roe* opinion states so, explicitly: *see supra*, text of *Conclusion* accompanying note 1). So, this Marshall memo "erodes one's trust in the fundamental fairness of our legal system" because it represents the exact opposite of "judicial impartiality" — "which goes to the very integrity of the legal system" (*Gray v. Mississippi* (1987), 461 U.S. 648, 668). It qualifies as nothing more than rank judicial advocacy emanating from one of the highest levels of our government. It is an abortion-access advocate masquerading as a Supreme Court justice. And it explains why the *Roe* justices inexcusably and unconstitutionally failed to appoint (sagacious) counsel to represent *Roe's* fetus in the course of holding that the fetus does not qualify as a constitutional or due process clause person. It is rule by men, and not by the rule of law. So, shame on the *Roe* majority and concurring justices, and on any and every person and organization who defends or supports *Roe*, such as the information media, Giuliani, the Kerrys, Cuomos, Bidens, Kennedys, Gores, Clintons, Obamas, Spectors, Boxers, Feinsteins and Pelosis, the Senate Judiciary Committee (which, under the guise of the defunct right of privacy (*see Rafferty supra* asterisk note (of *Side B*) at *paras.* 42-47) uses upholding *Roe v. Wade* as a litmus test for confirmation of a nominee to the Supreme Court), pro-*Roe* justices, such as Kennedy, Stevens, O'Connor, Souter, Ginsburg, and Breyer, pro-*Roe* legal scholars and law professors, such as Tribe and Chemerinsky, and legal organizations such as the ACLU. Not to be left out here is former President Jimmy Carter — unless he would claim nonculpable ignorance of the corruption of the *Roe* Court and of the lawlessness of the *Roe* decision. *See* J. Carter, *Our Endangered Values* 72 (2007): "As president, I accepted my obligation to enforce *Roe v. Wade*." The issue of executive enforcement of *Roe* has never even arisen. And what about a president's moral obligation to publicly trash a lawless decision?

Also, not to be left out here is the Democratic Party, the 2008 platform of which states in part that the Democratic Party "strongly and unequivocally supports *Roe v. Wade* ..., and we oppose any and all efforts to weaken or undermine [Roe]". This means, in effect, that the Democratic Party makes "upholding judicial fraud" one of its platform principles. And since President

Obama has repeatedly publicly stated that he will appoint justices who will uphold *Roe*, then the conclusion is inescapable that he supports judicial tyranny.

24  See, *e.g.*, *Co. of Sacramento v. Lewis* (1998), 523 U.S. 833, 845 (touchstone of due process is the prohibition of arbitrary governmental action), and *Oregon v. Mitchell* (1990), 400 U.S. 113, 246 ("Courts, no less than legislators, are bound by" the dictates of due process of law).

25  The *Roe* citation, here, is 410 U.S. at 158.

It is true that several justices in the lead opinion in *Casey*, and in reference to *Roe*'s selection of "fetal viability" as the so-called abortion cut-off point, noted that "we must justify the lines we draw". These *Casey* justices then proceeded to try and justify the *Roe* majority justices' not-until-fetal-viability, abortion cut-off line (505 U.S. 833, 870). This was nothing more than an attempt at diversion, because what must be justified here is not why the *Roe* justices selected fetal viability as the so-called abortion cut-off point (and, in any event, the *Casey* justices had no way of knowing the "why" here, for the simple reason that the *Roe* opinion is silent on this "why"), but precisely why and how the Constitution, itself, implicitly dictates this not-until-fetal-viability, abortion cut-off line.

In any event, neither *Roe* nor *Casey* justified *Roe*'s not-until-fetal-viability abortion cut-off point. All that *Roe* did was to define fetal viability. And all that *Casey* did was to simply repeat *Roe*'s definition of fetal viability.

To argue that the formed (post-embryonic) human fetus is not a human being because its organs (particularly its brain) are not yet fully developed, or because it is nonviable is the virtual equivalent of arguing that a newborn is not a human being because its brain is not yet fully developed (or that a young girl is not a human being because her breasts are not yet developed), or that no creature can be deemed the creature that it is unless it can live independently of its currently essential environment (and which would mean, of course, that no creature period could ever exist really).

26  416 U.S. 1, 8 n.5.

27    410 U.S. at 116.

28    478 U.S. 186. *Bowers* is cited as 539 U.S. 558.

29    *See supra*, text (of *Conclusion*), accompanying nn.22-25 & 32.

30    *Los Angeles Times*, Sunday, June 17, 2007, *Opinion* at M5 (last paragraph).

31    Justice William J. Brennan, Jr., *In Defense of Dissents*, 37 *Hastings L.J.* 427, 435 (1986). (*See supra*, text of *Conclusion* accompanying note 25.) Similarly, Justice Marshall observed: "'the validity and moral authority of a conclusion [or decision] largely depend on the mode by which it was reached.'" *Greenholtz, Nebraska Penal Inmates*, 442 U.S. 1, 34 (1979) (Justice Marshall dissenting in part) (quoting from Justice Frankfurter's concurring opinion in *Joint Anti-fascist Refugee Committee v. McGrath* (1951), 341 U.S. 123, 171). *And see Wisconsin v. Constantineau* (1979), 400 U.S. 433, 436 ("it is procedure that marks much of the difference between rule by law and rule by fiat").

32    *See Rafferty, supra* asterisk note (of *Side B*) at *paras.* 32-35.

## LONG CONCLUSION (TO SIDE B)

1    410 U.S. 113, 116 (1973).

2    E. Chemerinsky, *Rationalizing the Abortion Debate: Legal Rhetoric and the Abortion Controversy*, 31 Buffalo L. Rev. 107, 108 (1982).

3    550 U.S. 124.

4    Erwin Chemerinsky, *et al*, *Judges Know Best*, *Los Angeles Daily Journal*, Tues., May 5, 2007 at 6 (*Forum*).

5    Transcript: *Nightline: An Anatomy of a Decision: Roe v. Wade*, 6 (ABC television broadcast, Dec. 2, 1993) (on file with the author). *See also* J.C. Jeffries, Jr., *Justice Lewis F. Powell, Jr.* 346-47 (1994); and David Savage, *Roe Ruling: More Than Its Author Intended*, *Los Angeles Times*, September 14, 2005, at A1: "Powell firmly supported

a woman's right to abortion. He urged Blackmun to say it directly [which Blackmun subsequently did], rather than attack [the state's criminal abortion] laws as vague."

6     For the Powell quote, see John Jeffries, Jr., *Justice Powell Jr.* 341 (1994). *And see In re Murchison, supra,* note 5 (of the *Preface*). "The absolute worst violation of the judge's oath is to decide a case based on a partisan political or philosophical [or personal] basis, rather than what the law requires" ( Justice Antonin Scalia, *Are There Too Many Lawyers, Los Angeles Times Parade Magazine* (Sunday insert), September 14, 2008, p.9). *And see* the author's free online *Rutgers* article, *supra,* asterisk note (of *Side B,* p 195) at note 88 of paragraph 37.

    Suppose that the issue in *Roe* had been whether a Texas statute, outlawing consensual sex between an adult and a person under the age of eighteen, is unconstitutional in that an adult has a constitutional right to engage in consensual sex with a so-called "mature" minor who is at least sixteen years old. Suppose also that Powell related to Totenberg that an experience which strongly influenced him to join the majority of *Roe* justices who voted to find the Texas statute unconstitutional was an affair he enjoyed with his former law partner's sixteen-year-old daughter. Totenberg would have gone after Powell's hide.

7     *Cheney v.* USDC (2004), 541 U.S. 913. *And see, e.g.,* Steven Lubet, *The Importance of Being Honest: How Lying, Secrecy, and Hypocrisy Collide with Truth in Law* 127-133 (2008) (skewers Scalia's conduct in *Cheney's Case,* while failing to mention Powell's conduct in *Roe*); and Teresa Tomeo, *Double Standards, Our Sunday Visitor* 25 (October 4, 2009) (the media drooled over the killing of late-term abortionist, Dr. George Tiller by a fanatical pro-lifer, while virtually ignoring the killing of anti-abortion protester, Jim Pouillon by a fanatical pro-choice person).

8     476 U.S. 778-79.

9   *See* Goldering, *Development of the Human Brain*, 307 N. Eng. J. Med. No. 9 at 564, August 26, 1982; and the last paragraph of n.25 of *Side B.*

10   492 U.S. 490 at 566-69.

11   *See supra* text (of *Side A*) accompanying note 23. If Stevens' position here is sound, then, no less than thirty-six (36) states' fetal-homicide statutes are unconstitutional by virtue of the First Amendment's prohibition of religion in government. *See Curran, infra* note 14.

12   *Joint Anti-Fascist Refugee Committee v. McGrath* (1951), 341 U.S. 123, 171-72 (Frankfurter concurring.)

13   *Van Nostrand, supra* text (of *Side A*) accompanying note 23.

14   *Williams Obstetrics* 139 (17th ed., 1985).

You want to know what is (or should be) the greatest fear of pro-*Roe* supporters in the know? It is that the Supreme Court would agree to decide squarely the constitutionality of state fetal murder statutes. (*See Rafferty, supra* asterisk note (of *Side B*) at *para.* 72 — and its accompanying note 139.) The only thing that could be offered (or rather thrown) against the constitutionality of such statutes would be militant appeals to anti-religious prejudice. And once the constitutionality of these statutes is finally established, reasonable thinking persons would be forced to draw this conclusion: why, in heaven's name, should the mother of a human fetus and her doctor be constitutionally exempt from prosecution under such statutes simply because the mother desires to have her fetus destroyed? Should not she be its greatest protector? (The English common law on criminal abortion recognized no such exemption. *See Rafferty, supra*, asterisk note (of *Side B*) at *paras.* 12-27.) Or, what is the real worth of a document (in this case, the U.S. Constitution) which forbids a state from prohibiting a mother and some person in a white gown from obliterating the former's unborn child, and yet allows a state to prohibit a person from cruelly or unnecessarily killing, say, an opossum. Only an idiot could value an opossum more than a child in the womb of its mother. *See Los Angeles Times*, Sat., March 22, 2008, p.B4 (column

2): no charges in opossum attack due to insufficiency of evidence. *And see People v. Pool* (2008), 166 C.A.4th 904, 905; 83 Cal.Rptr. 186, 187 (Pool, unaware that his girlfriend is pregnant, strangles her, resulting also in the death of the woman's 10-weeks-old (conceptual age or 12-weeks-old gestational age) fetus. Held: fetal murder conviction affirmed. *See also* D.S. Curran, *Abandonment and Reconciliation: Addressing Political and Common Law Objections to Fetal Homicide Laws*, 58 Duke L.J. 1107, 1142 (2009) (as of 2009, 36 states have classified fetal or unborn-child killing as criminal homicide).

Here is another fear pro-*Roe* supporters in the know should have. How odd that the framers of our Constitution (who most certainly understood that abortion could be prosecuted as a despicable crime and "one of the worst known to the law"— *State v. Alcorn* (1901), 64 p.1014, 1019), intended to guarantee a right that would have been contingent upon the cooperation of a profession whose members swore an oath (the *Hippocratic Oath*) to have nothing to do with it. *See Rafferty, supra* (asterisk note of *Side B*) at paragraph 18.

Would not *Roe* dissolve in an instant if the medical profession decided to abide by its (original) *Hippocratic Oath,* and told the Supreme Court to go take a hike on abortion? (*See Connecticut v. Menillo* (1975), 423 U.S. 9, 10-11: notwithstanding *Roe v. Wade,* a state may continue prosecuting non-physician-performed abortions). So, how did Blackmun know (and he must have known this, or to be sure he would not have bothered to write the *Roe* opinion) that the medical community would cooperate with the *Roe* decision? And if that is true, then Justice Blackmun, former Counsel for the Mayo Clinic, must have possessed inside knowledge that the medical community would cooperate with the *Roe* majority justices' "determination" to make abortion not only legal but also safe, by in effect employing the use of judicial thuggery: slapping the faces of the several states for being overly concerned for the safe-guarding of the conceived unborn.

*And see* Henry Weinstein, *Doctors Appeal Ruling on Participation in Executions, Los Angeles Times* (Sat., Oct. 20, 2007) A13 (quoting Dr. Ross McKinney, Jr., Director of the Trent Center for Bioethics, Humanities and History of Medicine at Drake University: "It is hard for me to imagine someone saying that a doctor being there [i.e., at an execution by lethal injection] and contributing to someone's death is not a medical procedure that violates the *Hippocratic Oath*").

15  505 U.S. 833, 851 (Justices O'Connor and Souter joining).

16  Kennedy conveniently ignores here this observation of the Court in *Wisconsin v. Yoder* (1927), 406 U.S. 205, 215-216: "the very concept of ordered liberty precludes allowing every [or any] individual to make his own standards on matters of conduct in which society as a whole has important interests." *See supra*, text (of *Side B*) accompanying note 27. And, of course, in joining the majority opinion in *Glucksberg* (1997) (*see supra*, note 19 of *Side B*), Kennedy implicitly rejected, here, his *Casey*, hippy or new age babble.

The *Roe* majority-opinion justices, in their passion to add a new star (access to safely-performed abortion) to our constitutional constellation of individual ("fundamental") rights, "unwittingly" proved the non-existence of the very right (the so-called right of privacy) from which this new star supposedly emanates. *See supra*, note (of the *Preface*), and *Part II* of *Rafferty, supra*, asterisk note (of *Side B*), beginning at paragraph 42. Also, the only way this new star can be held to be constitutionally "fundamental" is if "judicial predilection" fundamentalizes it. *See id.* at paras. 48-71, & 89.

Justice Bork referred to *Roe v. Wade* "as the greatest example and symbol of the judicial usurpation of democratic prerogatives in this century." Robert H. Bork, *The Tempting of America: The Political Seduction of the Law* 116 (1989). During his confirmation hearings, Bork stated that the Constitution does not recognize a general or independent right to privacy. Because Bork spoke the truth here (*see supra*, note 10 of *Preface*), this highly qualified justice failed the Senate's litmus test for confirmation.

17  492 U.S. 490.

18  *See* David G. Savage, *Roe's Author Found Himself a Bystander in '92 Abortion Fight*, Los Angeles Times, Mar. 5, 2004, at A25, Linda Greenhouse, *supra* note 20 (of *Side B*) at 203, and J. Toobin, *The Nine: Inside the Secret World of the Supreme Court* 51-59 (2007).

19  *See* R. Reuben, *Man in the Middle*, California Lawyer, October, 1992, at 35.

20  1 *Coke's Institutes*, 970, (2nd ed., 1648).

21  1 *Blackstone's Commentaries*, 69 (1765).

22  *See* respectively, Charles Fried, *Order and Law: Arguing the Reagan Revolution: A First Hand Account* 75 (1991); and Richard A. Posner, *Judges Writing Styles (And Do They Matter?)*, 62 U. Chi. L. Rev. 1421, 1434 (1995).

23  Philip Bobbitt, *Constitutional Fate: Theory of the Constitution* 157 (3rd ed., 1984).

24  *Justice Brennan, infra*, note 25. In the case of Professor Tribe, an exception, here, is in order: he should be burned at the stake along with his numerous (discarded) pro-*Roe* commentaries. Bopp and Coleson observed of Tribe that he "is the embodiment of the confusion created by *Roe's* poor reasoning. He has developed and discarded several alternative justifications for *Roe* in the past thirteen years." James Bopp, Jr. & Richard E. Coleson, *The Right to Abortion: Anomalous, Absolute, and Ripe for Reversal*, 3 BYU J. Pub. L. 181, 189 (1989).

25  Justice William J. Brennan, Jr., *In Defense of Dissents*, 37 *Hastings L.J.* 427, 435 (1986). In *Roe*, Brennan failed to heed his own admonishment here. There, he urged Blackmun to adopt fetal viability as the abortion cut-off point. *See Balkin, supra* note 21 (of *Side B*).

26  The citation to *Casey* is 505 U.S. at 867.

Here is *Casey* in its essence: it adopts all of *Roe's* central holdings, while implicitly rejecting all of *Roe's* reasons given in support of those holdings, and then fails to set forth so much as a single dot of recognizable, constitutional reasoning in support of its adoption of all of *Roe's* central holdings. And somehow that is supposed to convince the *Casey* critic that what is operating in *Casey* is, not an exercise in judicial predilection, but rather a true exercise of impartial, judicial adjudication. I propose that *Casey's* acronym be deemed *cpsd*: clinging pathetically to *stare decisis*.

27    David Gelernter, *Let's Take Abortion Away from the Court*, *Los Angeles Times*, September 23, 2005 at B13.

28    *See* the April 4, 2006 House subcommittee hearing on the Court's budget request.

29    *Rom.* 12:2. *See supra* text (of *Side A*) accompanying nn. 34 & 35, as well as that note 35.

# A SMALL MATTER
# OF PROCEDURE

Sleeper Law Student (SLS) to his law professor (PROF): Tell me
professor: do you agree with this statement from *Wisconsin v
Constantineau*, 400 U.S. 433,436 (1971): "It is significant that
most of the provisions of the Bill of Rights are procedural, for it is
procedure [as in procedural due process] that marks much of the
difference between rule by law and rule by fiat [including rule by
tyrannical, judicial fiat?]"

Professor (PROF): I do.

SLS: Professor, do you agree that *Dred Scott* is widely recognized as the
worst decision ever handed down by our Supreme Court?

PROF: Yes, that's true, and I agree with that description of *Dred Scott*.

SLS: Professor, it's true, is it not, that in *Dred Scott*, Scott (the slave) was
at least given the opportunity to be heard on the issue of whether
or not he has a right to sue to be relieved of his status as a slave?

PROF: Yes, that is true, he was indeed given or afforded procedural
due process.

SLS: Professor, tell me - yes or no: in *Roe v Wade*, is it not true that,
unlike in *Dred Scott*, *Roe's* fetus was not given an opportunity to
be heard on the issue (decided there) of whether or not he has a
right —as a 14th Amendment person not to be obliterated by his
mother?

PROF: Ah-ah, aaaaaah-ye—y- e- s, I suppose that's true.

SLS: Professor, now, I am not comparing a fetus living in the womb of his
mother with a walking around, living human being; but it's true, is
it not, that for all you or any other person really knows, or thought
(such as our Founding Fathers, the Signers of the *Declaration of
Independence*, and the Framers of the *5th Amendment*), a human
fetus living in the womb of his mother is no less a human being
than a walking-around one?

PROF: Yes, that's true.

SLS: Professor, I maintain further that almost by definition "fundamental" or "inalienable rights" are complimentary and that, in any event, they can never collide on a constitutional plane? Do you agree?

PROF: Yes.

SLS: Professor, I maintain also that the Constitution is "no respecter of persons," and by that I mean one person's constitutional rights are not subservient to another's? Do you agree?

PROF: Yes.

SLS: Well, then, Professor, unless you assume that such a fetus is not a constitutionally recognized person (which is the very issue under consideration), then are you not compelled to agree that _Roe v Wade_ is a worser decision than even _Dred Scott_?

PROF: I wouldn't know, because worser isn't a word - so shut-up and sit down.

SLS: O.K. Professor. Thank you. I will shut up. But, here is my mid-term paper. I wrote it up as a "_Fetus as Person Manual_". And it refuses to be shut up:

# A FETUS-AS-PERSON LEGAL PRACTICE MANUAL FOR PRO-LIFE ATTORNEYS AND LEGAL ORGANIZATIONS

This manual has been prepared in response to this message (marked urgent) from the conceived unborn:

> Greetings to you, our lawyers, and other supporters. We hear that you are saying that, from a constitutional standpoint, we are persons no less than our mothers, and that because the Constitution (following the lead of our good and providential Creator) "is no respecter of persons," we are entitled to be protected constitutionally no less than our mothers. Our losses (although conveniently not counted as such by many) already exceed fifty million. Therefore, we implore you: LET OUR SIDE BE HEARD, put on the law, and proceed 'shrewdly as serpents' (*Mt.* 10: 17).

A renewed effort to overrule <u>Roe</u>, and to establish the human fetus as a constitutionally recognized and protected person, does not require a constitutional amendment, state or federal legislation, a long period of time, or massive litigation and briefing projects. All that is required is "pointed" briefing and "immediate" court action in the state and federal trial and appellate courts. Costs, here, would be negligible given <u>pro-bono</u> legal representation and waiver of court filing fees on the grounds of "fetal indigency". And know that after you have suffered defeat after defeat in those courts, that to get a hearing before the Supreme Court, it takes but the votes of four (4) of the justices to get you there. If the state and federal trial and appellate court judges and justices ask you "who do you think you are"(?), tell them you are "the persistent widow" in *Luke* 18: 1-8, and that you will persist in filing a petition for issuance of fetal-protection orders one bloodied, discarded fetus at a time until the Court grants the requested hearing which its own founding documents say that it should do.

The pro-fetal petition, in addition to relating the court jurisdictional grounds, and the material facts of the case, need relate only the following three (3) legal points:

## (1)

Elementary principles of procedural due process dictate that both sides of a disputed legal issue be given a meaningful opportunity to be heard. *Roe's* fetus was one side of the "both sides" of the *Roe* issue of whether *Roe's* fetus qualifies as a constituional person (within the meaning of the word "person" in the 5th (14th) Amendment due process clause). However, *Roe's* fetus was incapable of defending itself, and was appointed neither a guardian ad litem nor an attorney. Therefore, *Roe's* fetus was denied procedural due process. This constitutes, perhaps, the most egregious judicial error in the history of Anglo-American law. Of the thousands of Supreme Court cases (including, and especially *Dred Scott* – who was at least given the "opportunity to be heard" on the issue of whether he could sue to be relieved of his status as a slave), no one can cite a case other than *Roe* (and perhaps also *Planned Parenthood v Danforth*: see Rafferty, infra, at pp. 197-198) wherein one side of a disputed legal issue decided by the Court was not afforded an opportunity to be heard on the issue. The essence of due process does not consist of the fair presentation of the legal issue under consideration, although judges and justices do a great disservice to the principle that "justice achieved requires that it can be seen as so," when they manipulate an issue under review (as did the *Roe* majority justices on this issue of "fetal personhood": see Rafferty, infra note 4 of Side B at pp.196-97) so that it provides them with a way to where they want to go. And it does not consist of a fair presentation of the pros and cons of deciding the issue one way or the other. It consists of nothing less than that one whose interests (particularly, those interests that can be defined properly as "vital") are directly and materially affected or impacted by how the issue may be resolved, is provided with an opportunity to be heard on how that issue should be decided. Putting this another way, "mandated due process not afforded equals decision voided." The _Roe_ Court, in electing to weigh in on the question or issue of Fourteenth Amendment fetal personhood or the right of _Roe's_ fetus not to be deprived of his right to continue living in the absence of first being afforded due process of law, had an absolute Fifth Amendment, due process-mandated duty to ensure that _Roe's_ fetus was given an opportunity to be heard, and to defend his asserted right not to be obliterated, by appointing him a guardian ad litem, who would seek out sagacious counsel to defend and to assert the "vital" interests of _Roe's_ fetus. In its rush to judgment declaring access to physician-performed abortion to be a woman's fundamental right, the Court failed to execute the constitutionally mandated duty that it owed to _Roe's_ fetus. All this dictates that, as a matter of constitutional law, _Roe's_ fetal non-person holding is, on its face, void ab initio, and so it is not the law of the land, is not binding on the states, and can be decided anew at the trial court level. See, e.g., _Gardner v. Superior Court_ (1986), 182 C.A. 3d 335, 339; 227 Cal. Rptr. 78: "in the development of the common law, the analysis of printed decisions of appellate courts is only part of the show. Development of the law begins in the trial courts." This would not be an instance of a lower court refusing to be bound by a legally-binding higher court decision because, in this instance, the higher court decision is not binding legally since it is void ab initio. (See _Burgett v Texas_ (1967), 389 U.S. 109: Gideon - denial of right to counsel-error renders criminal conviction "void ab initio" and subject to being attacked as so, collaterally: meaning, a party need not seek to void it (if it is asserted either by the respondent or the bench judge) in the rendering court and can, instead, seek to void it in the court where his current case is being heard).

(2)

_Roe v. Wade_ holds expressly (410 U.S. 113, 156-57) that if the fetus qualifies as a 14th (5th) Amendment due process clause person, then _Roe_ collapses absolutely and totally.

(3)

There is now no question that the fetus qualifies so. (Philip A. Rafferty, Roe v. Wade: Unraveling the Fabric of the America 49-54, Tate Publishing & Enterprises, LLC., 2011 (Revised and Expanded, 2012). (Hereinafter, cited as Rafferty.)

To create a "real case or controversy" pro-life lawyers and organizations would have to do the following:

> Convince a husband or unwed father-to-be (prefer-ably a slew of them) whose wife or mate is going to seek an abortion, to go into state or federal court and seek orders barring his wife or mate (and her doctor) from killing or destroying a constitutionally protected fetal person and having himself appointed as guardian ad litem for the fetus, and also having himself found to have "standing": See the last paragraph of Rafferty, supra, p. 197. These husbands and unwed fathers-to-be could be located via ads in religious newspapers, etc.

Nothing more need be done, said, or written about _Roe v. Wade_. (Ignore the ideological patronizing of the Court by the Erin Chemerinskys of the world: E. Chemerinsky, The Conservative Assault on the Constitution 175 (2010)). What is needed is "in-court" action. Inaction, here, by pro-life lawyers and legal organi-zations equates with no less than fleeing the battlefield.

I will, in closing, be crystal clear about what is being stated in this manual: a state or federal bench judge is "not" prohibited by _Roe v. Wade_ from ruling or deciding that the human fetus qualifies as a due process clause person. And should such a judge decide so (and issue an order prohibiting a fetal abortion in the case at hand), then he or she would not be acting against _Roe v. Wade_; for that decision, itself, dictates that it collapses totally if the human fetus qualifies as a constitutionally recognized person. And although _Roe_ holds that the human fetus does not qualify so, that _Roe_ holding is "void ab initio", and so is "not" binding on a state or federal bench judge (and for that matter on any judicial officer or court of appeal period).

Should the issue of whether or not the human fetus qualifies as a due process clause person be put properly before a bench judge, and should that judge protest that it is not for him or her to set forth new law or precedent, then counsel for the fetus should cite _Gardner_, supra, and inform the judge of the following: by refusing to decide this issue, you are, in effect, denying the fetus's protection petition, and, therefore, you are, in fact, making new law or precedent: In this case, that the human fetus does not qualify as a (5th) 14th Amendment due process clause person. And if the bench judge responds with this broadside:

"Counsel, that's not true. Don't tell me what I have decided; I decide what I have, or have not decided. But if I were to rule on your issue, I would rule against you, if only for the reason that long before, as well as around the time (1868) the 14th Amendment became law, American women enjoyed a substantial liberty or right to abort their unwanted children. And so says Eric J. Segall in his Supreme Myths (2012) at p. 52, and I quote: "Few people realize that, prior to the mid-19th century abortion was legal until quickening – the moment when a woman could first detect fetal movement (usually around 16 weeks) .... Thus, prior to the Civil War a woman could legally secure [by virtue of her state's reception of the English common law] an abortion in the United States."

Counsel, then, should respond by letting go with this volley of legal and historical truths:

"Then how come: (1) If a woman (whether or not she was pregnant, let alone had reached quickening) killed herself in the course of trying to self-abort, she was deemed guilty of felony suicide (see Rafferty, supra at pp. 53, 204 (n.16), and 159 - Russells' Case) and, (2) if she died, here, at the hands of another person, then that person was launched into eternity at the end of a rope? (See the cases set forth in Rafferty, supra at Appendix 3, p.89). (3) Quickening played no role period in abortion prosecution at the common law until the 1st decade of the 19th century (and this came about through nothing more than a judicial error in misinterpreting "quick with child" which referred not to the onset of quickening, but rather to the onset of completed fetal formation.) Samuel Johnson's preeminent A Dictionary of the English Language (1755), defined "quick with child" as "the child in the womb after it is perfectly formed," (later as "pregnant with a live child".)   And although the OED has erroneously equated "quick with child" with "quickening," this error has been corrected in the later SOED editions (wherein "quick with child" is defined as "pregnant with a live fetus [or young child].) (See Rafferty, supra at pp.52, 199-203, and 155-158 – Phillips' Case.) (4) The common law born-alive rule, which disqualified children, who died "while" still in the wombs of their mothers, from being legally recognized as victims of unlawful homicide (and which probably did not become accepted or settled law until approximately the advent of the 17th century) did not derive from perceived difficulties in determining the cause of fetal death, but derived rather from nothing more than another error in judicial interpretation. Some early 14th century wording contained in an incomplete and defective reporting on a 14th century, double-homicide prosecution in Bourton's Case (1326-27), aka., The Twins–Slayer's Case (specifically "and for the reason that the justices were unwilling to adjudge this thing [i.e., the alleged felonious destruction of unborn twins] as felony," and which means no more than that the justices were "preliminarily" of the opinion that this admittedly double "homicide" was not "committed with felony or malice aforethought," and therefore would qualify as a "bailable" and "pardonable" homicide) was misinterpreted by leading 16th (17th) century legal commentators and compilers (such as Staunford and Coke) to mean that the "felonious" killing of an unborn child was not a "felony" or hanging offence - which it most certainly was when done "feloniously" or with "malice or felony aforethought". (See Rafferty, supra at page 126 – Bourton's Case.) Staunford and Coke, in support of their commentaries on the common law rule that a child killed in his mother's womb cannot qualify as a victim of unlawful homicide (these commentaries are reproduced at www.parafferty.com, infra at pp. 605 and 161-162, respectively), cite not only Bourton's (Twins-Slayer's) Case, but also R. v. Anonymous (1348). In point of fact, it seems almost certain that R. v. Anonymous was not even a case. It appears to be nothing more than a hypothetical question posed by some attorney who answered erroneously the very hypothetical question that he posed to himself. (See Rafferty, supra pp. 143-149.) Those persons who maintain that then perceived difficulties in determining the cause of fetal death is what gave rise to the born-alive rule have not produced so much as a single dot of evidence to support this theory. And available evidence indicates that coroners, grand jurors, and jurors who set on criminal trials, did not find it to be an insurmountable difficulty in determining what caused an unborn child to die in his mother's womb. See e.g., Rafferty, supra p. 102 (Code's Case.) And see id at 143-149 - Anonymous' Case. See also www. parafferty.com, infra at pp. 180-185 and 193-194. (5) Pre-quick with child abortion was prosecuted as a serious misdemeanor offence. See Rafferty, supra at page 70 - Beare's Case. (6) To accuse a woman of having an abortion constituted criminal libel/slander. (See www.parafferty.com, click on Roe V. Wade, and scroll to pp.130 (Eighth Rule), 383 (n.42), and 725 - Cockaine's Case.) (7) At common law one could be said to have a right to do this or that thing only if the law provided a means or legal procedure for vindicating the right or remedying its hindering or violation; and no such means or procedure for accessing abortion (for obvious reasons) existed at common law (See www.parafferty.com, supra at pp. 218-220.) (8) All licensed physicians, midwives, and apothecaries or druggists had to take an oath not to have any thing to do with abortion other than trying to prevent it from even happening. (See www.parafferty.com, supra at pp. 223-224.) (9) No person under the sun can cite to so much as a single particular period, time, place, or location in pre-20th century England, the United States, or Colonial America, etc., where abortion was practiced in the open, let alone that it was practiced so because it was thought then and there to be legal. Any such place or location would have been immediately shut down as a "public nuisance". (See www. parafferty.com supra at pp. 130 (Ninth Rule), and 382 (n.43).) (10) As soon as a state legislature got wind (usually through a published decision of one of the state's appellate court's decisions) that pre-quick with child abortion was not criminalized in their state, the legislature almost immediately criminalized the same statutorily. (11) If abortion was a woman's right at common law, then how is it that every person, who lived under the jurisdiction of the common law, and who wrote on the subject of voluntary abortion, understood it to be an unspeakable crime and indistinguishable from murder or infanticide? I am referring here to judges, legal commentators, medical-legal writers, physicians, philosophers, natural scientists, social commentators, and authors of midwifery books. (See www.parafferty.com, supra at pp. 223-224.) And finally (12), if abortion was a liberty at common law, then why, well into at least the 19th century in England, did so many unmarried, pregnant women, year after year, opt for taking the risk of being launched into eternity at the end of a rope for killing their newly born children, rather than opting to kill them while they were still in the wombs of their mothers? Infanticide prosecutions exceed abortion prosecutions here by a thousand (1,000) or so to one (1). (See Rafferty, supra at pp. 170-171.)"

It is, here, no wonder, then, that neither Segall nor his sources cite so much as a single dot of legal authority in support of their proposition that abortion was a woman's common law liberty. But, for what I maintain here, I cite an abundance of primary and secondary authorities. See, generally, Rafferty, supra text of Side B accompanying notes 13-18 (as well as those notes), and Rafferty, supra Appendices 1-6. And see (online), Philip A. Rafferty, Roe v Wade A Scandal Upon the Court, 7 Rutgers Law Journal (2006) at paras. 12-27, and www.parafferty.com (click on Roe v Wade and have at it.)

# POSTSCRIPT

What can be stated truly about the so-called fundamental right to have an abortion can be said of no other fundamental right: It is a practice that may very well consist in the killing of an intact or existing, innocent human being (and to which the many - some 35 plus - state, fetal murder statutes attest: see Unravelling, supra, pp. 218-219 (at note 14) and also at pp. 27-29.) No unbiased, reasonable person can say that this is not so. To maintain, as did the *Roe* majority justices, that a concern for whether abortion kills an intact human being can be simply arbitrarily excised from the constitutional equation of whether abortion access qualifies as a fundamental right is the equivalent of arguing that a concern for human safety can be arbitrarily excised from the building equation for a new superhighway. With that consideration removed, nothing, here, is left really to consider. And it is that judicial mindset which undoubtedly caused the Roe majority justices to commit due process error in failing to appoint constitutionally mandated legal representation to Roe's fetus in the arguing of the issue of whether he (a human fetus) qualifies as a 5th (14th) Amendment, due process clause person.

The Roe majority justices would, of course, deny that their conclusion that procured abortion qualifies as a "fundamental right" was arrived at without consideration for the aborted fetus. They would have said that "we gave it the same consideration which, according to the late renowned legal scholar, Cyril Means Jr., it was given at the English common law; and we expressly acknowledged as much in our opinion in Roe v. Wade: 'our holding [that a woman has an unfettered "fundamental," constitutionally guaranteed right to procure an abortion of her non-viable fetus]...is consistent with the lenity of the [English] common law on [abortion.]'" (See Roe v. Wade, 410 U.S. at 165). The exact opposite is the truth: What Roe held to be a "fundamental right" because it was recognized as such at the English common law (and therefore is established as one of the most sacred of all constitutionally guaranteed rights), was "murder" at the English common law. And the trial court judge ruled so in <u>Queen v. West</u> (1848 – Cox's C.C. 500, 503; 2 Car & K 785, 175 English Rpt. 329), in the course of instructing the jury on the common law crime of the murder of a non-viable human fetus or human being:

> The prisoner is charged with murder: and the means stated are that the prisoner caused the premature delivery of the witness Henson, by using some instrument for the purpose of procuring abortion: and that the child so prematurely born was, in consequence of its premature birth, so weak that it died. This, no doubt, is an unusual mode of committing murder...; but I am of the opinion (and I direct you in point of [the common] law), that if a person intending to procure abortion does an act which causes a child to be born so much earlier than the natural time, that it is born in a such state that it is less capable of living [meaning that the child "became nearer to death or farther from life"], and afterwards dies in consequence of its exposure to the external world [<u>i.e.</u> because it was aborted alive in a non-viable state], the person who by her misconduct so brings the child into the world, and puts it thereby in a situation in which it cannot live, is guilty of murder.

Blackstone, in no uncertain terms, has, from his grave, deemed our <u>Constitution</u> (which includes the Court's holdings in <u>Roe</u> and in <u>Casey</u>) as tyrannical to the highest degree (1 <u>Blackstone Commentaries</u> 129 (1765):

> This natural life [i.e. the life of a human being, which "begins in contemplation of law as soon as an infant is able to stir" or is organized into a recognizable human form - at which stage it receives its human or rational soul: <u>see</u> <u>Unraveling</u>, <u>supra</u> p. 52 at text accompanying note 13] being, as was before observed, the imme-

diate donation of the great creator, cannot legally be disposed of or destroyed by any individual [particularly its very own mother: see id p.53 at text accompanying note 16]....merely upon their own authority....Whenever the Constitution of a state vests in any man, or body of men, a power of destroying at pleasure, without the direction of laws, the lives or members of the subject, such constitution is in the highest degree tyrannical.

mL        8 - 13